AUDEN

An Introductory Essay

"False, . . . but no falser than the world
it matches."

(*Poem 9—'Look Stranger'*)

". . . thanks to your service,
"The lonely and unhappy are very much alive."

(*'The Sea and the Mirror'—Ch. 1 stanza 1*)

W. H. AUDEN

AUDEN

AN INTRODUCTORY ESSAY

By

Richard Hoggart

1965

CHATTO & WINDUS

LONDON

PUBLISHED BY
Chatto & Windus
LONDON
★
Clarke, Irwin & Co. Ltd.
TORONTO

First Published 1951
Second Impression 1961
Third Impression 1965

COPYRIGHT 1951 BY
RICHARD HOGGART

Printed by the Replika Process
in Great Britain by Lund Humphries, London and Bradford

For

Valentine and Bonamy Dobrée

"But always there are such as you..."

(Last stanza, 'New Year Letter')

Contents

CONTENTS

PREFACE

THE reader might well ask three questions before consenting to look at this essay—why should another book on poetry be written? why should it take this form? and why should it be about Auden?

Poetry puts us into contact, to a degree not possible in other forms of literature, with a sensitive personality exploring, and trying to put in order, its experience. Since we can all read today, the potential audience for poetry should be larger than it has ever been. Some of the reasons why it is not will emerge in the course of this book. Two are worth emphasis here: firstly, the novel is now so much the dominant literary form that many a 'common reader'—whose grandfather read Tennyson as well as Thackeray—would regard an excursion into poetry as slightly bizarre; secondly, not all modern poems are easily understood by the most willing layman. And if he turns to works of criticism, he finds that they are often highly allusive and technically formidable studies, which demand from their readers an apparatus, and a readiness of knowledge, which few can have.

This essay is addressed to people with no special literary training, but with an interest in the quality of our lives today, and a readiness to examine whether the reading of poetry has an important relation to that interest.

Auden's poetry is particularly concerned with the pressures of the times. It may be roughly divided into that written in England during the 1930s and that written in America afterwards. The earlier work is, on the whole, easier to understand than the later, and in part helps to explain it. It seems likely that most people who read this book, if they have any prior knowledge of Auden, will derive it from that earlier work—perhaps through some poems which they have met in anthologies. So this book moves, in general, from the earlier towards the later work. Such reference is made to what was loosely termed 'the Auden group' in the 'thirties as has seemed helpful. For to consider Auden's first phase in isolation would be to distort one's findings; he was then very much of the 'thirties. The poetic movement which we associate with that decade began at Oxford in the late 'twenties and faded at the beginning of the last war. It forms a peculiarly complete block in our recent literary history; for those of us who were adolescent during its progress, it has the nostalgic appeal of something involved with our own development. So one of the reasons for writing this book is personal.

This essay is meant to be an introduction only, a running of the finger down certain aspects of Auden's verse, so that the general reader may turn to it more readily. When he does, he will find that this is a very partial account, that I have not understood some things, and have, no doubt, misinterpreted others. He may also find that, in the attempt to clarify, I have abstracted too much and consequently distorted.

But in the end we discover our literature for ourselves. The reader should go to Auden's poems, not once but several times, before and after reading this book. After being thus used, it should be discarded; the end is to read poetry, not books about poetry.

I have acknowledged those of my many debts which I could name, but have unfortunately forgotten some creditors and have come to regard their opinion as my own. This is middleman's work, and is sure to have many echoes.

November 1950   R. H.

Acknowledgements

My deepest thanks are due to J. M. Cameron, G. E. T. Mayfield, C. F. Waldron, and, most of all, my wife Mary. Without their constant and detailed corrections and suggestions it would not have been possible for me to write this book.

Grateful acknowledgement is also made to the authors, translators, executors, editors and publishers for permission to quote from the following works. The source of each separate quotation is given in the notes:

From volumes of poetry by W. H. Auden. Faber and Faber Ltd. London. Random House, Inc. New York.

The Descent of the Dove by Charles Williams. Faber and Faber Ltd. London. (1939.)

The Poems of Emily Dickinson edited by M. D. and A. L. Hampson. Jonathan Cape Ltd. London. (1937.) Little, Brown & Co. Boston. Copyright 1914 by Martha Dickinson Bianchi.

Anglo-Saxon Poetry translated by Prof. R. K. Gordon. J. M. Dent and Sons Ltd. (1927.)

The song 'There comes a Time' by Michael Carr and Horatio Nichols. The Lawrence Wright Music Co. Ltd. London.

Rainer Maria Rilke; Poems translated by J. B. Leishman. The Hogarth Press Ltd. London. (1939.)

New Introductory Lectures on Psycho-Analysis by Sigmund Freud. The Hogarth Press Ltd. London. (Editions of 1933 and 1946.)

Introductory Lectures on Psycho-Analysis by Sigmund Freud. George Allen and Unwin Ltd. London. (Impressions of 1922 and 1936.)

Talks to Parents and Teachers by Homer Lane. George Allen and Unwin Ltd. London. (1930.)

The Modern Theatre by Eric Bentley. Robert Hale Ltd. London. (1948.)

English Blake by Bernard Blackstone. Cambridge University Press. (1949.)

Søren Kierkegaard by Melville Chaning-Pearce. James Clarke and Co. Ltd. London. (1946.)

Types of Modern Theology by H. R. Mackintosh. James Nisbet and Co. Ltd. London. (1937.)

The Shorter Oxford English Dictionary and H. W. Fowler's *Dictionary of Modern English Usage*. Clarendon Press, Oxford.

ACKNOWLEDGEMENTS

'The American Scene', introduction by W. H. Auden to *The American Scene* by Henry James. Charles Scribner's Sons. New York. (1947.)

'Squares and Oblongs', essay by W. H. Auden in *Poets at Work*. Harcourt, Brace and Co. Inc. New York. (1948.)

'Mimesis and Allegory', essay by W. H. Auden in *English Institute Annual (1940)*. Columbia University Press. New York.

Review of Rilke's 'Duino Elegies' by W. H. Auden in *New Republic*, Sept. 6th, 1939. New Republic. New York.

I have also to thank Eric Bramall, A.R.P.S., for permission to reproduce his photograph of Auden which appears as Frontispiece to this book.

CHAPTER I

FIRST IMPRESSIONS

(1) *Fertility and Wit*

THE reader who plunges directly into Auden's work may well recoil from the variety and force of the impressions he derives. He will find competence and virtuosity; carelessness, cliquishness and obscurity; interest in people, anxiety to reform and concern over the fate of society; impersonality, clinical analysis and drum-beating; he will meet boyishness succeeding maturity, the formal laced with the idiomatic, brilliant diagnosis succeeded by the slapstick of a buffoon, controlled exposition contrasting with slipshod chatter.

This barrage of epithets is introduced to draw attention at the start to the protean character of Auden's verse, to that quality which *New Verse* meant to indicate when it declared in November 1937: "He is the first English poet for many years who is a poet all the way round." In those early poems in particular Auden is exciting to read, and, through all the obscurity, he promises a good deal. His sympathies and interests are wide; he is witty and inventive; he writes with gusto and fluency. So much so that, looking at, for instance, 'The Orators', written when he was twenty-five, one may be slightly chilled by the cleverness. For although one may accept such an adroit and varied brilliance as a common form of early exercise by the born writer (Auden's handling of his material never has an amateur air), at times it is merely slick. Auden has much of the exhibitionist in him. He has frequently written outside his range.

But if much of Auden's work is wasteful and lumpy, it is rarely dull or laborious. In the 'thirties this exuberance, the free play of so energetic and curious a mind, had the effect of a stimulant on English verse; and like most stimulants, it did not do good to all who received it. It set in motion a reaction from Eliot's austere poetic example, a reaction with its own dangers, as Auden has since admitted:

> "Time and again have slubbered through,
> With slip and slapdash what I do,
> Adopted what I would disown,
> The preacher's loose immodest tone. . . ."

In part the diffuseness is caused by the spongelike nature of Auden's imagination; he can quickly pick up another's mannerisms and as quickly drop them, though not, usually, without modifying and assimilating some. At school he imitated Hardy; in the early 'thirties he was doing no more than his contemporaries in imitating Hopkins, though few did it so easily:

> "Me, March, you do with your movements master and rock
> With wing-whirl, whale-wallow, silent budding of cell."

Or

> "Good to a gillie, to an elver times out of mind
> Tender, to work-shy and game-shy kind
> Does he think?"

Throughout his verse, echoes from Anglo-Saxon and the Icelandic sagas are placed alongside snippets from the popular Press and the music-hall; odd items from scientific textbooks or from musical analysis are mixed with debts to Eliot, Owen, Housman and many others. The sonnet sequence in 'Journey to a War' and many subsequent sonnets have been greatly influenced by Rilke. The later Henry James helped to form the manner of Caliban's speech in 'The Sea and the Mirror'.

Sometimes Auden is doing little more than writing pastiche and enjoying it, much as he enjoys playing at word-games. It is this side of his character which produces the four bright cabaret lyrics for Miss Hedli Anderson, the parodies of national anthems, children's patriotic ditties and soldiers' marching songs, and which prompts the often obscure wit-writing, and the word-drunk passages such as these from a recent poem:

"For us the mornes and motted mammelons,

. . . .
                     . . . Yet the jussive
Elohim are here too . . ."

This is, or was, the Auden of whom Louis MacNeice wrote:

"But your lust for life prevails—
Drinking coffee, telling tales."

It is the Auden who thinks joking a release, a protection against morbid self-regard, who loves fantastic, slightly surrealist fun, is especially fond of Lear, Carroll and Firbank, and likes the jibe with a moral point. All this helps to account for Auden's occasional refusal to help the less-alert reader, for that knowing assurance which can be so overbearing. There may be, too, something of the intellectual's intolerance of the merely ordinary or dull. There may be a touch of hardness, a lack of sympathetic response in one part of the character, for the vitality seems now and again arrogant. This shows itself in several ways, from the studiedly careless tossing at the reader of concepts from Groddeck—"a slight proneness to influenza"; "the liar's quinsy"—to an occasionally almost insoluble concentration of style. There is also a little of the émigrés' pride, that pride which is the self-defence of the outsider and rebel. For though Auden is sometimes only out to shock the bourgeoisie, that fact does not altogether account for his violent tactics. He is using shock treatment because he has a sense of great urgency. The manner of 'The Orators' is in many places wilful, but its themes are by no means trivial. (It is ironic that the 'Letter to a Wound', which was attacked for perversity rather more than other parts of 'The Orators' when the book first appeared, should be felt by the much more restrained

Auden of the mid-'forties to be the only part of that curious production worth a place in the collected edition of his work.) In all his early work Auden shows a strong sense of social responsibility and great purposiveness. But he knows that it is difficult for the poet to communicate widely today.

(2) *Early Obstacles*

We cannot seriously consider these difficulties of communication until we have examined the related charges of carelessness, cliquishness and obscurity, which are so often levelled at Auden.

Certainly Auden is often careless and untidy: he may, as Isherwood describes in *Lions and Shadows*, make up a poem from odd lines which he particularly likes; and he often repeats favourite phrases. So, Mr. and Mrs. A., in 'The Ascent of F.6', say: "For Monday returns when none may kiss", and one of the lyrics written for the film 'Coalface' has: "For Monday comes when none may kiss"; in 'The Orators' there occurs: "Some blazers lounge beneath the calming tree . . . too much alone"; and in the Prologue to 'Look Stranger': "The ladies and gentlemen apart, too much alone." 'Letters from Iceland' introduces: "again the driver pulls on his gloves", and he returns in 'The fruit in which your parents hid you, boy', as "The mad driver pulling on his gloves"; the same "experienced matron" taking care of the diet of schoolboys occurs in 'The Dog beneath the Skin' and 'The Letter to Lord Byron'; and the same "banks of roses" appear in several places as an image of the wish for ease. In the 'Letter to Lord Byron', which forms chapter two of 'Letters from Iceland', Auden originally wrote:

> "And the traveller hopes: let me be far from any
> Physician; and the poets have names for the sea."

In transmission 'poets' became 'ports' by error; Auden was happy to leave it thus, finding the chance version more evocative. I mention this to stress the ease with which Auden writes, not to wag a pedantic finger over it. Dryden, too, confessed that a rhyme had often helped him to a thought.

Sometimes the ease becomes slackness, as in those almost automatic catalogues of clever images which possess little imaginative connection. This is not to object to a legitimate use of freely associating imagery but to an unselective use, and to verse which sounds like a collection of tags from a well-informed mind, as here:

"... the intolerable neural itch,
The exhaustion of weaning, the liar's quinsy."

The reader may be in danger of regarding as an extension of subtlety what is really carelessness disguised by technical skill. He may mistake an almost insolently smart incantation or a rhetorical flourish for the assured movement of a major poet. All this is most in evidence in the very early work; it is what tempted so many knowledgeable young men to imitate Auden without having his fundamental seriousness.

Auden, at least, is usually suggestive; he does see a connection, realise a nuance or note a revealing correspondence. But in these early poems he often writes too hastily; he may baffle his reader by changing his symbols abruptly, or produce an exercise in one mode when a little thought would have warned him of its unsuitability. He is so responsive to fragmentary experience that he finds it difficult to withdraw. He is today much more disciplined to withdrawal. Fifteen years ago, he says, he "rioted with irrelevance" and wrote much "pure rubbish", which he now regrets ever having conceived. He calls 'The Orators', "a fair notion fatally injured", one of that painful class of good ideas which "incompetence or impatience prevented from coming to much."

Before looking at Auden's much-discussed obscurity, it may be useful to recall some simple and general considerations on the subject. Firstly, then, we must distinguish between an unnecessary obscurity caused by the inefficiency of the author, in which the effort of disentanglement is not justified by the final reward, and, on the other hand, a necessary complexity arising from the nature of the experience to be expressed—to appreciate which the reader must be capable of feeling with a sensibility equal to that of the writer; i.e. we have to distinguish between a piece of string carelessly tangled and the same shaped into a complex but significant pattern. It follows that for literary communication of any value, we need an efficient reader as much as an efficient writer.

In Auden's verse one finds obscurity which arises from an unusual handling of language—from ellipsis (the omission of minor parts), oddnesses of construction, experiments with new forms and so on; obscurity caused by private references—mainly jokes; obscurity from carelessness and the desire to be fashionably difficult—e.g. the poems made up of fragments; obscurity from allusions not likely to be recognised by more than a handful of readers—e.g. references, not so much to Freud's work as to that of Groddeck, or the use of set phrases from psychology; and lastly, that obscurity which some readers find because they are unfamiliar with the experience expressed. It need hardly be said that several of these characteristics may appear in one poem.

Of carelessness something has already been said. Of that obscurity which is caused by the reader's failure to catch allusions we hope to speak later. There remain the oddnesses of construction, the extreme compression and the private references.

Auden's 'telegraphese' style—the epithet is, I think, Louis MacNeice's—is distinguished by its omission of articles, relatives, connectives, personal, demonstrative and other pronouns, and auxiliary verbs. It occurs predominantly in the early work and most evidently in the charade 'Paid on Both Sides'; but is to be found as late as 1935 in 'The Dog beneath the Skin', and recurs in 'The Age of Anxiety'. The very early work has a stark air, caused both by the ellipsis and by heavy debts to Anglo-Saxon and Icelandic verse. It grates badly except when very well-handled, and is likely to sound like nothing so much as the draft of an executive's report, jotted down by headings. If it avoids that, it may issue as a sort of muscle-bound mutter:

> "Can speak of trouble, pressure on men
> Born all the time, brought forward into light
> For warm dark moan."

It is the verse of a young man prepared to experiment widely with forms and manners of expression, but particularly suspicious of lushness, and anxious to evolve a hard, cerebral style: at its best it is taut, bare and cogent.

At its worst it may leave the reader feeling, among other things, that he does not belong to the right set; and so, to look farther than the very early elliptical verse, may the allusive asides and the oblique comments. Even the fact that periphrasis has a long literary ancestry does not justify lines like these; they are, in the bad sense, smart:

> ". . . the peace which that old man provided,
> Of the sobriquet of Tiger senilely vain."   (Of Clemenceau.)
> "the naughty life-forcer in the Norfolk jacket."   (Of Shaw.)
> ". . . the neat man
> To their East who ordered Gorki to be electrified."
>   (Of Lenin.)

And who were "the Bavarian cyclists"? and what was "Coghlan's coffin"? And what was the ordinary reader to make of the full parade of private references and group paraphernalia?— the boys' school and guerilla warfare props (sudden raids, frontiers, ambushes and treason, fortified farms and first elevens); the privately weighted symbols and the general air of a Boy Scout patrol. These were characteristic of all members of the group: in Auden himself they appeared in special form, and particularly in 'Paid on Both Sides' and 'The Orators'; there the group afflatus was from the leader himself, the head prefect, the cock of the patrol. It all intensifies our suspicion of occasional attitude-striking: we find, not so much a social, as an intellectual cliquishness, and a touch of moral heartiness. Auden was aware of the exclusiveness and its affectations, and of the obscure guilt from which it might have sprung:

> "Pardon the studied taste that could refuse
> The golf-house quick one, and the rector's tea:
>
> . . . .
>
> Yet answered promptly the no subtler lure
> To private joking in a panelled room.
> Pardon for these and every flabby fancy."

I do not know enough about psychology to attempt an explanation in its terms of this pervading sense of inadequacy in certain matters, or of the great interest in childhood and school. The reader feels it in the background of the early work of the whole group, as well as in contemporary prose writers such as Connolly, Isherwood and Upward. Why, for instance, were they all so interested in the apparatus of the spy story? How does one account for the whole setting of Edward Upward's 'Journey to the Border'?

In some degree the fondness for the climate of war arose from the sense of menace which all had in the 'thirties, from the sense of being in enemy country. Briefly, these poets felt that they did not properly belong, that in this century less than ever the poet is able to assume an audience or his own place in society. The impression of isolation from the stuff of society was acute, and so was the desire for reintegration:

> ". . . however far we've wandered
> Into our provinces of persecution
> Where our regrets accuse, we keep returning
> Back to the common faith from which we've all dissented,
> Back to the hands, the feet, the faces."

In "the destructive element" a small group of friends could be a useful centre. The scattered points of light, to use a favourite image of Auden's, might exchange frequent messages. Such an attitude can quickly degenerate into a pettish assertion of clique-values, but short of that it seems a legitimate reason for group solidarity. Helping to strengthen it was the members' very urge to reform. They wanted to challenge many of their society's guiding assumptions, but thought themselves in an important respect cut off. Their occasional perversity sometimes arose from the tension between these two poles of their thinking: their realisation of the vast indifference of society to the creative artist, and their great desire to change that society. And they did try to help, with earnestness and great expense of spirit. Whether the effort was wasted will be a later question. For the moment it will be sufficient to remember that the strain of "maps and chaps" on the not normally gregarious person can be great, and that therefore the occasional indulgence in clique-snobbery may be viewed with sympathy.

(3) *Self-awareness and Perception*

These poets, then, were all extremely aware of themselves in society and acutely self-conscious. They tried to be aware of their own historical and sociological position. They tried to assess and counteract the forces which had produced the isolation they felt. Their concern was not only philosophic—to analyse the culture in which they lived—but technical—to find effective methods of communicating that analysis. Of the best-known figures in the group, only Auden omitted to write a book explaining his poetic purposes: Spender wrote *Life and the Poet*, Day Lewis *A Hope for Poetry*, and MacNeice *Modern Poetry*; all wrote articles on the poet's place and purpose. Auden made his views clear in several articles and in personal statements scattered throughout his verse—in particular in 'Letters from Iceland'. Since the war the theme has become one of those he most frequently treats.

This awareness—especially of his own historical position and of his situation in a society towards which he has responsibilities—is possessed by Auden to an unusual degree. Informing it are an intelligence and an intuitive perception of exceptional keenness.

By intuitive perception I mean that quality, possessed by all in some measure but in particular by the creative writer, often very generally described as 'insight'. Auden has called it the power of the "naïve observer" as contrasted with that of the "learned observer", though the two are not mutually contradictory. Both methods of approaching experience, the intuitive and the objective, are valuable, nor can they really be separated. Some of the truths which Blake grasped intuitively were arrived at a hundred years later, and from a different route, by Freud. Auden holds the not uncommon view—his particular creditors are Blake and D. H. Lawrence—that since the Renaissance we have valued reason (in our sense of the word, not in the classical or medieval sense) at the expense of imagination, and so neglected an important manner of apprehending experience. For:

"In grasping the character of a society, as in judging the character of an individual, no documents, statistics, 'objective' measurements can ever compete with the single intuitive glance. Intuition may err, for though its judgment is, as Pascal said, only a question of good eyesight, it must be good, for the principles are subtle and numerous, and the omission of one principle leads to error; but documentation, which is useless unless it is complete, must err in a field where completeness is impossible."

It is this kind of perception which allows Auden to pass his eye over a situation, a web of relationships or a complex of emotional nuances, and select the typical feature, the important connection. One sees it particularly in the main choruses to 'The Dog beneath the Skin', and in the poems at the beginning

of 'Journey to a War'. Its lucidity is both exciting and liberating
to the reader, presumably because it sets some part of what has
previously seemed amorphous into a highly selective but
revealing pattern:

> "And nervous people who will never marry
> Live upon dividends in the old world cottages
> With an animal for friend and a volume of memoirs."

It is shrewd and pat; it makes a pithy comment about a
social feature—and it gains its power from the significance of
the selection, from the finding and fixing in communicable
form of a situation of great suggestiveness; that suggestiveness,
that symbolic quality, is hidden from most of us by the dis-
jointedness and incoherence of everyday life. Sociological and
psychological knowledge, though they may be useful here,
count for less than the ability to select the salient detail, the telling idiosyncrasy. Auden's perception is informed by an acute
and vigorous, though perhaps not profound, intelligence, as
well as by great pity and charity. It showed itself effectively as
early as 'Poems 1930' (see 'Watch any Day'), and is today as
sharp as ever, as Caliban's speech in 'The Sea and the Mirror',
and parts of 'The Age of Anxiety' demonstrate.

CHAPTER II

SETTING AND STANCE

(1) *Setting and Symbolic Landscape*

AUDEN'S scenery is either a backcloth against which some human situation is considered or a symbol for some activity of the psyche; in neither case is it regarded as of much interest in itself. Auden has no trace of anthropomorphism and could never draw a moral from the contemplation of nature in the way that Wordsworth did:

> "To me art's subject is the human clay,
> And landscape but the background to a torso."

He will spot the human addition to a natural scene, refer to his resources of information and make a terse comment. Louis MacNeice says: "He likes the human element. His favourite landscape is the Black Country." His first line on the Chinese port of Macao is typical: "A weed from Catholic Europe, it took root." When he mentions the pollen finding the pistil, he compares it to a burglar making an entry; and wild animals interest him chiefly as reminders, by contrast, of human guilt. There is the Auden view—the pervasive human interest and the comment informed by it. The title-poem of 'Look Stranger' is one of his few poems of natural description, and even there humanity's errands obtrude at the end.

Auden's geography, then, is always political or economic, the geography of the Prologue to 'Look Stranger', the opening chorus of 'The Dog beneath the Skin' and Poem 29 of 'Poems 1930', where the wealthy residents of the Sport Hotel are envisaged:

"... constellated at reserved tables
Supplied with feelings by an efficient band
Relayed elsewhere to farmers and their dogs
Sitting in kitchens in the stormy fens."

Auden is aware of the geographical pattern mainly as it rein-
forces his sociology. So, in 'Spain'—before reaching the poorer
final section—his glance traces this:

"On that arid square, that fragment nipped off from hot
Africa, soldered so crudely to inventive Europe,
On that tableland scored by rivers,
Our fever's menacing shapes are precise and alive."

This wide-ranging eye, this preoccupation with what is
happening in the fastnesses of Abyssinia or the ghettoes of
Poland, give him a width of allusion which most of his contemporaries lack. Whatever happens, he cannot forget that
he is implicated in the sickness of Western civilisation;
he must help where he can. And so he writes to Christopher
Isherwood from Iceland: "We are all too deeply involved with
Europe to be able, or even to wish, to escape. The truth is, we
are both only really happy living among lunatics."

Auden's particular settings, whether urban or natural, are
usually stark. He likes all places in which are shown with
special clarity the curious distortions of personality that a
mechanical civilisation produces, all places heavily engraved
with the tortuous manifestations of social activity—"My heart
has stamped on / The view from Birmingham to Wolverhampton"—and especially with that activity in decline, with "dis-
mantled washing-floors", "ramshackle engines", "disused fac-
tories, worked-out mines," "derelict ironworks on deserted
coasts", "tramlines and slagheaps, pieces of machinery".

His natural scenery is volcanic or glacial, the land of the
Icelandic sagas and of much Anglo-Saxon verse, the land of the
moraine and the glacial flood, a region whose barrenness is

broken only by rocks, the Northern Pennine country of his early fell-walking, the uplands.

Such regions are not usually backgrounds to human activity but symbols, translations of abstract ideas. His shorter metaphors are very often drawn from climate and environment, thus:

> "village of the heart";
> "map of desolation";
> "birth of a natural climate and of love";
> "noons of dryness";
> "our climate of silence and doubt";
> "The provinces of his body revolted,
> The squares of his mind were empty."

Sometimes the image is extended over a long passage or a whole poem, as for example in Part 3 of 'New Year Letter' and that fine poem 'In Praise of Limestone'. To turn abstractions into terms of an allegorical landscape seems indeed to be characteristic of Auden's mind. Conversely, a landscape can bring to mind, sharply and symbolically, some abstract comment on life or the psyche. Gonzalo, in 'The Sea and the Mirror', likens himself to:

> "Some ruined tower by the sea
> Whence boyhoods growing and afraid
> Learn a formula they need
> In solving their mortality."

The four characters in 'The Age of Anxiety' describe the seven ages of man predominantly in landscape-imagery, and the seven stages which follow are stages through various landscapes. One of Auden's favourite images, which he uses more than once in the 'Quest' sequence of sonnets, is of country children (innocence) being beckoned to make the journey to town (knowledge; sin). He refers frequently to the child's acceptance as one of the whole of its experience, natural objects along with human. In the wilder parts of Northumbria he first felt, he says, the urgent questionings which have never since been stilled. Those bare and wild uplands, yielding to a "green and civil life" below, symbolise man's original savagery and his "faulting into consciousness". On the way down, the lower outcrops and occasional relics of human activity represent his myths and art, his taming of nature and his failures, and his renounced techniques ("Their tramways overgrown with grass"). Always the main interest is in man's attempt not simply to tame a savage nature but to understand himself. So the abandoned mine-shafts signify this urge:

> ". . . that drives
> Us into knowledge all our lives,
> The far interior of our fate
> To civilise and to create,"

and to know,

> "Self and not-Self: Death and Dread."

Since the later 'thirties, the influence of Rilke has greatly strengthened and extended Auden's manipulation of abstractions through allegory:

> "One of the constant problems of the poet is how to express abstract ideas in concrete terms. . . . Rilke is almost the first poet since the seventeenth century to find a fresh solution . . . [he] thinks of the human in terms of the non-human, . . . one of [his] most characteristic devices is the expression of human life in terms of landscape. It is this kind of imagery which is beginning to appear in English poetry."

(2) *Objectivity and Optimism*

Auden's bare, upland regions provide a particular view of the world below, a panoramic view, the view of the hawk or the airman. He introduces these figures, whose recurrence has already been noted by Stephen Spender as early as 1930, when he talks of looking at society "as the hawk sees it or the helmeted airman", and begins another poem:

"From scars where kestrels hover
The leader looking over
Into the happy valley,
Orchard and curving river,
May turn away to see
The slow fastidious line
That disciplines the fell. . . ."

In 'The Orators' the important figure of the Airman sym-bolises the forces of release and liberation. Obvious charac-teristics are his position above, and slightly apart from, the situations he observes, and his ability to take a wide, bird's-eye view. He has a good command of the salient detail in the scene below him; he experiences that sense of control which comes from the ability to trace some pattern in the mess which, to those involved below, seems overwhelming.

The Airman, well-equipped with scientific knowledge and confident, makes a general survey and comes down to heal. There is something of the pedant about him; he intends to teach and reform; his moralist's eye sweeps widely, selecting the typical images he needs:

"Here on the cropped grass of the narrow ridge I stand,
A fathom of earth, alive in air,
Aloof as an admiral on the old rocks,
England below me:
Eastward across the Midland plains
An express is leaving for a sailor's country;
Westward is Wales."

The lushness of a Mediterranean climate would not be suit-able here: a northern setting is needed, the severe, strict region of "The slow fastidious line / That disciplines the fell". Clearly, discipline and strictness are particularly admired by Auden: he talks of "the strict beauty of locomotive", of a "strict and adult pen", and asks, in the dedication to 'Look Stranger', "What can truth treasure or heart bless, / But a narrow strictness?"

In one of his direct statements of purpose Auden said that a poet must preserve a "necessary impersonality". But that impersonality is not meant to narrow or restrict: its scope is as wide as Keats's "negative capability", although—and the difference is illuminating—it does not imply the immersion in sensuous experience which Keats required, and is meant always to be charged with active intelligence and purposiveness. For Auden the first step towards such an impersonality is submission to a discipline, the training of the mind to its task. Thus, whilst they were at Oxford he tried to dissuade Spender from attending concerts of classical music; such visits were a weakness, a falling away from the prescribed regimen. He has always suspected the formless overflow; he mistrusts the unpruned personality in a work of art and hates what has been called 'gutspinning'. The artist is the selector, the communicator, whose main pleasure comes from the selection and communication, not from the exposure of his fascinating dark subconscious. Spender says of Auden at Oxford: "Another word he often used was 'clinical'. The poet's attitude must be absolutely detached, like that of a surgeon or a scientist." So very few of Auden's poems betray personal emotions or fears. He has decided—helped by his natural bent—that he has no right to take up the time of his readers with his own heart-searchings. He rejects the conception of the poet as a tortured, self-centred neurotic: neurotic, perhaps, but one who cures himself by working out that neurosis in artistic creation, who makes himself as informed as possible, who is concerned with others and especially with others in society. He has therefore never been in danger, in his philosophic thinking, of solipsism.

One may appreciate the attitude better by comparing Auden's 'Musée des Beaux-Arts' with Spender's 'The Sad Standards' (sometimes called 'The Past Values'). Spender, reflecting that the standards implied in the work of the old masters startle us who live in a valueless age, makes his comment by concentrating on one incident, "the freshly dead young / Sprawled in the mud of battle"; he pours out his pity on them, and on their "dreams of girls":

> "Alas for the sad standards
> In the eyes of the old masters
> Sprouting through glaze of their pictures!"

It is wholly characteristic of Auden that what should seem to him admirable in Brueghel's 'Icarus' is that the painter has shown normal life going on steadily and unwittingly all around whilst Icarus falls. He comments appreciatively that it is this very contrast between the personal horror and the ceaseless, unknowing stream of life which gives to such an event its peculiar pathos:

> "About suffering they were never wrong,
> The Old Masters: how well they understood
> Its human position; how it takes place
> While someone else is eating or opening a window or just
> walking dully along."

Whereas Spender is terribly involved in it all, Auden watches with the disciplined artist's and notetaker's eye, to which "a stranger's quiet collapse in a noisy street is the beginning of much lively speculation". His vocabulary abounds in terms used with that care and fondness which a craftsman reserves for his more specialist tools. Wyndham Lewis, after a visit from Auden in the early 'thirties, noted the impersonality along with the virtuosity: "He is all ice and wooden-faced acrobatics."

There are, of course, some poems in which Auden is more personally involved. One thinks at once of his love lyrics. But even here the experience is usually related to its social setting:

> "Certainty, fidelity
> On the stroke of midnight pass
> Like vibrations of a bell,

And fashionable madmen raise
Their pedantic boring cry:
Every farthing of the cost,
All the dreaded cards foretell,
Shall be paid, but from this night
Not a whisper, not a thought,
Not a kiss nor look be lost."

So, though the poem tells of a night of love, the beauty of that night is made perilous by the poet's consciousness that it has been snatched from disorder, that it is one of the few 'wide', 'serene', 'tall' moments. It becomes, too, an earnest of what might be more generally possible if we learned to rid ourselves of our "narrow days".

These love-poems do not neglect the sensuous resources of language . . . the above quotation, for instance, evokes an atmosphere of calm, gentleness and joy asserting itself in spite of the knowledge of human frailty; but their appeal is also intellectual, to our minds as well as to our senses. And their sensuous appeal is mainly aural. In this respect a comparison of the styles of Auden and MacNeice, when they are dealing with roughly similar themes, is revealing. MacNeice's sensuous responses are particularly strong; he is acutely aware of sights, sounds, smells and tastes.

We have said that this objectivity (using the word in a different sense from that employed at the end of Chapter I) comes in part from Auden's position *above* the scene he describes, from his appearing to look *at* the object without being himself fully involved. It is the position of Ransom, the mountaineer in 'The Ascent of F.6'. Auden's work, therefore, has often the air of an aside, a comment on the text; one feels that he may be, in the last resort, a little cold. The hard brilliance suggests a failure of imagination at some important points. The impression is heightened by the fact that Auden's energy and technical skill have sometimes set him to write when he had little to say. If we recall a point made earlier—that his use of language is predominantly conceptual—we may understand why some of his verse seems brittle. And the fact that one tends to remember his work by odd lines and phrases rather than by whole 'experiences' of poems, supports this. The occasional lack of contact shows in, for example, Mr. and Mrs. A., the "ordinary people" of 'The Ascent of F.6'; it shows, too, in Auden's over-readiness to see by types, by his itch to label and classify "all types that can intrigue the writer's fancy". There is an unpleasant separation from the subject in that line.

On the other hand, we have evidence of Auden's warmth, friendliness and quick sympathies, not only from the record of his friends, but from occasional moving verses such as those on the simple pleasures of evenings at school:

> "Equal with colleagues in a ring
> I sit on each calm evening,
> Enchanted as the flowers
> The opening light draws out of hiding
> From leaves with all its dove-like pleading
> Its logic and its powers."

Yet Auden likes to feel that he is helping to put things in order. In his youth he was reputed to be harsh if he felt it necessary. Isherwood says he used to be afraid of Auden's hard, analytic and surgical comments on him. Spender, talking of the same brutality and of the kindness which informed it, says:" What to me was most terrifying was the way in which those like Gabriel Carritt, who knew him well, would say, 'Really, Auden is very kind and quite simple'."

He shares with the novelist an absorbed interest in the involutions of the human condition, in tangled motives and complex relationships; he has the novelist's eye for scenes made alive by the play of human conduct ("novel writing is a higher art than poetry altogether"). The most interesting subject for him is self-doubting man, suffering, the cause of suffering, and the bearer of a moral sense which drives him to question everything: "Yet we must kill and suffer and know why."

And though his view is often generalised, Auden delights also in the particulars of human activity. He likes even to be 'in the know', to be able to make the informed comment, reveal the eclectic interest, the racy angle. This probably accounts for some of his liking for Hardy; they share an interest in the apparently trivial—the telling gesture and the little give-away movement—and the ability to draw significance from it. The police-court-news side of 'Satires of Circumstance' would appeal strongly to Auden. The hotch-potch of notes to 'New Year Letter' shows that the interest has remained as strong as ever.

It is important to keep fluid in our assessment the apparently contradictory elements in Auden's character; to remember that his social interest, though detailed and often gossipy (again, how easily he could pick up the jargon of trades), is informed by wide and strong sympathies (although neurotics and psychotics with well-defined drives are of special interest). And although he may tend to look at people as types and with what occasionally seems a cold detachment, his concern is intense; he is not driven simply by a passionless curiosity.

He is, indeed, an incorrigible and energetic optimist, always setting off for frontiers or sailing for islands or heading for mountains. He is a positivist, calling out "Repent—Unite—Act", who never omits that third injunction. That spirit remains in the later work, not expressed so haphazardly as during the 'thirties but still powerful:

> "O once again let us set out
> Our faith well balanced by our doubt,
> Admitting every step we make
> Will certainly be a mistake,
> But still believing we can climb
> A little higher every time,
> And keep in order that we may
> Ascend the penitential way
> That forces our wills to be free,
> A reverent frivolity."

It may be that Auden's fondness for wide and spacious scenes, for broad uplands, for large and generous movement, is inspired by their suggestion of strength, absence of fear, assured action, a freedom which "solitary man sat weeping on a bench" has lost. In the "traffic of magnificent cloud / Moving without anxiety on open sky", he sees the power, the serene, unfussed, positive action of "the truly strong man". He uses, as commonly as 'strict', epithets such as 'wide', 'tall', 'generous', and, particularly, 'enormous'. They suggest the "spacious days" he hopes for.

Meanwhile, strict discipline is needed, objectivity, analysis. So Auden is at the simplest level of his work a social commentator. He adjured his friends to learn first to be good reporters: Geoffrey Grigson, expounding the early Auden æsthetic, says: "Report well; begin with objects and events."

(3) *The Preacher, and the Uncertainty of Tone*

Auden, then, is vigorous and constructive; he aims at a synthesis; he looks towards "the directed calm, the actual glory". But he has never thought social ambulance work sufficient. He is, finally, a moralist, concerned with the problem of human guilt. Of that his own guilt, the guilt of the comfortably reared Englishman, is only one form:

> "Nor ask what doubtful act allows
> Our freedom in this English house
> Our picnics in the sun."

The fact that Auden largely fails as a satirist, though not as an ironist, may be attributed to this insistent practical sense. He is so anxious to effect an improvement that he is disabled for the more violent kinds of satire.

He sees society as sick; not only as sick politically, so that she throws up such monstrous growths as Fascism, but as revealing, by these outward symptoms, an inner ailing. He insists on the need for both political and psychological healing;

he addresses himself to sick creatures of a sick society (he, too, is a sick creature). This special quality of the relationship between artist and audience determines the manner of most of his work.

Politically and economically, Auden might have said in the 'thirties, we move from slump to strike to war to slump and so on; psychologically we are assailed, with the help of scientifically applied mass-suggestion, by the creeping secret diseases of civilisation. We are a society of out-of-work and frustrated persons. More, we are without belief, without organic unity; we are "depressed in the vale of no faith". Our world is cold, inhibited, out of balance, all brain and no heart:

> "Never before was the intelligence so fertile;
> The heart more stunted: the human field become
> Hostile to brotherhood and feeling like a forest."

We should distinguish between Auden's concern for society and that of the writers usually associated with him. Like them, he is concerned at the disintegration of modern life; he lays more stress than they on the fact that that disintegration comes from an inner sickness which starts with the individual. As a result, he is on the whole less susceptible than his colleagues to vague idealised hopes.

It follows that Auden's field of action as a preacher is a two-fold one: political reform, through exposition and action—in common with some others he joined movements, attended committees and wrote an occasional "ephemeral pamphlet"; and psychotherapy, through the spreading of the findings of psychology and the awakening of a sense of its importance. For Auden the psychological reformer, as Louis MacNeice said, almost anything will become (a) an example or symbol of a neurosis demanding cure, or (b) an example or symbol of how a neurosis produces good (since Auden believed, in the middle 'thirties, that all progress is due to neurotic restlessness). For Auden, the political reformer, almost anything will be (a) a product of the enemy, of reaction, and therefore bad; or (*b*) a relic of the obsolete past, perhaps once good but now to be deplored; or (*c*) an earnest of better things, a pioneer of the future. This view is most crudely and, in parts, most brilliantly expressed in 'The Orators'. It derives partly from Blake's idea of the tension of contraries:

> "Without contraries is no progression. Attraction and Repulsion, Reason and Energy, Love and Hate, are Necessary to Human Existence. From these contraries spring what the religious call Good and Evil."

It probably derives also from Prinzhorn, a psychotherapist whose work Auden much admired.

If all progress is due to neurotic restlessness, the artist himself is a self-cured neurotic. His neurosis has been of the second type; it has produced good. (Readers of Freud will recognise a debt to the *New Introductory Lectures on Psycho-Analysis*.) Auden adds: "There must always be two kinds of art, escape art, for man needs escape as he needs food and deep sleep, and parable art, that art which shall teach men to unlearn hatred and learn love." That sentence is particularly interesting: it expresses both Auden's sense of responsibility and his urge to amuse; it uses the word 'love' in a special way; it suggests one reason for Auden's attempt to write popular verse.

Auden has subscribed to Wilfred Owen's statement: "All the poet can do today is to warn": he understands by 'warn' something very wide. His constant comment, analysis and assessment are informed by a sense of urgency, of crisis and of responsibility, by an anxiety to improve society:

> "We pray the power [for men of goodwill—R. H.]
>   to take upon themselves the guilt
> Of human action, though still as ready to confess
> The imperfections of what can and must be built,
> The wish and power to act, forgive, and bless."

So, deliberate and widespread preaching is essential. To realise that "kindness to ten persons" is not enough may cause us great "metaphysical distress", but is necessary. A mind of this sort is never likely to regard art as an end in itself.

But in talking of the moral ends of art, one presupposes the existence of an audience able to appreciate the manner in which art works. Each generation has to rediscover the nature and value of the artistic process. In literature, to be still axiomatic but more precise, each generation must think back to first principles if meaning and content are to be kept fresh and significant, and language to be revivified by being brought into fresh contact with meaning. In a period when art is widely disregarded, the artist's audience will be small, since it can consist, in the main, only of those who are out of sympathy with their society's prevailing attitudes. Auden may on occasion hopefully address himself to "writers and shopgirls"; but in the nature of the case, his shopgirl readers can be no more the average shopgirls than he can be Ethel M. Dell. And even to those who might have listened, nothing came over, in most cases. The gap hindering communication was not often bridged, and never on a large scale.

For here is a primary problem. The phenomena of modern life—the super-cinemas, the barnyard press and all the rest—are known to everyone. To the writer who is also a moralist they have a significance—as the symptoms of a profound disease—which he must strive to make clear to his audience, an audience which is itself implicated in the cancerous state of affairs. But most people have lost the habit of listening, indeed the ability to listen, to their parable writers. And too often the writer's convenient technical shorthand (e.g. political and psychological phraseology) will dismay even the best-intentioned amateur. So somehow the writer, spread-eagled between the two worlds, has to evolve understandable signals, has at the least to communicate with that small proportion from all grades of society which feels in some way as he does.

This state of affairs, Auden seems to have decided in the 'thirties, demands all kinds of adjustments from the writer who sets out to bridge the gap; it demands, for instance, that he learn something of sociology and psychology, the better to analyse with their tools; it demands that he be allusive, trying all the time to relate his knowledge to the dilemma which he is considering; it demands many adjustments in form and technique. I leave aside for the moment the question of the high cost to the writer of thus applying his gifts.

In all this we may find reasons for the varied and surprising tones of voice used in Auden's early verse. He wants to find and speak positively to an audience (all the more because he is reacting from the disillusionment common among writers in the 'twenties). But he is far from clear as to whom he is addressing himself: there may be several possible audiences, though they can scarcely be addressed all at once. This dubious relationship to his audience—and the technical decisions which were taken in an attempt to resolve these doubts—largely account for the inconsistency of his attack. One need only compare the confidence in the voice of, say, Jane Austen when she discusses her characters—the assurance with which she lays down her counters of communication, knowing that a large number of meanings are shared with her readers, that there is firm ground between them—to appreciate the case of the writer in this century. So Auden often wobbles from the ironic to the portentous ("In the hour of the Blue-Bird and the Bristol Bomber, / His thoughts are appropriate to the years of the penny-farthing: / He tosses at night who at noonday found no truth")—from the pally to the patronising, from the intellectual to the over-obvious, from the consciously rhetorical to the flatly idiomatic:

> "Creatures of air and darkness, from this hour
> Put and keep our friend in power.
> Let not the reckless heavenly riders
> Treat him and us as rank outsiders."

Sometimes it seems as though he cannot sustain an attitude to his audience for long; he is not sure how they are thinking: perhaps they have ceased to listen.

This kind of uncertainty can prevent a poet from singing freely about the things he finds worth praise: we affect cynicism towards those with whom our relationship is insecure; we enthuse with friends. It is true that Auden's irony is partly inspired by his perverse wit, by a wish to attack pomposity and pretension, and to debunk the grandeur raised on false assumptions, and the 'face' which hides a disinclination to examine one's own shortcomings. But he is ironic primarily because that manner is one of the most suitable, under present conditions, for verse of the kind he felt impelled to write. He learned something from Langland about the use of irony for commenting on a wide area of public and private life; he learned something from T. S. Eliot about the special uses of irony for the modern urban poet.

But irony is too oblique in its manner to satisfy Auden for long at a time; he usually has to change to a more direct approach, to find an outlet for his strong sense of purpose. Hence the assertiveness, alternately pleasing and annoying, the frequent exhortation and invocation, the talking at the reader (again, after the style of Langland), the rashes of imperatives and vocatives. Sometimes the attack may be sharp and invigorating:

> "What do you think of England,
>   This country of ours where no one is well?"

At other times it is the voice of doom—"The game is up for you and for the others"; "Know then, cousin, the major cause of our collapse"; or a magisterial laying-down of the law—"It is time for the destruction of error"; or a warning finger—"The dancers do not listen; but they will". At its worst it becomes drum-beating, button-holing, cheer-leading; it has something of the "I'm saved, are you?" air, the manner of the muscular moralist and ethical bruiser, the bright gusto of the gymnast of the psyche:

> "Drop those priggish ways for ever, stop behaving like a stone;
> Throw the bath-chairs right away and learn to leave yourselves
> alone.
> If we really want to live, we'd better start at once to try;
> If we don't, it doesn't matter, but we'd better start to die."

Certainly Auden does not allow himself to be carried away by such enthusiasm as swept some of his friends into dynamo-and-allotment imagery. But, though he may not hail new dawns quite as frequently as most, much of his political verse —in particular the earliest, and that contained in *New Signatures* (1932) and *New Country* (1933)—already has a strong period flavour. Both those anthologies, looked back at from across the war years, seem as dated as *The Yellow Book*, and the nostalgia which the reading of them can produce is probably similar to that which the earlier collection induced in our uncles. Part of the regret is for adolescence in a period when enemies seemed conveniently well-defined, and which had, behind all its excited denunciations, a sense of 'history on the move', a sense still of progress, and that through a fairly clear-cut struggle. The strangely complete confidence in some matters, the lack of further doubts about some areas of our life, the slogan-bandying and naïve red-flag-wagging seem comparatively prosperous in these more doubtful times. That all the best-known poets of the 'thirties feel this today is clear from their recent verse.

Auden could make play on occasion with the familiar properties of the progressive afflatus, e.g. with dawns and poets, both exploding; with frontiers, spies, airmen, power-stations; with floods, upthrusts, and any other abstract or concrete noun for a 'forward movement'. Often, after commending the force of his analysis, one is discouraged, as Mr. R. G. Leinhardt has pointed out, by an over-easy optimism. After the force of:

"The old gang to be forgotten in the spring
The hard bitch and the riding master. . . ."

he drops to: "the lolling bridegroom, beautiful there"; after
the acute detail of 'Sir, no man's enemy', he ends on a plea for:
"New styles of architecture, a change of heart". Similarly, in
the Prologue to 'Look Stranger', he rounds off some competent analysis with a vision of the future, driving: "For the vir-
gin roadsteads of our hearts an unwavering keel."

Many factors have led Auden to the soap-box and pulpit;
the sum of them may reduce, but does not entirely remove the
force of the assertion that he often, and particularly in his first
volume, hectors and nags, that the reader is too often given
strong propaganda in verse which is competent but careless.
But through it all, and driving him to these expedients, there
runs a deep concern and humility. That humility may be seen
—after all the various attitudes have been discarded—in the
whole manner of 'Sept. 1st, 1939'. Today the drumbeating has
almost disappeared; the irony remains, along with the more
direct verse whose object is to examine the nature of the truths
to which Auden now subscribes. And the concern will never
be lost, for:

"We are created from and with the world
To suffer with and from it day by day." (1946)

CHAPTER III

TECHNIQUE

AUDEN'S most immediately noteworthy characteristic as a craftsman is his consistent high efficiency. Much of his verse appears to have been written almost laconically, and yet has great surface brilliance. For example, the sonnet which dedicates 'Journey to a War' to E. M. Forster seems in some ways casual; yet it is neat, perceptive, informed; references to Forster's books are woven in smoothly and appositely; the technique is enormously assured. The same qualities are to be found in the occasional poem contributed to a symposium published for T. S. Eliot's sixtieth birthday. Or one may recall the skill in handling many different forms which is shown in 'The Sea and the Mirror' and 'For the Time Being', or the boldness of the title-poem to 'Look Stranger', which I take to be primarily an exercise in virtuosity, an attempt—in the tide's movement, the gull's flight, the ship's saunter—to marry movement and sound to mood and sense in an unusually direct way.

Or one may consider, as a particularly striking instance of Auden's technical versatility, his supple accommodation to the influence of Rilke, and especially his adaptation of Rilke's kind of sonnet, which he now seems able to produce with ease. A poem as early as 1935 has all the apparent marks of Rilke's influence ("Just as his dream foretold, he met them all: / The smiling grimy boy at the garage / Ran out before he blew his horn; . . ."). But it was the 'In Time of War' sequence in 'Journey to a War' (1939) which first showed a deep assimilation, and the influence was extended in the cameos of 'Another Time' (1940) and in the 'Quest' sequence of 'New Year Letter' (1941). There is the same clear symbolisation in landscape and incident of abstract problems otherwise difficult to express;

the same unheralded jump into the narrative which requires
the reader to pick up the legend as he goes along (e.g. Rilke:
"They sit and watch it playing at his feet / Half consciously...",
and Auden: "They wondered why the fruit had been forbidden / It taught them nothing new . . ."); there is the same
air of quiet control, the same unhurried and largely unrhetori-
cal assurance of tone, which comes mainly from having firm
symbols to manipulate. Thus Rilke, in 'The Unicorn' (not a
sonnet, but too valuable an example of Rilke's influence to
ignore):

> "And then the saint looked up, and in surprise
> The prayer fell back like a helmet from his head:
> For softly neared the ne'er accredited
> White creature, like a hind the unmerited
> Loss of her fawn lamenting with sad eyes.
>
> The ivory framework of the limbs so light
> Swayed like a balance delicately deflected,
> There glided through the coat a gleam of white,
> And on the forehead where the beams collected
> Like a tower in moonlight stood the horn so bright,
> With every footstep proudly re-erected.
>
> Its mouth was slightly open, and a trace
> Of white through the soft down of gray and rose,
> Whitest of all, the gleaming teeth described;
> Its nostrils snuffed the air and sought repose.
> The while its glances, keen, uncircumscribed,
> Projecting pictures into space,
> Brought a blue saga-cycle to a close."

And Auden:

> "They noticed that virginity was needed
> To trap the unicorn in every case,
> But not that, of those virgins who succeeded,
> A high percentage had an ugly face.

The hero was as daring as they thought him
But his peculiar boyhood missed them all;
The angel of a broken leg had taught him
The right precautions to avoid a fall.

So in presumption they set forth alone
On what, for them, was not compulsory:
And stuck half-way to settle in some cave
With desert lions to domesticity;

Or turned aside to be absurdly brave,
And met the ogre and were turned to stone."

Sometimes it seems as though Auden has become so skilled in this form during the last few years that he has produced it out of habit. Many of the examples have a suspiciously glossy finish. So have most of the derivatives, from Rilke through Auden, which now appear frequently in the reviews.

The same slick reliance on great facility is to be seen in the poems in memory of Yeats, Toller and Freud respectively, which are printed towards the end of 'Another Time'; each is in parts excellent, in parts perfunctory. And there is the over-working of certain favourite movements, such as the triple epithets or nouns:

"The friend, the rash, the enemy,"
"The enchanted, the world, the sad"
"The Soft, the Sweet, the Easily Accepted."
(there, too, are the capitals which Auden uses very readily)
"The Rich, the beautiful, the peculiar"
"The melting friend, the aqueduct, the flower";

and the pat ending on a line of two or three phrases:

"And watched the country kids arrive, and laughed."
"And plunged into the college quad, and broke."
"And wept, and grew enormous, and cried woe."

Most of these examples are from 'In Time of War' and 'The Quest', each of which shows the competence and the over-competence more clearly than any other group of poems.

(1) *Some General Characteristics: Associative Flow, Rhetorical Imagery, the Audenesque Simile*

Auden's use of everyday detail is not very different from that of other members of the 'pylon' school, although he does not reveal quite the same determination to drag it in at all costs. One should distinguish, for clarity, between items drawn from the surface phenomena of the times—the power-house, the dole-queue, the arterial road, the hiker, and, of course, the electric pylon; and those which are top-dressing to the mind of any informed contemporary—the death-wish, the dialectical struggle, the withering-away of the state, neuroses (various) and so on. As one might guess, Auden prefers the latter. But neither in this nor in the associative flow of the images are he or his colleagues innovators: in both Eliot had shown the way.

One reason for the use of associative flow helps to underline a recurrent sociological theme of this essay. The poet is trying to communicate, let us say, a mood of anger and pity at some aspect of the life around him. If he is fairly sure that he and his readers hold common moral standards and common linguistic counters, he will be able to make his statement firmly, using the accepted abstractions. Again, to refer back to an earlier illustration, consider the ease with which Jane Austen—writing for a comparatively small audience—can move into a scene big with "moral questions". It is scarcely possible to speak so confidently today. Since the breakdown of patronage, says Auden, the artist is an extreme case of the free individual, for whom society is open; but, he continues, "since art by its nature is a shared, a catholic, activity, he is the first to feel the consequences of a lack of common beliefs, and the first to seek a common basis for human unity".

One way in which the poet deals with this difficulty is to offer the reader a series of magic-lantern slides—"as if a magic-lantern threw the nerves in patterns on a screen"—each enshrining one aspect of the situation which has aroused this mood of anger and pity. Thereby he may, cumulatively, recreate and transmit his mood, although a direct moral comment drawn from it at the start might have been unacceptable. The slides are held up successively for the reader to feel their associated emotional charges; they affect one another by juxtaposition; they form parts of a suggestive whole and build up a subtle, complex mood. But they are presented one by one: "Look first upon this picture—now on this—and, again, on this"—(and then the general statement drawn from the whole) —"I am moved by fancies that are curled / Around these images and cling"—but there follows immediately: "Wipe your hand across your mouth, and laugh. . . ."

The example is taken from one of those early poems of T. S. Eliot in which he first showed in this century what the method might achieve. Nevill Coghill, Auden's tutor at Oxford, says that Auden announced one day that he had torn up all his poems because they were based on Wordsworth and that henceforth Eliot would be his model. He recited two new poems, of which Mr. Coghill says, "I was brought up to demand a logical as well as a sensual meaning in poetry, so his recitation was completely incomprehensible to me, though I was struck by some of the images that had a sudden but seemingly irrelevant force. . . . Auden explained with clarity and pity that to 'understand' a poem was not a logical process, but a receiving, as a unity, a pattern of co-ordinated images that had sprung from a free association of subconscious ideas, private to himself. He again recommended the works of Mr. Eliot." The results of that influence can be seen particularly in the images—by no means "private to himself" except in a few cases—in the poems of sociological reporting which appear in the 1930 volume and in 'Look Stranger'. Their use requires a keen eye for the significant image, since so much depends on the suggestive power and the ordering of the separate items. By using this method, Auden developed his naturally powerful selective eye and his ability to make 'objective' and epigrammatic social comment.

To say that Auden's expression is often dramatic is not to imply that he is a good dramatist, that, for instance, he can show character developing in action. It is to draw attention to his habitual transformation of his material into terms of 'dramatic gesture', to use G. S. Fraser's expression. It implies as well Auden's love of incantation—which he exercises in the last Hidden Chorus of 'The Ascent of F.6' and in 'O who can ever praise enough' in 'Letters from Iceland'; it implies the rhetorical swing we meet throughout the verse and also in the considerable body of declamatory prose.

Auden is addicted to the bold 'theatrical' flourish, the flourish of "the governess in the dead of night giving the universe nought for behaviour", and of Michael Ransom's "I thought I saw the raddled sick cheeks of the world light up at my approach as at the homecoming of an only son". It is a quality which helps to give his verse its characteristic vigour; when successful, the images condense, highlight and force the meaning on the reader's attention. Thus, in the fifth age of 'The Age of Anxiety', after a comparatively generalised contribution by Malin on the prosperous middle years of life, Emble suddenly gives freshness and contemporaneousness to his young man's sense of threat:

> "Why leave out the worst
> Pangs of youth? . . .
>
> . . . .
> . . . To be young means
> To be all on edge, to be kept waiting in
> A packed lounge for a Personal Call
> From Long Distance, for the low voice that
> Defines one's future."

47

This is a further aspect of that allegorised manipulation of abstractions which Rilke assisted. It provides another approach to the problem of communication with an audience to whom bare abstractions would be often meaningless or of various meanings. The result is sometimes strange, often brilliant, always forceful:

[Prospero is apostrophising the imaginative sympathy of the creative artist:]
". . . For all things
In your company, can be themselves: historic deeds
Drop their hauteur and speak of shabby childhoods
When all they longed for was to join in the gang of doubts
Who so tormented them; sullen diseases
Forget their dreadful appearance and make silly jokes;
Thick-headed goodness for once is not a bore.
No one but you had sufficient audacity and eyesight
To find those clearings where the shy humiliations
Gambol on sunny afternoons, the waterhole to which
The scarred rogue sorrow comes quietly in the small hours:
And no one but you is reliably informative on hell."

But the melodramatic is often substituted for the dramatic; the generous swing is merely aped by the journalistic sweep; we hear the dreadfully modernistic voice of the cosmic travelogue as "stars cool" and "the planets rush towards Lyra". This was most frequent in the mid-'thirties; it mars the last few stanzas of both the Prologue to 'Look Stranger' and 'Dover'. Or skittishness intervenes:

"Abruptly mounting her ramshackle wheel,
Fortune has pedalled furiously away."

"Fortune" is only one among a host of personified abstractions which haunt Auden's verse. He learnt something of their use from Langland, but would have arrived at it had he never read 'Piers Plowman'. He is, in fact, too easily tempted by this kind of allegory.

One special kind of simile is so much used by Auden as to be almost a mark of identification. At its best, as a simile should, it heightens the meaning of what is being said, e.g.:

> "Will Ferdinand be as fond of a Miranda
> Familiar as a stocking?"

> "Problems like relatives standing";

> "The sky is darkening like a stain."

And better:

> "From gradual ruin spreading like a stain";

> "They emptied out their memories like slops."

More frequently, it seems simply a matter of habit:

> "Fascinating like a tie";

> [of children's conspiracies] "weak like the vows of drunkards" and also "easy as a vow";

> "Here war is simple like a monument";

> "Observant like a beggar";

> "The cities hold his feeling like a fan";

> "Incapable of evil like a star";

becoming, on occasion, a bad habit:

> "Packed with meaning like a van";

> "Intrusive as a sill";

> "The winter holds them like the opera";

> "Desire like a police-dog is unfastened";

or a ridiculous one:

> "The poets exploding like bombs."

The common qualities are pungent conciseness and a start-ling contrast—a shock of surprise at the incongruity of the relationship called up. This is usually produced by mating the abstract with the concrete, the idea or quality with the strikingly contemporaneous visual image. The effect can be sharp and stimulating; in addition, it can easily sound rather desperate and bitter. It is probably this quality which particularly attracted writers in this century (the simile does occur in some earlier writers). T. S. Eliot has streets "that follow like a tedious argument"; E. V. Swart, in 'Casey Jones', has "vague as a bandage the infected go"; Graham Greene's *Ministry of Fear* begins: "There was something about a fair which . . . called him like innocence" (Auden might certainly have produced "innocence called him like a fair"). In the 'thirties the simile was over-used and echoed from one poet to another, mainly under Auden's influence. Spender has "intangible as a stock-exchange rumour", and Auden "impalpable as rumour"; Day Lewis has both "familiar as sunlight" ('A Time to Dance'), and "familiar as working-clothes" ('The Stand-To').

Auden is not so addicted to the technique today, though he still finds it useful, e.g. in 1947:

> "As a trombone the clerk will bravely
> Go oom-pah oom-pah to his minor grave."

One cannot regret the present economy; more than half of the similes scattered throughout the verse of the first dozen years might profitably have been omitted.

(2) *Conversational and Popular Metres : Myth and Epigram*

Auden's most characteristic manner is the conversational. He began early to hammer out for himself a supple and discursive style, capable of very wide variation. One may see the process beginning in such a poem as Poem 22 of 'Poems 1930' ("Get there if you can and see the land you once were proud to own"), and in the Prologue to 'The Orators'; some of its variations occur in such poems, otherwise very different, as 'Out on the lawn I lie in bed', the 'Letter to Lord Byron', 'New Year Letter', and the 'Quest' sonnets; some measure of the development in Auden's command may be obtained from a comparison of "Get there if you can . . ." with 'The Managers' (1948).

What one means to indicate by 'conversational' is largely a matter of the manipulation of speech rhythms to produce a distinct tone of voice in the verse, a tone which may be racy, persuasive, cool, dramatic, easy, unfussed and unhurried, but is always there. It is significant that much of Auden's later work reads better with an American intonation than with an English. Both the movement and the idiom of this ballad from 'The Sea and the Mirror', for example, are more American than English:

> "Sing first that green remote Cockagne
> Where whisky-rivers run,
> And every gorgeous number may
> Be laid by anyone."

To the development of the manner Langland, Skelton and some of the Middle English poets are the earliest contributors. Spenser and Dryden—"the master of the middle style"— helped, as did Hopkins' practice in the use of speech rhythms; Whitman, D. H. Lawrence and Wilfred Owen contributed something, and Eliot supplied the most contemporary models. For the more sophisticated variants of the style, Byron—"the master of the airy manner"—was the principal teacher; the Auden who believes that "chat" was an important function in life would be naturally attracted to the Byronic critical autobiography. The 'Letter to Lord Byron' is in a modified form of Byron's *ottava rima*. Auden has caught Byron's jauntiness and facetiousness; he uses similarly invocation, parenthesis, a wide, idiomatic and often superficial sweep, and the emphatic close on the final couplet.

Auden himself acknowledges a considerable debt to Yeats,

who, he says, "released regular stanzaic poetry from iambic
monotony . . ." (his experiments allowed) "freedom for the
most lucid speech with the formal base remaining audible";
later, discussing Yeats's 'In Memory of Major Robert Gregory',
Auden adds, "It never loses the personal note of a man speaking about his personal friends in a particular setting—and at
the same time the occasion and the characters acquire a symbolic public significance."

The verse which has resulted is flexible yet firm, and useful
in many ways. It takes wit well, and especially the occasional
ironic aside; it allows oblique comment in which two or three
lines sketch out a character or situation before the eye changes
direction; it can be an excellent form for knowledgeable
gossip:

> "I want a form that's large enough to swim in,
> And talk on any subject that I choose,
> From natural scenery to men and women
> Myself, the arts, the European news."

It may offer a useful mould for occasional subjects, as in 'The
Unknown Citizen'; or it may serve as a ground pattern to
support dramatic gesture:

> "Around them boomed the rhetoric of time,
> The smells and furniture of the known world
> Where Conscience worshipped an æsthetic order
> And what was unsuccessful was condemned;
> And, at the centre of its vast self-love,
> The emperor and his pleasures, dreading death."

It may be grave, friendly, unpretentious:

> "I sit in one of the dives
> On Fifty-Second Street
> Uncertain and afraid
> As the clever hopes expire
> Of a low dishonest decade:

Waves of anger and fear
Circulate over the bright
And darkened lands of the earth,
Obsessing our private lives."

It can, in short, suggest that direct conversation between reader and writer which Auden admired in Yeats. Since the matter of his verse, the prose meaning, is so important to Auden—he once used "memorable speech" as a definition of poetry—it was natural that he should set himself to acquire such a style. For a poet with his gifts and weaknesses the danger, which he has not altogether escaped, is that the conversational rhythm may sometimes degenerate into a sort of loosely regulated gossip.

Although his verse-rhythms are so often conversational, Auden frequently needs, in the longer poems and the verse-plays, the greater freedom which prose can give, and especially its licence to suspend a mass of detail from one small verb, or to be loosely discursive, or to build up to colloquial climaxes. He therefore favours the more baroque prose styles, those in which the lucid transmission of information is not the primary aim. He enjoys imitating the more declamatory manners, and does it skilfully, as in the 'Address for a Prize-Day' and the confidential girlish letter of 'The Orators', the high-powered shock-sermon in 'The Dog beneath the Skin', the radio topical talk and several other forms in 'The Ascent of F.6'. More interesting are such passages as Michael Ransom's soliloquy—at the opening of 'The Ascent of F.6', Herod's in 'For the Time Being', and Caliban's speech to the audience in 'The Sea and the Mirror'. It would be a mistake to say of Caliban's speech, for example—ah, just another prose pastiche; Henry James this time. Obviously, and for obvious reasons, Auden has closely modelled this particular passage on James; more importantly, it has the same general characteristics as Michael Ransom's and Herod's soliloquies, neither of which immediately suggests James, though both owe something to him. The manner is, like that of James, capable of bearing a heavy weight of material, of taking subtle strains and complex suggestion. In addition, it has almost invariably a touch of panache, an air of the theatre. Its origins may be found not simply in the demands of the material. They rest partly in the writer-to-audience relationship which has already been indicated; they rest, too, in the bent of Auden's character. When he is writing 'creatively', Auden is always something of an actor. His essayist's, critic's and lecturer's style is, comparatively, flat, rather too tightly packed, and unusually free from tonal variations. It is as if, once he is out of the 'creative' atmosphere, Auden loses his literary personality and remains erudite, intelligent and suggestive, but not very imaginative in his use of language.

To say that Auden wrote some popular verse is not to repeat in another way that his manner is often conversational. Verse in conversational rhythms is not necessarily popular; it may make considerable demands on the intelligence and sensibility of the reader; popular verse does not. Auden's exercises possess the traditional characteristics of all popular verse from the ballads to the contemporary jazz-song. Such verse is usually clear and easy to understand; it may be emotional, but is not emotionally subtle; it has a straightforward beat and progress, and makes much use of simple mnemonic and incantatory devices such as repetition, pronounced and regular rhythm, and a well-marked rhyme-scheme. It is assured, 'big-hearted', free and easy; it is out for a laugh ("Over the heather the wet wind blows / I've lice in my tunic and a cold in my nose"); it takes you by the ear with the 'I've got a horse' or the Casey Jones touch ('Come all you rounders, if you want to hear'); it is boisterous, slangy and abusive ("Beethameer, Beethameer, bully of Britain, / With your face as fat as a farmer's bum"); it banters, hectors or simply rollicks (as in 'It's farewell to the drawing-room's civilised cry'; Auden is not simply drum-beating in such cases—he is also writing in a traditional manner). The verse-forms vary greatly, although the common ballad stanza, rhyming *abcb*, with the established tropes is probably Auden's most common single form. Some poems restrict themselves to driving home one or perhaps two points, and there is often a moral, put over with either sentimentality or cynicism ('There's a moral to this story and the moral is this' is the classic close), a simple, 'human' moral, well 'plugged'. So Auden's 'James Honeyman' celebrates the inventor of a poison gas who brings about the death of his own family, and 'Victor', the nice young lad with a faithless wife whom he finally kills.

Auden has drawn freely on both English and American ballads, on nursery rhymes and doggerel, on modern popular songs and less-modern music-hall songs, and on Kipling. He has always been interested in what he would call 'light' verse, and has carried on a minor campaign to reawaken the taste for it. He thinks there is a place in the canon for verse which chiefly entertains and amuses ("the pious fable and the dirty story / Share in the total literary glory"), and once asserted that poetry;

> "If it doesn't start there,
> Ends at least, . . .
> In an attempt to entertain our friends."

He would perhaps not be so indulgent today; much of his light verse is loose, slipshod and juvenile, and he has omitted the larger part from his collected poems. But his taste, if it is not now as wide as *The Poet's Tongue* and *The Oxford Book of Light Verse* indicated, remains catholic. His competence, his touch of bravura and his sense of irony and fantasy ensure that he enjoys using the manner. He has written some excellent ballads, notably, 'O, what is that sound?' and the pastiche, 'O, where are you going?' The former catches the sense of wonder and horror peculiar to one type of ballad; the latter—the Epilogue to 'The Orators'—uses Anglo-Saxon alliteration and half-lines inside a nicely balanced stanzaic construction, and in its final stanza draws together the parallel threads of the simple moral: that the first positive step against frustration is not to give in to fear.

The most interesting examples—such as 'O, for doors to be open and an invite with gilded edges', and 'George, you old numero'—use the basic devices of the genre, but carry a weight of suggestion which a truly popular song dare not approach. Nor is the moral they so often point sufficiently generalised to command easy assent. The well-tried selling-tricks are there, but Auden is persistently warning and enlightening. His ballads may be loose, extended, dramatic, but they will also make a therapeutic comment on, say, some aspect of personal maladjustment. Thus, Poem 26 of 'Another Time' begins:

> "As I walked out one evening,
>   Walking down Bristol Street,
>   The crowds upon the pavement
>   Were fields of harvest wheat."

But includes:

> "In headache and in worry
>   Vaguely life leaks away,
>   And Time will have his fancy
>   Tomorrow or today."

And ends:

> "O stand, stand at the window
>   As the tears scald and start;
>   You shall love your crooked neighbour
>   With your crooked heart,
>
>   It was late, late in the evening,
>   The lovers they were gone;
>   The clocks had ceased their chiming
>   And the deep river ran on."

It has been suggested above that Auden and his contemporaries were trying to do something, in the 'thirties, to bridge the gap between them and their potential audience, and that their difficulty was increased because today the poets and the public use different languages:

> "The important thing to notice, though, is this:
> Each poet knew for whom he had to write,
> Because their life was still the same as his."

Thus Auden of the Augustans. A supporting statement in 'Letters from Iceland' asserts that the poet belongs to the whole of society, and is not, or should not be, a solitary antic condemned to a clique life: he has a duty to counter those forces which steadily push him into isolation. So most of Auden's friends practised in the same popular manner, though only Louis MacNeice approaches Auden in facility; his 'Bagpipe Music' is as good as any of Auden's light verse. Cecil Day Lewis, although some parts of 'Overtures to Death' are effective, cannot carry jocularity as comfortably as Auden. The late Michael Roberts, the most active publicist of the group, said, in the introduction to *New Signatures* (1932), that they were trying to create a "popular, elegant and contemporary art".

In common with the others, Auden here wants his work to reach places to which it would not normally penetrate. Thus 'Refugee Blues' 'plugs', in "buddy, can you spare a dime" fashion, the fate of the expatriate German Jew. Sometimes, too, the cheap, easy and trite forms are echoed so that the attitudes they embody may be the better exposed. Auden is trying to put the poet in place again, not only as an entertainer, but also—perhaps more importantly to him—as a widely accepted parable-maker; he wants to catch the ear of some who would not normally dream of reading poetry, and he will use almost any tried technique to succeed. He therefore employs, in addition to the popular verse properties already mentioned, approaches to which people today have shown themselves

particularly susceptible; e.g. the sporting reference and the
ready scientific allusion. He wants to remove as many 'literary'
hindrances to the making of contact as possible. He knows too
that wide contact is possible only at certain levels, that if he
makes too many demands he will not be read. Nevertheless, he
seems to have felt in the 'thirties, the times do not allow writers
of his kind to neglect any possible approach. The parable-
maker is a society's myth-maker. But in what condition are our
myths today?

By myth I mean a story or group of stories which is the
common property of a society, contains some general human
experience and implies an attitude to it. Thus, though the
properties of mythology change from age to age and from
culture to culture, its basic themes are constant—as a glance at
the recurrence of, say, the Grail legend in different societies
will show. The themes are constant because the main human
dilemmas do not change, though their presentation does; and
the attitudes taken towards those dilemmas vary within certain limits.

The writer of myth works by using figures and situations
whose suggestive force makes them bigger than themselves.
Most people may be unconscious of the exact nature of the
appeal being made to them; they none the less feel that the
pattern of the story means more than the series of incidents
composing it. The patterns suggest a possible order out of
what at first seems a formless mass. So the myth-making of the
creative writer can help to suggest some way of bringing together the disparate features of our experience. A mythology is
a collection of tales, socially and individually symbolic.

It follows that an existing mythology presents a writer with
a recognisable stock of images which he can manipulate symbolically for his readers, and that a live mythology will only be
found in a society with some cohesion. Equally, no matter
what condition a society may be in, those of its writers who are

not simply entertainers will always be trying, by the use of symbol, to create that relationship between them and their readers which a myth implies.

Literary myth helps, therefore, to give coherence to a society, and also reveals the character of that society. Healthy myths are only likely to exist in societies with some communal health; if the tradition shows sickness, that sickness will be the society's. It may be that in a society so large and specialised as ours such common legends are no longer possible. This seems to be Auden's opinion: he refers at one point to "the wounded myths that once made nations good", and later adds: "Myths are collective creations; they cease to appear when a society has become sufficiently differentiated for its individual members to have individual conceptions of their tasks."

Nevertheless, says Auden, the poet has a moral purpose, he is a maker of parables:

> "You cannot tell people what to do, you can only tell them parables; and that is what art really is, particular stories of particular people from which each, according to his immediate and peculiar needs, may draw his own conclusions."

But if it is true that, in the increasing complexity of our lives, we find it difficult to recognise any generally valid symbols, if, instead of a mythology, we have only a "tradition sick at heart", what can the poet do about it? If certain technical and administrative problems were solved, should we then be nearer recovering the tradition? In the 'thirties some thought so:

> "The solution of some too insistent problems may make it possible to write 'popular poetry' again; not by a deliberate patronising use of, say, music-hall material, but because the poet will find that he can best express his newly found attitude *in terms of a symbolism which happens to be of exceptionally wide validity.*"

I take it that Michael Roberts, from whose introduction to

'New Signatures' the above quotation comes (the italics are mine), was thinking chiefly of the results of solving certain political problems. It seems to me improbable—and I believe that Michael Roberts later came to think in this way—that political changes would do any more than restate, in another form, the central problem—that of large numbers of people living close together but with little sense of community and with their imaginative responses distorted.

We have already referred to some of the difficulties before of the moralist who tries to adapt genuinely popular forms. His efforts have little chance today of competing with that kind of song of which Auden made a direct parody in 'The Dance of Death':

> "You were a great Cunarder, I
> Was only a fishing smack,
> Once you passed across my bows
> And of course you did not look back."

Or with this actual example:

> "There comes a time when clouds must fade away,
> There comes a time when tears are laid away
> And there are rainbows over country lanes again
> And happy Bluebirds sing their gay refrains again.
> There may be times we have our cares, but then
> There is a tide in the affairs of men,
> And this old world will be in perfect rhyme
> Because there comes, there comes a time."

In the 'forties a group of younger poets have made synthetic attempts to create 'a modern mythology'. Auden would never have been likely to think such a thing possible. But he was undoubtedly in sympathy with the general aims expressed by Michael Roberts and others, and let them affect his verse. Today he writes little of this particular kind of popular verse. He has had to leave the field to *There comes a Time* and its counterparts.

Yet it would be a pretentious error to think that such productions give, in their crudity and tawdriness, an accurate idea of the nature of the lives of those who hum them. Our society has only the ghost of a mythology—one compounded largely of visually presented figures—the Little Man, Jane, Popeye and others. They are the pseudo-mythical figures of a society both specialised and uniform (all are separate and therefore all are united at least in their sense of loss and inadequacy); they are the parts of a pseudo-mythology of longings and yearning, which puts some landmarks into life, but suggests neither its true complexity nor any difficult moral demands.

In some degree our popular songs perform the same service, of course, but by no means so successfully. For several reasons, the song writers have much less confidence in their appeal than the cartoonists. That failure of spirit may seem a cause for hope to more serious versifiers, but is, in fact, further proof of their difficulties. It points to the fact that popular verse has lost even its unconscious hold (which visual figures still largely retain), and is regarded with a sort of affectionate cynicism, as something marginal, a harmless narcotic. Life, lived on the whole much more sensitively than such popular songs would lead one to expect, goes on elsewhere:

"What is real
About all of us is that each of us is waiting

. . . .

That is why you should not take our conversation
Too seriously, nor read too much into our songs."

There is today no correspondence between the good and the popular in literature. Robert Burns, says Auden:

"came from . . . a genuine community where the popular tradition in poetry had never been lost. In consequence Burns was able to write directly and easily about all aspects of life, the most serious as well as the most trivial. He is the last poet of whom this can be said."

61

In short, popular poetry cannot today be adult. Before it can be, a change will have to come, not only in society, but in society's attitude to verse. Thereafter common myths might once more emerge in our literature. Meanwhile, no poet can sing for a society, only for fragments of it. He may be glad that at least his audience is not from one class only, but from the concerned in all classes.

It may be possible to make a fairly wide appeal with cynical verse of the kind most often produced nowadays in the only real communities of our time—those of the services in time of war. Auden calls this kind of 'debunking' verse 'comic art':

"From now on the only popular art will be comic art . . . and this will be unpopular with the Management. . . . It is the law which it cannot alter which is the subject of all comic art. What is not comic will either be highbrow art or popular or official magic."

This is too pessimistic a view—'comic art' is essentially negative and popular art may be more than that—but it does underline the practical impossibility of creating myth today. A poet such as Auden appeals to those who have moved outside whatever there is of folk-life in their time, and turned to comment on that life. His appeal to them is the stronger because his imagination is diagnostic rather than descriptive. It is a proof of the difficulty of the situation and the inadequacy of 'comic art' to meet it that the more vivid of Auden's light poems often became simply the amusement of the minor intelligentsia, and the pert allusions to the death-wish and the withering away of the state corresponded for them to the variety comic's cracks at the nagging wife and the hire-purchase collector.

There is, then, a place for 'comic art', though not a central one. More importantly, certain aspects of the myth-making process are still open to the poet. Auden's practice shows that he knows this, in spite of such statements as the above. He knows, for instance, that he has to create symbols recognisable to his scattered anonymous audience, symbols which, by their force and suggestion, will help towards order, clarity and unity. Other aspects of myth will be less open to him, no matter how much he may want to use them. Thus Auden is attracted to ritual—"the acknowledgment that there are relations which are obligatory and independent of our personalities"—but cannot often use it. He employs it somewhat artificially in the plays and more successfully in 'For the Time Being'. But the audience who respond to the 'comic art' which he thinks so important today are not likely to have much taste for ritual and incantation. They *will* respond to telling symbols.

The most difficult task of the writer will be to find comprehensive symbolic patterns capable of embodying the major situations of the day. The problem is not peculiar to poets: Kafka tried to solve it in *The Trial* and *The Castle*. Auden's nearest approach to Kafka in this (and the connections in this case are numerous) is in the 'Quest' sequence of sonnets. He is examining there, in symbols, the extraordinary difficulty of finding the Way. Thus sonnet eight, dramatically and idiomatically, treats one aspect of the main theme, that of the special temptations in the path of the sensitive, intelligent man —how his intelligence and sense of concern set him industriously examining his experience, only to conclude that love and pity are false values; how he reacts reluctantly into pure egotism and acquires great power; and of the panic and emptiness inside. This is a sonnet which shows, not only the effort at some sort of myth and the great skill with which it is conducted, but also the faults which so often appear in Auden's sonnets modelled on Rilke:

> "He watched with all his organs of concern
> How princes walk, what wives and children say;
> Re-opened old graves in his heart to learn
> What laws the dead had died to disobey.

And came reluctantly to his conclusion:
'All the arm-chair philosophies are false;
To love another adds to the confusion;
The song of pity is the Devil's Waltz.'

And bowed to fate and was successful so
That soon he was the king of all the creatures:
Yet, shaking in an autumn nightmare, saw,

Approaching down a ruined corridor,
A figure with his own distorted features
That wept, and grew enormous, and cried Woe."

Most successfully this search for the beginnings of myth
caused Auden to develop his command of detailed, representative image. If a poet is to find symbols, he must have a wide
knowledge of the scattered phenomena of modern life, and
must make so careful and significant a selection that he is able
to elevate everyday items and particular instances into the
general and symptomatic. "The poet fetches / The images out
that hurt and connect": he must turn his concepts into images
of force and immediacy; the ordinary must be heightened and
shown to embody a way of life, a system of values. This kind
of writing predominates in Auden's verse from the beginning
of his work (the passage on excessive lovers of self in the
'Address for a Prize Day' from 'The Orators' is particularly
striking) to 'The Age of Anxiety'. Its development may be
traced in the recurrence of typical human figures—from the
'Insufficient units / Dangerous, easy, in furs", or "The old
gang to be forgotten in the spring "of 'Poems 1930', through
those "standing on these impoverished, constricting acres, /
The ladies and gentlemen apart, too much alone", and the
holiday-making city-dwellers who "play leap-frog, enter cafés,
wear / The tigerish blazer and the dove-like shoe" of 'Look
Stranger'. Or the variations of one image might be noted—
that for those who lead a closed, inhibited, tight and tidy life.

In the opening chorus to 'The Dog beneath the Skin' it appears as:

"And nervous people who will never marry
Live upon dividends in the old-world cottages
With an animal for friend and a volume of memoirs."

The chorus to scene 5 mentions:

"Those whose houses are dustless and full of Ming vases."

More than ten years later the image recurs, not so vividly, in the euphoria scene of 'The Age of Anxiety':

"Lesser lives retire on their savings,
Their small deposits of starches and nuts."

The figures are not equally successful, but they are all symbolic.

To write in this way, then, requires the poet to find what Mr. Eliot has called "the objective correlative", and to fix it in concise and pithy phrases. The pungent, compressed phrasing encourages what may be called the "sociological or psychological epigram". This manner, which produces so much 'memorable speech', in phrases if not in whole poems—one does not forget "the sallow oval faces of the city", or "the tigerish blazer and the dove-like shoe"—probably did as much as any other quality to give Auden his public in the 'thirties. It may be seen at its fullest in 'August for the People', but had appeared earlier in poems like 'It was Easter as I walked in the public gardens'; it developed along with the power of finding apt symbols, and is, indeed, a part of that process.

The epigrammatic manner applied to individuals reached its peak in 'Another Time', where are collected poems on Pascal, Voltaire, Arnold, Lear, Housman, Rimbaud and others. In these individual cameos the figures are not dramatic in the sense that Eliot's 'Prufrock' is. They are not called up in appearance, movement and speech: Auden is primarily concerned to examine the psychological make-up of his characters; he analyses them, and comments, but does not describe; he is conceptual, not dramatic; analytic, not narrative. So he often writes of general types—'The Composer', 'The Novelist'—rather than of particular people.

The bold selection and succinctness of these poems bring them close to good caricature (Auden's favourite type of picture). Of Housman he says:

> "Deliberately he chose the dry-as-dust
> Kept tears like dirty postcards in a drawer;
> (Food was his public love; his private lust
> Something to do with violence and the poor)."

Before long he could produce this verse with little apparent effort, and always with a high degree of competence.

'Another Time' has a section entitled 'People and Places': it might have been called simply 'People', since all the places —hence their interest for Auden—are remarkable for their human associations. These poems give a good introduction to the epigrammatic manner used sociologically. 'Dover' is one of the best; in its fifty lines Auden touches on a wide number of related themes. For Dover is a place of special significance; it is both an end and a beginning. It is the last point in the territory of "the old gang to be forgotten in the spring", and echoes their seediness and hollow pretension; it is also the point from which the migrants set out for new countries. So Auden comments on the condition of Europe and England's relation to it; he mentions the character of frontier towns, and the psychology of migrants (he has always been attracted to the 'wanderer' theme), and makes subsidiary allusions to the social function of the soldiery and the economy of England; and he talks, as so often, about the attraction of the childhood dream and about the 'lonelies', the frightened souls behind the façades, the sea of personal unhappiness and misery . . . "each one prays in the dusk for himself".

TECHNIQUE

That 'Dover' manages to handle so much matter in so little space is due to its clean outlining of sharply perceived detail, the picking out from above of the significant fact from the ordinary—the soldiers' pub manners, the seaside-cum-port-cum-county-town architecture—the interplay of allusion, and the dry ironic strokes of the statements:

"Steep roads, a tunnel through the downs, are the approaches;
A ruined pharos overlooks a constructed bay;
The sea-front is almost elegant; all this show
Has, somewhere inland, a vague and dirty root:
                    Nothing is made in this town.

. . . .

Here live the experts on what the soldiers want
                    And who the travellers are,

Whom the ships carry in and out between the lighthouses
That guard for ever the made privacy of this bay
Like twin stone dogs opposed on a gentleman's gate;
Within these breakwaters English is spoken;
                    without
Is the immense improbable atlas.

. . . .

And the old town with its keep and its Georgian houses
Has built its routine on these unusual moments;
The vows, the tears, the slight emotional signals
Are here eternal and unremarkable gestures
                    Like ploughing or soldiers' songs.

. . . .

And the cry of the gulls at dawn is sad like work:
The soldier guards the traveller who pays for the soldier;
Each one prays in the dusk for himself and neither
Controls the years. Some are temporary heroes:
                    Some of these people are happy."

There are few obscurities once the reader is accustomed to the pithy item-by-item detail and comment, and to the concentration of the epithets. It is a pity that two of the later stanzas are slack: in each Auden makes grandiose gestures:

"The tides warn bronzing bathers of a cooling star";

and:

"High over France, the full moon, cool and exciting,
Like one of those dangerous flatterers one meets and loves."

But 'Dover' recovers in the last verse (quoted above), and ends, as it has been for most of its length, suggestive, rooted in its period, epigrammatic and stimulating verse.

Both the fact that the contemporary atmosphere is favourable to this kind of writing, and the existence of certain tendencies in Auden's character, make him often over-use or misuse it. He sometimes offers as a significant symbol what is really a private reference, or gives a high epigrammatic finish to what does not warrant it. Or the highlighting becomes routine: so Yeats's death takes place on "an afternoon of nurses and rumours". The polish glitters too much, especially in some of the psychological cameos. We turn away from the fixing of a character by one obsession or in one line, from Matthew Arnold explained by his father, Pascal by his mother, from Lear as "a dirty landscape painter who hated his nose", and Rimbaud summed up in "the cold had made a poet"; we consign much of this to the part of the mind which is tickled but put on its guard by the 'New Yorker' profiles.

For the form is almost too accommodating; the favourite tricks are too often repeated. There is, for instance, the over-indulgence in that primary resource of the epigrammatist, the see-saw line, with its balancing nouns and epithets:

"The expansive moments of constricted lives."
"The frantic washing of the grimy fact."
"The simple act of the confused will."
"The glib justification of the sorry act."

All these lines illustrate another characteristic—not peculiar to Auden's verse but very common there—which G. Rostrevor Hamilton, I think a little harshly, has examined. That is the special use of the definite article. T. S. Eliot uses it freely:

> "The distraction fit, lost in a shaft of sunlight,
> The wild thyme unseen, or the winter lightning
> Or the waterfall. . . ."   (*The Dry Salvages.*)

And:

> "There is a time for the evening under starlight,
> A time for the evening under lamplight
> (The evening with the photograph album)."
>   (*East Coker.*)

Auden's use has shown itself incidentally in several previous quotations. Sometimes he builds up a catalogue:

> "The boarding-house food, the boarding-house faces,
> The rain-spoilt picnics in the windswept places,
> The camera lost and the suspicion,
> The failure in the putting competition,
> The silly performance on the pier. . . ."

A kind of knowingness between writer and reader can be implied; this is not just 'a' certain and particular camera lost, it seems to say—it is 'the' camera which is any lost camera and yet all cameras lost in such circumstances, to those of us who have the eye for such significances. So flattering and yet narcotic is the catalogue that the reader may accept some items which have no particular import. But this is to say that the method must be used with restraint, as Auden often and Eliot almost always does. In Auden's case, even the group feeling which can be induced, suspect though it may sometimes be, is partly inspired by the wish to create a community in some things—in analysis if not in affirmation.

But Auden rarely fails to be acute and penetrating at some

point. Whatever may be the contemporary circumstances prompting his use of the method, he has a natural inclination towards it. Stephen Spender says of him:

> "Auden has always had to a remarkable degree this capacity to think of everything and everyone as a cipher within a pattern which he has invented to explain life in his own mind. He also has a remarkable gift for inventing the most inclusive imagery to explain how the different factors round him fit into the general pattern which he sees so clearly."

In less competent hands the style becomes glib. It would not be useful to look at the efforts of those who imitated Auden's use of this idiom to the point of banality. There is more value in a glance at the work of some who are competent poets in their own right. 'This too I saw', from 'A Time to Dance', is one of several successful poems of the kind by Cecil Day Lewis. A comparison of Auden's 'Spain' with Spender's 'Vienna' gives a good idea of Auden's greater objectivity and power of selection, as well as of Spender's sensitivity. Louis MacNeice, though his impact is not as sure, and though there is a lot of "slack" in his verse, is often effective:

> "Old faces frosted with powder and choked in furs.
> The jut-lipped farmer gazing over the hump-backed wall.
> The commercial traveller joking in the urinal.
>
> . . . .
>
> The country gentry cannot change, they will die in their shoes
> From angry circumstance and moral self-abuse,
> Dying with a paltry fizzle they will prove their lives to be
> An ever-diluted drug, a spiritual tautology."

MacNeice shares Auden's love of the idiomatic, but has not the same degree of isolation; he mixes more easily, is fonder of personal sentiment; nor is he so much concerned about social reform, and he is too sophisticated to be a tub-thumper. He is

—and this most nearly explains why he has not the same clarity of outline as Auden—more sensuous and less clinical:

"They are cutting down the trees on Primrose Hill
    The wood is white like the roast flesh of chicken
    Each tree falling like a closing fan."

Thus MacNeice on the coming of war; Auden would probably have produced, instead of the two sensuous images, an epigram or two containing several generalised adjectives—a series of comments initiated by the tree-cutting incident; intellectual pronouncements rather than sensuous images. His epigrammatic manner allows him to present forcefully the *ideas* which a wide range of social and individual detail inspires in him.

(3) *The Plays, with Christopher Isherwood*

The three plays which Auden wrote in collaboration with Christopher Isherwood may be most usefully regarded as another part of his effort to gain a wider audience. The drama is the most communal literary form, and Auden turned to it at roughly the same time and, in part, for the same reasons as T. S. Eliot. Auden's main aim was to present dramatically issues which he thought important, and to make his audience feel the need to reach decisions, to admit themselves committed.

The plays were written specifically for Mr. Rupert Doone's Group Theatre, which was at the time experimenting with verse drama. In each, one or both of two fictitious European countries (Ostnia and Westland) figure; in each, prose alternates with verse often routine but occasionally good (e.g. the dirge for Lamp in 'The Ascent of F.6', beginning "Death like his is right and splendid"); each play uses choruses, derived distantly from the Greek tragic choruses, to define a background, a contrast or a moral; each of them is very topical and makes wide use of political and psychological knowledge, much of it commonplace; most of the characters are from stock; the enemies in particular are Aunt Sallies, easily knocked over because too easily conceived.

All the characters except Michael Ransom have the flatness and jerkiness of figures in animated cartoons. In 'The Dog beneath the Skin' the chief character, Alan, is a catalyst, a guide through events, a lay-figure to whom things happen. We do learn something of what is going on inside Michael Ransom, but he is not conceived in the round; he represents motive in action, the fight with the will; he is the embodiment of an internal struggle. One cannot be moved by the plight of any of these people as people; one is not, in that sense, involved.

Even if Auden wished to 'create character' in the usually accepted sense, it is doubtful whether he could. We have already suggested that he has an eye for critical gesture, that his imagination is in that way dramatic. But his analysing and abstracting quality ensures that, though he may see his figures in terms of significant actions, he is not able to let them develop in and through those actions: he presents them as abstractions from the beginning, and marshals them to illustrate his moral.

But it is probable that Auden does not aim at creating character, except perhaps with Michael Ransom, and that for personal reasons. He is trying to construct a theatrical form which will present certain problems vividly, and will quickly and sharply engage the attention of the audience. The English commercial theatre at the time could offer no models, but some of the experimental work going on here and in Germany indicated possible methods. Eliot's 'Sweeney Agonistes' suggested certain lines of work, and 'The Rock' and 'Murder in the Cathedral' were to suggest more. There was some vigour in what remained of the old idiomatic music-hall and variety tradition, and the cinema employed other possible techniques, notably the use of quick cuts from scene to scene, and associative linkage. Much farther back, the old morality plays could be drawn upon. 'Paid on Both Sides' (1928), with its alternating prose and verse, its stichomythia, chorus and startling interruptions, was an unsatisfactory first essay: 'The Dance of Death' looks forward more plainly to 'The Dog beneath the Skin', especially in its borrowings from music-hall and cabaret.

Auden's debt to the German experimental stage is probably most important of all. He almost certainly saw something of that stage during his stay in Germany just before 1930, as no doubt did Christopher Isherwood. Mr. Eric Bentley's book, *The Modern Theatre*, has some useful passages on German experimental drama. A comparison of the characteristics he describes with those of Auden's three plays suggests that, though Auden learned something from German expressionism of the 1920s (especially from its attempt to "work by lyricism and musical counterpoint", to be "an expression of the unconscious, dream world", and in its trick staging), his primary model was the German 'epic drama', whose leading exponent was Bertolt Brecht. Mr. Bentley goes so far as to call Auden's plays "imitations of Bertolt Brecht". To indicate the aims of 'epic theatre' as distinct from those of what he called 'dramatic theatre', Bertolt Brecht drew up this comparative table:

"*The Dramatic Theatre*	*The Epic Theatre*
The stage embodies a sequence of events	The stage narrates the sequence
involves the spectator in an action, and	makes him an observer but
uses up his energy, his will to action	awakes his energy
allows him feelings	demands decisions
communicates experiences	communicates pieces of knowledge
the spectator is brought into an action	is placed in front of an argument
is plied with suggestion	with arguments

sensations are presented	till they become insights
man is given as a known quantity	man an object of investigation
tense interest in the outcome	tense interest in what happens
one scene exists for another	each scene exists for itself
linear course of events	curved course of events
natura non facit saltus	facit saltus
the world is what it is	the world is what it is becoming
what man should	what man must
his instincts	his reasons
thought determines reality.	social reality determines thought."

So these are 'external' plays; they are purposive; they throw their beams outward, and invite action. The spectator is not required to submit himself imaginatively to the story, nor to identify himself internally with the characters. The emotions may be touched, but the mind should remain in command, stimulated, commenting, judging, criticising, deciding. The personality as a whole is not engaged or given up; there is no "willing suspension of disbelief".

The plays offer only a limited satisfaction, because even the tenets of 'epic theatre' do not allow Auden the kind of scope his mind requires. But in the 'thirties they were exciting to see; they were often amusing, and were at least attempting something, even though much of their energy was only superficially dazzling. Today, since they are unlikely to be seen on the stage, they offer a reader some invigorating verse, and some of the best contemporary illustrations of attitudes in the 'thirties. Their importance in the history of the modern theatre is negligible: they are sports—by German experiments and T. S. Eliot out of the political excitement of the time. In the body of Auden's work they may best be placed, we have suggested, with his more popular and purposive writing. No doubt Auden was interested in the technical challenge; no doubt he was glad of the scope for amusing games; chiefly he aimed at attracting and stimulating what he thought of as a growing audience. One could not argue that 'The Age of Anxiety' has a successful form, but its structure represents, at all events, one more attempt to solve the same problem which prompted these plays—how he could, with his abstracting mind, his power over dramatic image, and his sense of moral purpose, present a lengthy and arresting commentary on the contemporary situation. That 'The Age of Anxiety' is so much more difficult than the plays is not altogether due to Auden's perversity, or to a refusal any longer to grapple with the business of communication.

'The Dog beneath the Skin'

'The Dog beneath the Skin' is a boisterous and lively play, sometimes witty, often careless and boyish. It is a period-piece, attacking rather obviously the abuses of the time; it has not, and is not intended to have, any characters, nor any relationships between characters; the action does not develop, but, in Brecht's terms, "each scene exists for itself", and the course of events is curved. Alan, the central figure, sets out from home is caught up in several allegorical incidents, and comes back. The scenes are presented in the manner of a revue, boldly, at high speed, and with theme songs.

Sir Francis Crewe, the heir of the squire of Pressan Ambo, is missing, and each year one local youth sets out to find him. So far seven have failed to return. At a large meeting in the garden of Pressan Vicarage, Alan Norman, a well-meaning lad, is chosen as the eighth seeker. If he succeeds he will receive half the Crewe land and the hand of Iris Crewe, the only daughter. This and the final one are the only two scenes set in England; in it the figures of middle-class 'county' and rural England present themselves in Gilbert and Sullivan metres; they are one group of the 'enemy's' agents, the minions of "the genteel dragon"—the army, the Church, the landed gentry.

As Alan leaves with a stray dog he has called Francis, the chorus, which has introduced the first scene with a long social commentary, takes up that theme again. Throughout, the charade-like incidents and the choruses' commentaries alternate. The main choruses—although this is not a rigid classification—are long, full of social reference and direct:

"Follow our hero and his escort on his latest journey:
From the squares surrounded by Georgian houses, take the
    lurching tram eastward
South of the ship-cranes, of the Slythe canal."

The semi-choruses are in a different manner: they aim at incantation; they make an oblique comment on the action rather than direct statements about it:

"Enter with him
These legends, love,
For him assume
Each diverse form
As legend simple
As legend queer. . . ."

Crossing the Channel, Alan falls in with two abysmally cynical journalists who make the expected comments on the Press as a provider of fake but politically useful dope. The three reach Ostnia, a reactionary bourgeois country with a despotic monarchy—a kind of society still to be found in Europe a dozen years ago—just in time for one of the regular mass political executions. Thence Alan goes to the capital's Red Lamp Street, intent on his search for Francis: there he meets one of his own predecessors, Sorbo Lamb, now a confirmed drug addict. Sorbo has been sufficiently exceptional to break away from the life at home—only to fall into new false attitudes; he has exchanged one form of rigidity for another. So, more heroically, has Chimp Eagle, whom Alan meets later in the operating theatre of Paradise Park. Chimp has imagined that release could come simply from external political action; he has not seen deeply enough.

Westland's lunatic asylum, from which Alan is rescued by the journalists, symbolises the insanities of the fascist state, its hysteria, its denial of the personality, its cult of the leader, its race theories, its views of woman's province. As they leave there by train Alan meets Grabstein, a caricature of international capitalism, and here, as in other similar situations, the expected comments are made.

Paradise Park is appropriately introduced by a parody of a popular song. In it Alan sees various forms of escape from life—the æsthetic escape into 'art for art's sake'; the escape into love as a womb for two; the escape into hypochondria. After an interlude on the road, Alan reaches the Nineveh Hotel, with its five hundred bedrooms, three hundred bathrooms and three hundred and seventy-five w.c.'s, the type of all that is vulgar and brassy in megalopolitan culture. The cabaret scene, a skit on the fun-and-games of tired businessmen, is typically witty in parts, but on the whole obvious, e.g. a diner selects his own chorus-girl by pinching her leg as though she were a fowl. But the hostility of the highbrow-hating Destructive Desmond, his brutal assertion of the authority of the lowest common denominator in taste, is one of the few really effective pieces of satire in the play. Desmond is the new barbarian, the angrily baying vulgarian, furious at the discriminating, insistent that democracy means, not merely freedom to be a brute, but to admit no other standard. So values disappear under the necessity for conformity; so Destructive Desmond slashes a Rembrandt in a storm of rage and fear.

Near the end of his wanderings Alan is rescued from an affair with a cabaret-star by the dog, who now reveals himself as Francis, the long-lost heir. Until Alan set out to find him, Francis never left Pressan, but lived there in an unrecognisable shape, disgusted with all his new angle of vision showed him.

The implication is presumably that an essential stage in the growth to maturity is the realisation of the falsities of one's own society, and that in the process one becomes a changed person, a stranger in the midst, whom one's relatives feel they no longer recognise ("I don't know what's come over ——. He doesn't seem the same boy nowadays"). Francis's roots are up; he is "the truly strong man" who has made the decisive break. Alan too, it is implied, has been on a journey of discovery, a journey towards greater honesty through the experiencing of various forms of deception, and Francis welcomes him as a recruit for the new order—surprisingly, since Alan's reactions to events have been more those of the lamb than of the strong man. Together they set off for Pressan again.

In Pressan another celebration is on foot, opened by a vigorous, apocalyptic, nervous and rhetorical sermon on sin, of which Auden thinks highly enough to include it in his collected works. Into all this Francis is able to burst with thoroughly enjoyable denunciations, and thereafter there is much changing of sides, with "the old gang to be forgotten in the spring" breathing indignation, and some of the young defaulting into self-imposed exile with Alan. As they leave, the old gang turn into suitable animals and the chorus and semi-chorus invoke the vision of a country where:

> ". . . grace may grow outward and be given praise
> Beauty and virtue be vivid there.
>
> .   .   .   .
>
> And lovers by themselves forgiven
> The whole dream genuine, the charm mature
> Walk in the great and general light
> In their delight a part of heaven
> Its furniture and choir.
>
> To each his need: from each his power."

This is Auden's characteristic 'Love' again, allied to his leftism—a lyrical but vague coda to a slap-happy knocking-down of many old guys. But one cannot read 'The Dog beneath the Skin' for its message: one reads it for some good scattered verses, for some of the chorus's commentaries, for an occasional good parody and for the astonishing sermon.

'The Ascent of F.6'

'The Ascent of F.6', chiefly because it has a stronger central thread, is more worth study than either 'The Dog beneath the Skin' or 'On the Frontier'. One of the scenes—that between Ransom and the Abbot—has a force not approached in either of the other plays. There is the usual alternation of prose and verse, this time with some attempt at heightening the tension by moving into verse at moments of crisis—as when Ransom and his mother address one another in blank verse (actually, unimpressive), or when Ransom, on F.6, railing at the blizzard, echoes Lear confronting the storm; there are some incantatory passages and some striking dramatic gestures ("I have found a spider in the opulent boardroom. / I have dreamed of a threadbare barnstorming actor, / And he was a national symbol"); and there are some parodies of popular and cabaret songs, mainly by Gunn, though the best—"At last the secret is out"—is from the chorus.

In general, 'The Ascent of F.6' is not as careless as the other two plays. Its construction is tighter: after some simplified assaults on such things as the unscrupulous Press, the technique of sensation, imperialism and threadbare public-speaking, have been cleared out of the way, it concentrates on one main theme—the climbing of the mountain and its significance for Michael Ransom.

Ransom is a scholar and ascetic, sensitive and yet a man of action, whose greatest enthusiasm is mountain climbing. He is finally persuaded by his mother, after his statesman brother James and others have failed to move him, to lead an assault on F.6. The Ostnians are also preparing a party with the same object, since the natives of the region, which both countries want, believe that the first white man to conquer F.6 will rule them for a thousand years. By the time F.6 is finally climbed, three of Ransom's friends—Lamp, Shawcross and Gunn—have lost their lives. Just before the first death and in the very middle of the climb, Ransom has his interview with the Abbot, in which his dilemma is discussed at length but still not fully faced.

The dilemma arises from the realisation, by a man of exceptional gifts, that corruption seems inevitably to follow from the use of power, that the will is usually impure, but that to react therefrom into isolation may be itself another form of sin. By virtue of his qualities Ransom is potentially a man of power, and knows this; he is, in fact, obsessed with the problem of power, suspicious of himself, and yet unable to analyse his own motives satisfactorily. He has become profoundly mistrustful of his own driving force; he sees the mark of the serpent on all men's actions and on their relations one with another, and his mountain climbing, like his scholar's withdrawal, is in part an escape to a 'purer' battle with impersonal forces. We meet him first sitting alone on the summit of the Pillar Rock above Wastdale, telling the beads of his obsession in a rhetorical prose soliloquy, which begins by commenting on the selfish springs behind Dante's creative activity and widens to comment on the endlessness of self-deceit and self-justification, and on the impossibility of communication except with "the unqualified and dangerous dead", to whom alone Ransom will pay homage.

Ransom can detect the infection in the will of others; he recognises his brother's lust for power; he understands his friends (who are also his subalterns, since he is a natural leader) —he envies Lamp's simple singleness of purpose, but knows he could never possess it himself; he sees the value of a weak but comparatively uncomplicated youth like Gunn (a surface-sketch for Emble in 'The Age of Anxiety'); he is able to give good if unacceptable advice to the permanent head-prefect

Shawcross, who hides his refusal to face the weaknesses of his own character in homage to his ego-ideal Ransom. When Ransom finally removes his shadow and obliges Shawcross to face himself, alone, Shawcross realises that even his admiration for Ransom was "only another kind of conceit". He cannot meet the challenge of his new nakedness, and kills himself.

Ransom sees all this and sees some way into himself—but not far enough. He talks of "those to whom a mountain is a mother", but fails to apply the moral to himself; until the final dénouement at the top of the mountain he is trying to understand his personal dæmon, wondering whether the better course would be to turn back, but still, in all essentials blindly, going on. The Abbot presents him with a clear choice, but one which he cannot seriously consider, partly because he is not yet ready for those particular alternatives, partly because he already sees the insufficiency of the Abbot's choice. The Abbot's crystal shows Ransom the special form of his own temptation, in the pleading faces of the lost and lonely who want a healing god and ask Ransom to assume power over them: "Restore us. Restore us to our uniqueness and our human condition." Ransom is haunted by the vision; he has no lack of pity; but he knows that pity can betray, and so produce worse results than it sets out to cure. (Auden has talked of this same point recently: "The vice of pity, that corrupt parody of love and compassion which is so insidious and deadly for sensitive natures.")

The Abbot's call is direct: "The Dæmon is real. Only his ministry and his visitation are unique for every nature" (and, it is implied, are more complicated for those more complicated). The existence of the dæmon proves that life is evil and, since the dæmon works through the will, the will is always evil. One may try to evade the dæmon or to ignore it—like Shawcross, who tried to lose his personality in another's; or one may wrestle with it as Ransom is doing in trying to conquer F.6. All these ways, says the Abbot, are wrong: by opposing our will to the dæmon we bind ourselves more tightly to it. Even the sense of pity is the dæmon's ally; if Ransom thinks to climb F.6 and then descend to help the world, he will fail, for:

> "As long as the world endures, there must be order, there must be government; but woe to the governors, for, by the very operation of their duty, however excellent, they themselves are destroyed . . . government requires the exercise of the human will; and the human will is from the Dæmon."

So, in language reminiscent of Eliot's 'Ash Wednesday', the Abbot urges the cleansing of the will by the way of complete renunciation. But he finally admits that he is himself a man of power, and that even here, in this place of withdrawal, he is haunted by memories of the sensuous world. Ransom is muddled, but sees the inadequacy of a spiritual isolation which is also a form of spiritual pride and a refusal to be committed.

He only sees those motives more clearly at the very end. To each of his party the mountain has represented a different thing; they all came for the wrong reasons. But the others had come partly out of allegiance to Ransom; they die in part the victims of his pride and cowardice. His driving force may have been less obvious than his brother's, but is no more admirable. At the top of the mountain, in a scene silly with expressionist fancies, the symbolism is made manifest in the figure of the dæmon which has drawn Ransom to the climb. The dæmon is real, but is self-created, his own dæmon; it is finally revealed as Mrs. Ransom, ready to receive Michael on her bosom. She has always given her overt love to James, although her love for Michael was the greater. She wanted Michael to learn strength thereby, since "the truly strong man is he who stands most alone". But Michael was not sufficiently strong; in climbing the mountain, he expressed his desire to displace his brother and possess his mother's love for himself. So he lies destroyed, as the Hidden Chorus sings over him a fine rhetorical dirge on the weakness of man. The implications of this chorus, like those of the discussion with the Abbot, are a good deal wider than any suggested by the very crude Freudian symbolism of the final scene. A mother-fixation may properly be shown as part of the problem, but to make it the culmination of the whole climb and the climax of the play is to ignore the more complex problems already posed for the sake of a theatrically startling close.

Throughout the action two highly stylised citizens of a mechanical society, Mr. and Mrs. A., deliver choral commentaries on their own dreary lives. They derive a vicarious thrill from the newspaper accounts of Ransom's exploits; he is the dying god, not preaching at them, but doing dangerous things for them; and so they feel dashing too—and go to Hove for the week-end. They are relatives, much more shallowly conceived, of Quant, in 'The Age of Anxiety'. But their monotonous reels of rhyming couplets bore. And though the movement of the verse is meant to underline the monotony of their lives, one doubts whether those lives are by any means as dreary as Auden conceives them. Auden is so particularly—and personally—interested in the exceptional man that he too quickly classifies the unexceptional. He cannot see them as in themselves very interesting; they interest more as objects of pity and concern than as personalities whose richness is hidden under the humdrum. "Our moments of exaltation have not been extraordinary, but they have been real," say Mr. and Mrs. A.; but one suspects that, though Auden believes this, he does not really feel it naturally. It seems as though he has to remind himself at intervals that the lives of the ordinary obscure family, and of "the little men and their mothers, not plain but / Dreadfully ugly", can be anything other than deadly dull, a "closed life the stupid never leave". In Ransom, who has so much in common with Auden, the attitude breaks out in the exasperation of:

"Under I cannot tell how many of these green slate roofs,
    The stupid peasants are making their stupid children."

83

Much earlier in Auden there was:

> "Those shall be taught who want to understand
> Most of the rest shall love upon the land."

And:

> "All of the women and most of the men
> Shall work with their hands and not think again."

No doubt many people are dreary, perhaps more than most of us realise. But Auden too soon forgets that, though the most obvious characteristic of many people is their unlimited patience in 'putting up with things' as they come, most have moments of remarkable intuitive grasp, and the spiritual problems of the most ordinary are as pressing as those of the better-endowed. He seems too quickly willing to consign them—much as he consciously fights the tendency in his later work—to collective living in a state of childlike innocence, leaving the exceptional few to fight the battle of belief and grace.

But this is to be too harsh towards Auden. It over-emphasizes an impression one nevertheless gains from some parts of his work—that though he has a profound concern for ordinary people, he lacks certain insights into the nature of their lives; and that this lack is connected with his special regard for the Michael Ransoms, the exceptional men.

'On the Frontier'

The 'melodrama' 'On the Frontier' is, in contrast with 'The Dog beneath the Skin', a very tidy piece—and has much less sparkle. There are seven scenes in three acts, and five interspersed choruses, spoken by groups of workers, prisoners, dancers, soldiers and newspaper readers. The scenes are set either in Valerian's study or in the Ostnia-Westland room. Ostnia is the decaying democracy, and Westland the leader-stoated total state of 'The Dog beneath the Skin'. Most of the characters are the usual types in silhouette, and there is much social comment, sometimes vivid, sometimes banal.

We are presented with an animated cartoon on the quarrels of national states, the machinations of international capitalists, the deceptions of the Press, the psychology of fascism and the inner decay of the democracies. The Westland and international-capitalist armament manufacturer Valerian, for example, delivers set speeches as a bogeyman keeping the workers quiet with dope and welfare. What he says may be largely true, but sounds like a dramatised ABCA talk staged by a subversive subaltern. No matter what Auden's aim may be in these plays, he would have done better either to have omitted such things as Valerian's long soliloquy on the common man, cared-for and unfree, or to have realised them in terms of incident. Valerian's Leader is another puppet constructed from psychological jottings—the lonely little man with a tyrant's urge for power, inwardly gnawed by anxiety; calmed by music, because underneath, like everyone else, he wants love, but soon thrown into hysterical rage again.

Against these two are set, firstly, one bourgeois family from each country, the Thorvalds and the Vrodnys, expressionistically occupying opposite halves of the stage in the same scenes. Into each half the respective national broadcasting systems pour a barrage of hate when war breaks out; into each come the increasing miseries of war—and reach their climax when a starved Westland spinster, whose adoration of the Leader has been an outlet for her thwarted love, is smitten with a suitably Groddeckian disease. Eric Thorvald and Anna Vrodny, whose love has leapt frontiers, die on either side of the stage, asserting that their real enemies are not those they have been called upon to fight. Eric, who has been a pacifist, but finally fought, utters the main moral of the play—that the times demand active commitment:

> "Yet we must kill and suffer and know why.
> All errors are not equal. The hatred of our enemies
> Is the destructive self-love of the dying,
> Our hatred is the price of the world's freedom."

Behind the ordinary families are the representative choral groups, most of them extraordinarily dull. The newspaper readers speak in prose, and the soldiers sing a fine cynical ballad, but the rest make oversimple statements in rhyming couplets flatter even than their sense warrants:

> "Oil that bearing, watch that dynamo;
> When it's time to strike, brother, I'll let you know.
>
> Stoke up the fires in furnace number three;
> The day is coming, brother, when we shall all be free!"

It is this kind of ingenuous leftism which distinguishes 'On the Frontier' even from 'The Dog beneath the Skin'. It was written in 1938, specifically for a left-wing audience, and was by some rated the best of the three plays when first produced. This is probably because it is as bold as a poster, startling in its contrasts, obvious in its propaganda and unambiguous in its assaults. It remains one of Auden's most ephemeral efforts at popular writing. From it one remembers only some of the verse exchanges between Eric and Anna which, with their irregular rhythms and patterns of weak rhymes, strike a quieter, graver, as well as a deeper note than any other passages in the play.

(4) *Elliptical and Cerebral Verse*

At the very outset of his poetic career Auden's manner was by no means popular; he produced then some taut, cerebral verse:

> "To ask the hard question is simple;
> Asking at meeting
> With the simple glance of acquaintance
> To what these go
> And how these do:
> To ask the hard question is simple,
> The simple act of the confused will."

The language is bare and hard—MacNeice says that in this part of his writing Auden is trying to work towards the efficiency and virility of Dryden; Auden recalls that one of his slogans at the time was "good poetry should be classic and austere". The subject is usually an aspect of individual psychology, rather than anything of more general social interest or the expression of a mood. If the subject overrides the manner, a versified paragraph from Homer Lane or some potted psychologising from Groddeck results.

For this style, which is to be seen chiefly in 'Poems 1930', Auden owes debts to a large number of poets. Two or three years earlier he was imitating Wordsworth, Hardy and Edward Thomas. Then quite suddenly his interests, becoming more clearly defined, seem to have brought him under the influence of several writers who, though not a group in any way, shared some characteristics. And, as is so easily possible at that age, they quickly and radically altered his style. The debts to Mr. Eliot are mentioned elsewhere, as are those to Anglo-Saxon verse—though it is worth emphasising here that the tautness and ellipsis of the latter contributed importantly to the change we are now discussing. Other creditors are Skelton, Hopkins, Robert Graves, Laura Riding and Emily Dickinson.

Skelton's influence was predominantly on tone and movement; he showed especially how short, staccato, vigorous lines might be handled. Ode four from 'The Orators' is almost a straight parody of him. Here an extract from it is set alongside one from Skelton's 'To Mistress Margaret Hussey':

"O my, what keeps	Of Mirry Margarete
At disheartened sweeps	—As mydsomer flowre,
Fitters and Moulders,	Jentyll as fawcoun,
Wielders and Welders	Or hawke of the towre,
Dyers and bakers	As pacient and as styll
And boiler-tube makers,	And as full of good will
Poofs and Ponces,	As faire Isaphill,
All of them dunces	Colyaunder,

Those over thirty
Ugly and dirty."

Swete pomaunder,
Good Cassaunda;
Stedfast of thought,
Wele made, wele wrought."

Hopkins showed how the argument, the movement of the verse in the mind, rather than formal grammar, might decide its movement to the ear. His was a general and pervasive influence, but at least once he produced a fragment remarkably prefiguring these early poems of Auden:

"What makes the man and what
The man within that makes
Ask whom he serves or not
Serves or what sides he takes.

For good grows wild and wide,
Has sides, is nowhere none;
But right must seek a side;
And choose for chieftain one";

which might particularly be compared with Auden's:

"Simple to prove
That deeds indeed
In life succeed
But love in love
And tales in tales
Where no one fails."

During the nineteen-twenties Robert Graves and the American poet, Laura Riding, had been making similar experiments. From a volume published by Robert Graves in 1930 I quote parts of 'Nature's Lineaments' and 'Certain Mercies': from the first:

"Whose griefs are melancholy,
Whose flowers are oafish,
Whose waters, silly,
Whose birds, raffish,
Whose fish, fish";

and from the second:

> "Now must all satisfaction
> Become mere mitigation
> Of an accepted curse?
>
> Must we henceforth be grateful
> That the guards, though spiteful,
> Are slow of foot and wit?"

Laura Riding had been writing a dry, staccato, cerebral verse which Auden's even more resembles. In her, as in him, Skelton's energetic sequences sometimes become a sort of mental stutter; but the metrical similarities are less important and striking than those of tone and theme.

Some of Emily Dickinson's poems, a selection from which was published in 1924, have a gnomic concentration similar to that which Auden was seeking:

> "A deed knocks first at thought,
> And then it knocks at will.
> That is the manufacturing spot,
> And will at home and well.
>
> It then goes out an act,
> Or is entombed so still
> That only to the ear of God
> Its doom is audible."

They carry, too, the same startling, condensed images, as in the words italicised here:

> "Softened by Time's consummate *plush*,
> How *sleek* the woe appears
> That threatened childhood's citadel
> And undermines the years!
>
> *Bisected* now by *bleaker* griefs
> We envy the despair
> That devastated childhood's realm
> So easy to repair."

The early experimental poems of Auden deserve more attention than they have so far received. In them he was trying to
arrive at a manner which would convey difficult and subtle
ideas curtly, tightly and aphoristically. By 1936 he was using
the style much less; that date, too, marks his point of greatest
general popularity.

It is wholly characteristic of the bent of Auden's mind that
his adjectives—and we are not now referring simply to his
early verse—should comment rather than describe; that they
should, so to say, stand at the side of their noun and fit it into
relationship with something else, rather than, by description,
enlarge our apprehension of the noun itself. Others have, of
course, used the epithet in this way, but it is his predominant
use; as a result one remembers his epithets rather than his
verbs. In its crudest form this is what occurs:

> "Since the external disorder, and extravagant lies,
>   The baroque frontiers, the surrealist police
>   What can truth treasure . . .?"

Or, more effectively:

> "the mild and vegetarian beasts";
> "the made privacy of this bay";
> "the immense improbable atlas."

The effect of these epithets is primarily intellectual; they
set up a play of ideas, an excitement, in the mind of the reader.
So the force is often greater when more than one adjective is
used, as in some of the examples above, and as here:

> "impoverished constricting acres";
> "lucky guarded future";
> "intelligible dangerous marvels."

The juxtaposed adjectives reinforce one another, or, to change
the image, establish a series of poles across which the connota-
tive charges spark. It is by this means, rather than by the

sensuous manipulation of language, that the verse is given texture and tension. The evocations are largely controlled, the connotations comparatively limited. The reader must be alert enough to make the necessary connections. Sometimes part of the effect comes, too, from the unexpected ordinariness of the adjectives, as in "vegetarian beast", "made privacy", "pauper civilian future".

This play of cross-reference, this counterpointing of ideas, may be seen most directly and simply in a couplet such as:

> "And the active hands must freeze
> Lonely on the separate knees".

or at greater length in the love-song 'Lay your sleeping head'. There rhythm, assonance, pausing, deliberate cliché, all contribute to the total effect, of course; but it is the epithets which contribute most to the expression of this highly qualified love-relationship, a relationship that is intensely valued even though inevitably marred, a relationship that exists in spite of, and partly because of, all the limitations:

> "Lay your sleeping head, my love,
> Human on my faithless arm;
> Time and fevers burn away
> Individual beauty from
> Thoughtful children, and the grave
> Proves the child ephemeral:
> But in my arms till break of day
> Let the living creature lie;
> Mortal, guilty, but to me
> The entirely beautiful."

It has connections with the 'wit-writing' of the metaphysicals. Similarities with the dialectic of Donne's early love-poems have been discussed by others.

In the looser metres the concentration of adjectives used thus can help to prevent slackness. When it is misused the manner becomes an annoying mannerism—Auden is then using combinations of noun and adjective in which one is more aware of the novelty of the juxtaposition than of much heightening of meaning:

> "the peculiar tree";
> "the new imprudent year";
> "the panting unfair city."

We have already suggested that Auden's imagination works largely in terms of dramatic images. What has not so far been noted, except incidentally in the discussion of similes, is the fact that these images are often translations of abstract ideas. Thus Prospero's tribute to the creative imagination ("No one but you had sufficient audacity and eyesight / To find the clearings where the shy humiliations / Gambol on sunny afternoons," etc.) is a vivid metaphorical presentation of psychological concepts. Caliban's speech in the same work is histrionic, flippant, idiomatic, but works essentially in the same way:

(The Great Master's neglected 'id' admonishes him at the close of his creative life.) "Had you . . . really left me alone to go my whole free-wheeling way to disorder, to be drunk every day before lunch, to jump stark naked from bed to bed, to have a fit every week or a major operation every other year, to forge cheques or water the widow's stock, I might, after countless skids and punctures, have come by the bumpy third-class road of guilt and remorse, smack into that very same truth which you were meanwhile admiring from your distant comfortable verandah but would never point out to me.

"Such genuine escapades, though, might have disturbed the master at his meditations and even involved him in trouble with the police. The strains of oats, therefore, that you prudently permitted me to sow were each and all of an unmitigatedly minor wildness: a quick cold clasp now and then in some louche hotel to calm me down. . . ."

Some of the Quest sonnets are not so successful:

> "Enraged phenomena bear down
> In overwhelming waves to drown
> Both sufferer and suffering."

Auden feels the force of abstractions so powerfully that he immediately transforms them into concrete metaphors. But even when handling these often very lengthy and complicated images he is still doing that in which his mind feels most at home: he is manipulating ideas, making what Edwin Muir calls "a statement of relations". So strong is this abstracting quality that, if the image fails, he can be led to this kind of intellectualism in verse:

> "The freedom of
> The actually deficient on
> The justly actual."

In his prose articles Auden indulges his bent and often produces grouped notes of ideas rather than a fully written essay.

Auden combines, then, an unusually powerful image-making faculty with a persistent desire for geometric order. He is continually trying to abstract patterns from experience. He once remarked, according to Christopher Isherwood, that poetry should concern itself with "shapes and volumes". He was probably indicating there the quality one finds in so many of his poems—that they are, as it were, without colour and without smell, but that they have a sort of geometric form, produced by the tensions and interaction of the ideas manipulated in them. Auden has also said that he has not a strong visual imagination. Certainly some of the senses are starved in his verse. The exception is the aural sense; Auden's appeal to the ear is sensitive and skilful. There is no doubt that much of the early admiration of him arose from this, although it was not often mentioned as one of his outstanding qualities. We have become a little ashamed to admit our response to the poet as a singer. Auden's power is most strikingly, because unexpectedly, shown in some of those otherwise rather bare poems of the first volume:

> "This lunar beauty
> Has no history
> Is complete and early;
> If beauty later
> Bear any feature
> It had a lover
> And is another."

Later, in 'Look Stranger', the lyricism was given more scope, notably in the extraordinarily skilful title-poem. In 'Dover' (1938), the sensuous evocations induced by the sound reinforce the epigrammatic selection and the conceptual epithets:

> "The vows, the tears, the slight emotional signals
> Are here eternal and unremarkable gestures
> Like ploughing or soldiers' songs."

Yet, in spite of his brilliant eye for the melodramatically and metaphorically useful casual gesture, how rarely Auden communicates small, intimate, *felt* acts. From the moment he perceives them they seem to become revealing symbols, stimulating pointers: he begins immediately to generalise, abstract, classify. Stephen Spender has said somewhere that Auden lives very much in his own mental world, and that in reading him one misses much of the immediate sensuous response to ordinary life. It is true that Auden has written a fair number of lyrics—and continues to write them; one appeared in *Horizon* for November 1948—predominantly about love or friendship and very gentle in their manner. But he has developed his fine lyric gift less than he might have done, had he not been so gripped by the conviction that his period demanded more critical attitudes of the poet.

Auden is still in mid-career, and it would be premature to do more than suggest the rough line of his poetic development.

After being extremely difficult and elliptic, his verse gradually became much easier to understand. Most of the 'Poems 1930' are obscure, and they are sometimes tricksy; but the best have a fine, hard concentration. 'Look Stranger', printed in 1935 at the peak of Auden's left-wing period, is much more intelligible. It is not, I think, as has been frequently said, "the height of Auden's powers". It has fluency, wit and acute reporting; it is not unnecessarily difficult; but it lacks the precision and compression of the best early work. Some of the clarity of these middle-'thirties has been gained at the expense of the cutting-edge of the 1930 volume. 'Look Stranger' relies too much on virtuosity and is over-conscious of its audience.

'Another Time' (1940) is a transitional volume; it shows at their worst the slackness and overcompetence which mar 'Look Stranger', and the work between that volume and 1940; it indicates, both in themes and technique, the lines on which Auden would work whilst in America. It has been followed by four long works: 'New Year Letter', 'The Sea and the Mirror', 'For the Time Being' and 'The Age of Anxiety'. 'New Year Letter' (1941) is sometimes painfully slack and drumming, and one is jarred by the frequent mere cleverness; it is as though Auden is trying to write out of himself some of the more obvious weaknesses of the 'thirties (this is predominantly a technical comment; in themes, 'New Year Letter' is the first of the later group). But in parts of the 'Letter' and in the 'Quest' sonnets which follow it—as, too, in some of the sonnets from 'Journey to a War' (1939)—we find again poems which, although they do not entirely fulfil the promise of the early work, do confirm and develop some of their best characteristics—the compression, precision and intelligence.

One feels, in short, that although Auden was always developing certain of his powers, he neglected some of the most important—partly because he relied too much on his great natural talents, partly because he was unsure of his audience and his relation to it. 'The Sea and the Mirror' and 'For the

Time Being' revealed again some of those neglected qualities. Yet the 'Age of Anxiety' is perverse, brilliant, tortured, perceptive. Auden has not yet broken through to a manner adequate to convey his present material. He remains, technically, in the experimental phase which began just after the outbreak of war. His technical complexities reflect the spiritual difficulties with which he is now more than ever preoccupied

(5) *Commentaries*

In this section four poems are printed, each with a commentary. They have been chosen to illustrate different forms of obscurity, different types of poem and different periods in Auden's work. So there is an early elliptical poem and one from his Marxist period (it would be inadequate to call it a 'Marxist poem'), a song, and a later poem with a religious theme. Much of the poetry from the middle-'thirties would make pleasant material for comment, but is not really difficult.

The aim has been to clear away typical difficulties and to suggest an approach for those who find the poems, for both technical and other reasons, obscure. But to 'suggest an approach' is always a doubtful undertaking. Instead of helping the reader, one may prevent him from appreciating a poem fully, from allowing it to unfold itself at successive readings in the way best suited to his temperament. So I have tried to say enough to set the hesitant reader off on his own, by making the kind of remark which I think I should have found helpful in my own first approach. The main exception has been in the treatment of 'The Wanderer', where I have indicated something of Auden's indebtedness to other poets. And though critical analysis has not been an important part of my aim, I have said some things which seemed to introduce analysis such as the reader might valuably undertake himself.

The titles are those given in the *Collected Shorter Poems*, 1930–1944.

TECHNIQUE

THE WANDERER

(*From 'Poems* 1930')

"Doom is dark and deeper than any sea-dingle,
   Upon what man it fall
In spring, day-wishing flowers appearing,
Avalanche sliding, white snow from rock-face,
   That he should leave his house,
No cloud-soft hand can hold him, restraint by women;
   But ever that man goes
Through place-keepers, through forest trees,
A stranger to strangers over undried seas,
Houses for fishes, suffocating water,
   Or lonely on fell as chat,
   By pot-holed becks
A bird stone-haunting, an unquiet bird.

"There head falls forward, fatigued at evening,
   And dreams of home,
Waving from window, spread of welcome,
Kissing of wife under single sheet;
   But waking sees
Bird-flocks nameless to him, through doorway voices
Of new men making another love.

"Save him from hostile capture,
   From sudden tiger's spring at corner;
Protect his house,
His anxious house where days are counted
   From thunderbolt protect,
From gradual ruin spreading like a stain;
Converting number from vague to certain,
Bring joy, bring day of his returning,
Lucky with day approaching, with leaning dawn."

Here, very early in his poetic career, Auden is creating the
sense of threat, the threat which so often hangs over the sym-

bolic figure of the wanderer, the man setting out on some positive action, alone. The mood and the figure appear frequently in all his subsequent verse, in ballads like ' "O where are you going?" said reader to rider', and in various invocations, interjections and warnings; it is the 'Leave for Cape Wrath tonight' theme.

The call of 'doom' (judgment) comes in spring to a certain man, compelling him to leave his home and womenfolk and journey over seas and across mountains, lonely and in peril. This is, understandably, a situation not uncommon in Anglo-Saxon and Middle English verse. We may see Auden's aim more clearly by setting his poem alongside an Anglo-Saxon poem with the same title, which has obviously influenced him:

"Often the solitary man prays for favour, for the mercy of the Lord, though, sad at heart, he must needs stir with his hands for a weary while the icy sea across the watery wastes, must journey the paths of exile; settled in truth is fate! So spoke the wanderer, mindful of hardships. . . . He knows who puts it to the test how cruel a comrade is sorrow for him who has few dear protectors; his is the path of exile, in no wise the twisted gold; a chill body, in no wise the riches of the earth; he thinks of retainers in hall and the receiving of treasure, of how in his youth his gold-friend was kind to him at the feast. The joy has all perished. . . . Then the friendless man wakes again, sees before him the dark waves, the sea-birds bathing, spreading their feathers; frost and snow falling mingles with hail. Then heavier are the wounds in his heart, sore for his beloved; sorrow is renewed."

The parallels of mood and treatment are marked, and the variations interesting—as when Auden, no doubt with the aim of increasing the sense of loneliness, has, instead of 'the sea-birds bathing', 'bird flocks *nameless* to him'. One need do no more at this point than remark on the use of alliteration and of 'kenning' (poetical paraphrasing, as in 'houses for fishes' instead of 'sea'. 'Place-keepers' is a much less simple compound and has valuable modern associations).

There is a direct debt, also, to a Middle English West Midland homily, 'Sawles Warde', dating, it is believed, from the early thirteenth century. In it occurs the line:

> "His [God's] domes þe derne beot ant deopre þen eni sea dingle."
> ("His judgments that are secret and deeper than any sea-dingle.")

That line has clearly attracted Auden so much that he has used it almost unaltered. In 'Sawles Warde', too, a man has to leave his house and his womenfolk. But the spirit is farther from Auden's than is that of the Anglo-Saxon 'Wanderer'; it contains, for one thing, direct moralising drawn from the allegory. Auden has taken his lovely opening line and the central situation, of a man setting out on a journey from a house whose womenfolk miss him. He has been attracted, as always, by the figure of the lonely man carrying out a necessary but not clearly envisaged pilgrimage in a universe often hostile to him.

So he had to create, not only the sense of menace and of lonely pilgrimage ("a stranger to strangers over undried seas," which are "houses for fishes," but to him "suffocating water"), but the nostalgia, the longing for home. And the movement had to be simple, with no apparent sophistication. Hence, presumably, the use of only a few rhymes and those mainly weak, the short phrasing, and the recurrence of the short single-clause lines (although these may assist the sense too, as in:

> "There head falls forward, fatigued at evening,
> And dreams of home"

where the short clauses trace the movement of a head too heavy to hold itself up).

Although the use of alliteration to these ends is the most immediately obvious device, the interweaving of the vowel sounds is no less important. So, at the close of the second stanza, the vowels fall away to assist the 'm' and 'n' alliteration, as it suggests a homesick isolation and a longing for gentleness:

> ". . . sees
>   Bird-flocks nameless to him, through doorway voices
>   Of new men making another love."

But immediately after, in the invocation for the wanderer's safe return, the movement is energetic and decided, the sound loud and hard:

> "Save him from hostile capture,
>   From sudden tiger's spring at corner"

(the use of 'tiger's', with its suggestions of colour and the East, is faulty).

And there is the contrast of the darkness and heaviness of the opening, the beat of the 'd' alliteration and the run of long vowels, drumming out the threat:

"Doom is darker and deeper than any sea-dingle," with the light 'l' alliteration and the opening hopeful effect of the vowels in the final line:

> "Lucky with day approaching, with leaning dawn."

Auden so much liked the haunting simile of the moorland bird:

> ". . . lonely on fell as chat,
>   By pot-holed becks
>   A bird stone-haunting, an unquiet bird."

that he used it again a few years later, though he changed the bird:

> "Land of the ring-ousel; a bird stone-haunting,
>   An unquiet bird."
> ('Dog beneath the Skin', Chorus before Act II, Scene ii.)

The parallel list of three selected items in the second stanza points forward to the selective detailing of the mid-'thirties.

The common ellipses in Auden's verse at this time will already have been noticed, such as the omission of articles and connectives (e.g. in lines three and four of the first stanza). This style, as we noted earlier, is most common in 'Poems 1930': in that volume the new reader might perhaps turn first to Poem XIV, now called 'Shut Your Eyes and Open Your Mouth', which deals with the weakness behind a 'public face'.

OUR HUNTING FATHERS

(*From ' Look Stranger '* 1936)

"Our hunting fathers told the story
    Of the sadness of the creatures,
Pitied the limits and the lack
    Set in their finished features;
Saw in the lion's intolerant look,
    Behind the quarry's dying glare,
Love raging for the personal glory
    That reason's gift would add,
The liberal appetite and power,
    The rightness of a god.

"Who nurtured in that fine tradition
    Predicted the result,
Guessed love by nature suited to
    The intricate ways of guilt?
That human ligaments could so
    His southern gestures modify,
And make it his mature ambition
    To think no thought but ours,
To hunger, work illegally,
    And be anonymous?"

Auden may have little interest in pastoral things, but he frequently refers to brute beasts. He remarks—as Blake does in the 'Songs of Innocence and Experience'—on the animals' mental stillness, their natural goodness or neutrality, their moral calm as compared with the fever of the 'double man'. They remind him of the necessities of the human condition. In that we have reason and imagination, we are freer than the animals; but we also bear responsibilities, the inescapable obligation to make moral choices. We are capable of guilt, which they are not: "The animals, whose evolution is complete, whose knowledge of their relations with the rest of creation is fixed, can do evil, but they cannot sin."

In this poem, one of the best in 'Look Stranger', the condition of the beasts heightens by contrast a specific moral conflict, a conflict which, says Auden, the bourgeois intellectual must face and resolve when he becomes a Marxist.

Our fathers and grandfathers pitied the beasts for their lack of the faculty of reason, for their inability to 'progress'. In comparison, men were as gods, large, effective, liberal, reasonable, capable of 'southern' gestures, the gestures of 'love' from the morally secure. This fine tradition the middle classes handed on to their children through home, school and the older universities. But our generation feels guilty about the foundations of its inheritance, about the wrongs it ignores. The same sense of 'love' now leads us, more aware, into intricate acts of guilt, into wrong acts for right ends, into forsaking the liberal and humane in our social dealings for the evasive, the treacherous, the sly, into imitating *by choice* the cunning of the animals, a cunning which, it had seemed, would be irrelevant had reason been granted.

So the poem makes a comment (in the second stanza) on what, at this time, Auden held to be a moral necessity for him and people like him—that they had to reject even the 'decent' bourgeois values for the sake of a greater value. And the comment is introduced (in the first stanza) by means of an ironic yet regretful reflection on a tradition which he believed to have died; he points the change by reflecting on our altered relationship to the dumb creatures: ". . . our fathers, secure in their tradition, pitied the animals because they hadn't the gift of reason; we (for the sake of greater values) imitate the most *unreasonable* characteristics of the animals."

The comment is itself trite enough, and it seems probable that the reflection on it, not the straightforward Marxist assertion, initiated the poem. So the first stanza, besides *saying* what has already been indicated, contains a nostalgic music for the old peace and assurance. And the break is sharp. The second stanza is predominantly dry, clipped, heavily accented and closes briskly and firmly; it is, one may say, more 'conscious', more of a statement. The twentieth-century intellectual has uttered his regret at the coldness of his world and is deciding how best to face it.

But that comparison of the stanzas is a general one only, not accurate in detail. The use of the word 'southern' in the second stanza immediately disproves it. Only the word 'liberal' in the first stanza has anything like the same associative force: 'liberal' suggests, for example—to name only those associations which occur near the surface to one reader—the liberal spirit in public affairs, generosity and open dealing, Newman's idea of a liberal education, 'liberal' as the opposite of all that is intolerant and narrow, and as implying the assurance that comes from a position of authority and power, even though that power is used reasonably and humanely; and 'southern' suggests warmth and largeness, freedom, spaciousness, friendliness and frankness, the easy politeness which is popularly held to be characteristic of the American Southern States and the grace and ease of Italy.

It would be interesting, as an illustration of the changes in Auden's moral attitudes, to trace the use of the 'animal' comparison from 'Poems 1930' to 'The Age of Anxiety'. Variants of it may be found in the sonnet sequence 'In Time of War', in Poems III and XXXI of 'Another Time', and in the Alonzo and Ferdinand section of 'The Sea and the Mirror', which is quoted later in these commentaries.

SONG

(Poem XVI of 'Look Stranger')

"May with its light behaving
    Stirs vessel, eye and limb,
    The singular and sad
    Are willing to recover,
    And to the swan-delighting river
    The careless picnics come,
    The living white and red.

"The dead remote and hooded
    In their enclosures rest; but we
    From the vague woods have broken,
    Forests where children meet
    And the white angel-vampires flit;
    We stand with shaded eye,
    The dangerous apple taken.

"The real world lies before us;
    Animal motions of the young,
    The common wish for death,
    The pleasured and the haunted;
    The dying master sinks tormented
    In the admirers' ring,
    The unjust walk the earth.

"And love that makes impatient
    The tortoise and the roe, and lays
    The blonde beside the dark,
    Urges upon our blood,
    Before the evil and the good
    How insufficient is
    The endearment and the look."

Auden's lyrics or 'songs', as he now calls them, are of such
consistently high quality that it was difficult to know which to
discuss. 'Lay your sleeping head, my love' seemed at first the

obvious choice; too obvious, one finally felt, since it is already fairly well-known through anthologies and is by no means as obscure as some others. In the end 'May with its light behaving' was chosen because it very usefully illustrates both Auden's achievement in lyric and his occasional weaknesses.

The allegro opening expresses the pleasure of a May morning which urges even those fast-bound in the misery and iron of their own neuroses to expand, to be happy simply in *being*. Here is a moment of happiness, of lightness, of gentleness, evoked in part by the interplay of long and short 'i' sounds, by the 's' alliteration, and by the quiet echoing of the pattern of predominantly weak rhymes.

Thereafter the poem is sad. We respond to May much as the animals do; like them we are affected by deep instinctive forces. But we also stand in the hard light of consciousness; we know the unhappiness of the dual personality, which acts and questions its actions. 'Love', which prompts us as it prompts "the tortoise and the roe", also pushes us to the point where we realise its insufficiency. To our double condition Love conceived simply as "the endearment and the look" soon shows itself inadequate. Auden is already looking forward to the more complex view of Love which he examines in so much of his later work.

The third stanza, with its fragment from Freud and its sideglance at the exceptional man, is surely too bitty, has been overloaded with items, might even be omitted without great loss. It is largely responsible for the overbalancing of the poem: it contains too much staccato *detail*. And isn't 'vague' in the second stanza (Auden likes the word) so vaguely used as to be dangerous, an invitation to the reader to supply what evocations he pleases and ascribe them to the poem?

In contrast there is the economical charge of meaning in:

> "The singular and sad
> *Are willing* to recover",

and the fine conciseness of:

> ". . . to the swan-delighting river
> The careless picnics come",

and:

> "We stand with *shaded eye*
> The dangerous apple taken."

Among all the other songs, Poem XXX of 'Another Time' —'For us like any other fugitive'—might be read early. Some have been very successfully set to music by Benjamin Britten.

PART OF ALONZO'S LETTER TO FERDINAND
(*From 'The Sea and the Mirror'*, 1945)

"Dear Son, when the warm multitudes cry,
Ascend your throne majestically.
But keep in mind the waters where fish
See sceptres descending with no wish
To touch them; sit regal and erect,
But imagine the sands where a crown
Has the status of a broken-down
Sofa or mutilated statue:
Remember as bells and cannon boom
The cold deep that does not envy you,
The sunburnt superficial kingdom
Where a king is an object.

"Expect no help from others, for who
Talk sense to princes or refer to
The scorpion in official speeches
As they unveil some granite Progress
Leading a child and holding a bunch
Of lilies? In their Royal Zoos the
Shark and the octopus are tactfully
Omitted; synchronised clocks march on
Within their powers: without, remain
The ocean flats where no subscription
Concerts are given, the desert plain
Where there is nothing for lunch.

"Only your darkness can tell you what
  A prince's ornate mirror dare not,
Which you should fear more—the sea in which
  A tyrant sinks entangled in rich
Robes while a mistress turns a white back
  Upon his splutter, or the desert
Where an emperor stands in his shirt
  While his diary is read by sneering
Beggars, and far off he notices
  A lean horror flapping and hopping
Toward him with inhuman swiftness:
  Learn from your dreams what you lack,

.   .   .   .

"But should you fail to keep your kingdom
  And, like your father before you, come
Where thought accuses and feeling mocks,
  Believe your pain: praise the scorching rocks
For their dessication of your lust,
  Thank the bitter treatment of the tide
For its dissolution of your pride,
  That the whirlwind may arrange your will
And the deluge release it to find
  The spring in the desert, the fruitful
Island in the sea, where flesh and mind
  Are delivered from mistrust."

Alonso, the retiring King of Naples, on a ship bound for home from Prospero's island, is giving advice to his son Ferdinand, who will assume the throne.

The ground-theme is not an unusual one—the emptiness of kingship and worldly pomp and the uncertainty of human fidelity; the necessity for the elected to go through with the performance but never to allow their sense of its illusory nature to weaken, never to fail to set it against the background of man's loneliness and insufficiency; never to forget the enormous unknown outside—the desert, the vast kingdoms of inanimate nature—nor cease to be reminded by them of the mysteries which man's pomp does not touch nor his thought affect . . . "learn from your dreams what you lack".

Three centre stanzas which develop this theme have been omitted, and a final one, which is mainly narrative except for its close, when Alonso reveals that he is:

> ". . . now ready to welcome
> Death, but rejoicing in a new love,
> A new peace, having heard the solemn
> Music strike and seen the statue move
> To forgive our illusion."

(The last three lines refer to Act V, Scene 3, of Shakespeare's 'The Winter's Tale'.)

The dominant images are, then, impressive natural phenomena or particularly unpleasant brute creatures . . . the sea, the whirlwind, the deluge; the desert, that established symbol for the place where the will is purged; and the dumb things, careless of man, which inhabit these regions, and which, too, by being shark, octopus or scorpion, remind him of the hard facts which he tries to ignore.

The twelve-line stanza, of two rhyming couplets followed by eight lines with interlaced rhyming (*aabbcddefefc*), is unusual. The line is generally nine-syllabled, but its accents are those of speech not of foot measurement. The advantages of the form are shown best in the first stanza, where the closely woven rhymes and the polysyllables, the assonance, the '*s*' and '*sh*' alliteration, and the strong beating of the frequent accents right through to the curt last line, suggest not only the swaying fall of objects through the sea, but the element of dream. This is in keeping with the whole tenor of Alonso's advice: he is hovering between two forms of reality, between the life of everyday and the life which is a part of God's larger purpose and which we sense only momentarily and occasionally.

One notices—in the fish swimming unconcernedly past while the signs of worldly pomp float down—the modulation of an earlier theme (see the notes on 'Our Hunting Fathers'). But whatever its metaphysical implications, such a situation would appeal to Auden; it would excite his dramatic imagination in the same way as Brueghel's 'Icarus' did, when that picture initiated 'Musée des Beaux-Arts'.

The rest of the poem does not reach the same high level, though it illustrates the tone of much of Auden's later work. But imaginatively it moves on a different plane from the first stanza. Compare, for instance:

> "But imagine the sands where a crown
> Has the status of a broken-down
> Sofa or mutilated statue"

with:

> "The ocean flats where no subscription
> Concerts are given, the desert plain
> Where there is nothing for lunch."

In saying that there has been a drop, one is not objecting simply to a change of tone, nor simply to the introduction of idiomatic images; one is saying that to switch into perky idiom is faulty, and that the gift for dramatic imagery has been allowed to riot. And "sneering beggars" in the third stanza is careless, a use of the first words that came to mind.

The last stanza begins jarringly, with a great gulp of a parenthesis in the second line. It goes on to introduce too many symbols, most of them unrealised. One may compare the use of similar symbols in the 'Four Quartets', as well as some of Eliot's earlier work. Indeed, Eliot's influence is surely apparent here (in general his influence on Auden seems to me greater today than ever before), not only in the symbolisation, but in similarities of rhythm, tone and content. There are strong similarities between this last stanza:

> "But should you . . . [come]
> Where thought accuses and feeling mocks . . ."

and the Brunetto Latini episode of 'Little Gidding' (Part II), in particular where it refers to:

> ". . . the shame
> Of motives late revealed, and the awareness
> Of things ill done and done to others' harm."

CHAPTER IV

EARLY THEMES

(1) *Politics and Commitment*

IT is possible, for clearer understanding, to separate the main themes in Auden's work before 1940 from those now preoccupying him. But it would be wrong to imply a sharp break in his view of life just after his emigration to America. Throughout the 'thirties he was slowly but continuously moving towards his present position. The ideas which he is now examining in America are developments, extensions, prunings of his views of ten years ago: those views have, in fact, been continuously scrutinised and modified by an acute, enquiring and sensitive personality. There has been a change, at first glance a radical one, but it has been brought about by innumerable subtle shifts of balance and emphasis rather than by any abrupt reversal of opinion.

The sense of social commitment, the conviction that "we are conscripts to our age", the belief that today many people lead lives which are, for all kinds of reasons, unnecessarily restricted—these views are by no means peculiar to Auden and his contemporaries. Blake is one of their most important ancestors here. But there was a succession of writers with similar views in the 'twenties and not long before—in particular after the ending, in thunder and lightning, of the Edwardian summer afternoon. There are direct connections between what Auden and his group were doing in verse during the 'thirties and what Aldous Huxley and others had done in the novel during the previous decade. In condemning a joyless society which seems to have lost its guts, Auden follows Lawrence: in his pity and anxiety to help he echoes the tone and the technique of Wilfred Owen. Eliot showed those young intellectuals who were beginning to write at the turn of the decade how the medium of verse could be used to talk about their own times and problems; he "found the language for the crime", Auden says in his poem for Eliot's sixtieth birthday. In an article written for the same occasion, Louis MacNeice enlarged on the point:

> "However sheltered our young lives, however rural our normal surroundings, however pre-Industrial-Revolution our education, we knew in our bones, if not explicitly, that this which Eliot expressed so succinctly and vividly, this was what we were up against."

Auden's normal surroundings were not rural; they were those of the industrial Midlands, and there he was able to see very clearly the economic disorder of the 'thirties. For however much we may feel that Auden and others sometimes took a boyish pleasure in crying woe, the period was in a particular sense one of "crisis and dismay," one which saw "a boom in sorrow". This is not to agree that Auden's was "an unlucky generation"—all generations have to face specific forms of recurrent problems. It is to say that at this time the signs of material collapse were more than usually evident—in the physical misery of large numbers of people.

In England, it was a seedy era, the era of the newspaper canvassers and the cut-price stores, the era of the insecure and threadbare common man "begot on Hire-Purchase by Insurance", the messy period described in the opening chorus of 'The Dog beneath the Skin', the period of recurrent depressions, strikes and mass unemployment, of (though this is over-dramatically selective):

> "Smokeless chimneys, damaged bridges, rotting wharves and choked canals
> Tramlines buckled, smashed trucks lying on their sides across the rails."

Abroad, these were the years which saw the giant's progress to September 3rd, 1939, a progress whose centre and symbol was and remains the outbreak of war in Spain. This was a period when to talk about "the baroque frontiers and the surrealist police" was not simply to express oneself in a rather 'clever' way, but to be ironic about a real horror, as Erika Mann, to whom Auden addressed that line, knew as well as most.

It is not surprising, then, that Auden should cry more than once "no policy of isolation is possible", or should become, as it now sometimes seems to us, rather theatrical—as in the refrain to 'Spain':

"Tomorrow the rediscovery of romantic love
BUT TODAY THE STRUGGLE."

After all, most people refused to reflect on whether there might be any connection between their personal troubles and the wider political scene.

Hence the one-sidedness of Auden's near-Marxist writings, of which 'The Dance of Death' is the most extreme. He was drawn to Marxism all the more because it offered a strict intellectual discipline, a creed apparently untouched by 're-ligiosity'. Like many morally concerned intellectuals, he had his Marxist period in youth, and the training was not wasted. But he was not in the orthodox sense a Marxist; he never regarded man as a creature whose morals are socially induced and therefore, in the last analysis, not absolute; nor would a Marxist recognise Auden's conception of 'Love'.

More important than the approaches of Auden and his friends to Marxist philosophy are the decisions which they took about their art, as a result of their political convictions. Most of the poets have explained in detail the reasons for the restrictions which they imposed upon themselves. The basis of all the explanations is their analysis of the state of culture in this century. Cecil Day Lewis, in his preface to *The Mind in Chains*, said that collection "could never have been written were it not for the widespread belief that the mind is really in chains today . . . and that we can only realise our strength by joining forces with the millions of workers who have nothing to lose but their chains". The appearance of such novels as Rex Warner's *The Wild Goose Chase* showed that the assertion was more than a gesture. In the dedication to his translation of the 'Georgics', published in 1940, Day Lewis added:

"We were the prophets of a changeable morning
Who hoped for much but saw the clouds forewarning

. . . .

Spain was a death to us, Munich a warning."

It is true, and has been often remarked, that the Auden 'group' were all of middle-class origin, and that a good deal of their political enthusiasm seemed to be that of the sensitive middle-class boy who has just discovered that the charwoman is a person. The guilt was obtrusive:

"Louder today its wireless roars
Its warnings and its lies, and it's impossible
Among the well-shaped cosily to flit. . . ."

But this is no more reprehensible an origin for a social conscience than the working-class boy's revulsion from poverty: both are emotional starting-points and cannot legitimately be introduced to judge the final achievement.

So these poets deliberately declared "poetical martial law"; for although the best form of action might be hard to discover, something had to be done, and action itself was valuable:

"For men are changed by what they do;
And through loss and anger the hands of the unlucky
Love one another."

They believed some public action to be necessary and undertook it: Auden, Spender and other poets went to Spain during the Civil War; Auden went to China during the war with Japan.

Of the writer's situation in the 'thirties, Auden wrote an oversimple allegory (the villagers are those who make up the body of a society, the sportsmen are artists):

"The villagers replied that the first thing necessary was to fell the trees and clear away the undergrowth, and they suggested that the sportsmen should lend a hand with this. A few thought this a reasonable suggestion, but the greater part were alarmed and offended."

The analogy, as no doubt Auden knew, will not bear examination. But it gives evidence of the sense of urgency which was driving these writers. Unless we appreciate the force of that feeling of approaching ruin, we can hardly assess fairly the decisions which were taken as a result of it. It was, to these men, a time of war, in which the enemy was winning on all sides against a moribund opponent. This belief runs through the literature of the time from 1930 onwards. In the introduction to *New Signatures*, for instance, Michael Roberts had said much what Auden says above:

"Poetry is here turned to propaganda, but it is propaganda for a theory of life which may release the poet's energies for the writing of pure poetry."

Again, the assumptions will not bear close scrutiny, but the mood is clear.

Although Auden was not often as politically naïve as Day Lewis and Spender, he was sometimes inept. On at least one occasion he produced the bourgeois idealisation of working-class life:

"The missus came in with her hair down, a-crying,
Stay at home, George, stay at home, for baby's dying."

And his address to the workers could be very stiff-collared:

> "Brothers, who when the sirens roar
> From office, shop and factory pour
> 'Neath evening sky:
> By cops directed to the fug
> Of talkie-houses for a drug
> Or down canals to find a hug
> Until you die:
>
> . . . .
>
> We know, remember, what it is
> That keeps you celebrating this
> Sad ceremonial; . . . "

The last half-line, slightly literary and condescending, is particularly unfortunate.

Such political preaching as Auden did came to him, it would seem, more easily than it came to Day Lewis or Spender. These two had to abuse their natural gifts so as to produce informed political verse, and the strain to which they put themselves often told in disappointing fashion. In Spender the constant and deliberate externalising of a mind by nature uncommonly introspective produced a mass of tortured, unrealised verse. In this period Spender the political poet was only successful, to my mind, in 'Trial of a Judge', a play with many excellencies as well as many faults. In his foreword to *The Still Centre* (1939), Spender stated that he would henceforth abjure non-personal subjects. In an article written some years later he added:

> "There is no use any longer in taking sides with those politicians who seem a little nearer the truth than the others."

Auden could attack political fascism, not from a fully engaged interest in politics, but because he held that particular social eruption to be a symptom of forces which are against life; he was more interested in psychotherapy than in social mechanics: the former precedes and, in large measure, contains the answer to the latter.

(2) *Psychology*

Auden combines, we have stressed several times, an intense interest in the human heart with a desire to reform society, and he thinks our psychological ills greater than our political. It is important to see the two elements separately and to note the greater importance of the former to Auden. He is naturally attracted to the study of the human psyche, and especially of that psyche when it is twisted; he finds the minor obsessive rituals of neuroses fascinating. When we recall the powerful moralist in him, we find his anger at mental sickness, at the waste in the twisted lives around, at the increase in the number of those who find it impossible to adjust themselves, easily understandable. He is convinced of the urgent need for mental therapy; he believes that the spread and assimilation of the findings of psychology can help society towards health; he is sure that such action is morally desirable; he thinks it is owed to "the human creature we must nurse to sense and decency".

We have all to face and destroy the adversary, the dragon, the devourer, the hump-backed scissors-man, "the formless terror in the dream, the stooping shadow that withdraws itself as you wake in the half dawn". All these are images for the Enemy, the destroyer of life and love, whose agents are malaise, cowardice, inability 'to cope', inertia, the longing for death, frustration, the ingrown will, reason without emotion, self-regard; the Enemy is all the fear and negation which helps to dry and deaden. His qualities and his disguises are exhaustively enumerated in 'The Orators'.

So are those of his opponent, the Airman, the Healer, the truly strong man, the friend of life and of creation, the symbol of the refusal to be afraid, of the ability to rise to a large gesture. He is all those ancestors who stood firm for life-values, and whose memory gives strength against the enemy; he is all those healers, and especially the poets and psychologists, who fought the adversary in one way or another. Among these, for Auden, are "Freud and Groddeck at their candid studies / of the mind and body of man", and "Lawrence, Blake and Homer Lane, once healers in our English land"; so are Klages, Prinzhorn and many others.

Auden's psychological interest has been consistent, and though it may be eclectic, it is not dilettante: he knows a good deal about the subject and has read widely and carefully in it. That he sometimes used its jargon rather glibly, and was on the whole a Freudian (at a time when many were Freudians to be fashionable), does not detract from his seriousness. Freud's influence on him was greater than that of any other psychologist, but Auden does not make sustained use of Freud's theories. He thinks Freud's 'map of the mind' largely correct, and finds the cross-reference between his own imaginative perceptions and the findings of the psychological scientist stimulating and fertile. Obviously a creative writer must, by definition, have acute psychological interest and insight. And as an intelligent moralist, with wide interests and a special leaning towards science, Auden readily studied the findings of psychology and made use of its terms and definitions. Sometimes the training helped to give point to his statements and to strengthen the abstract and analytical qualities of his verse. It gave more assurance to the preacher in him. What he sensed as wrong the psychologists diagnosed as wrong; both orders of perception gave the same or very similar answers. Auden would have said much the same things about human beings if he had never read Freud. But he would have said them less boldly—and sometimes rather better, for on occasions, over-fed, he wrote 'psychologese' in poor verse. He has never been an out-and-out Freudian—he would not so completely discount myth, for instance, nor be satisfied with the Freudian interpretation of the artist. But there are large areas of agreement: Freud's lecture 'A Philosophy of Life', which ends the *New Introductory Lectures*, and in which Freud defines an attitude to science, to Marxism and to religion, would be a good introduction to many of Auden's attitudes in the early 'thirties.

Auden's special interest is in what the psychologists generally call 'anxiety' or 'dread'. He refers continually to "the lost, the lonely, the unhappy", the "*lonelies*", the sick souls, self-imprisoned, time-obsessed, subsisting on "aspirins and weak tea", those for whom "it is not good to be alone". This is the neurotic loneliness one finds in Eliot's 'Waste Land' ("My nerves are bad tonight. Stay with me"), and throughout modern literature; but it is much more pervasive in Auden than in most other writers. The displaced persons of the heart are everywhere: "No wonder then so many die of grief, / So many are so lonely as they die." From all around arises the "heavy breathing of the lost", and their public masks (assumed to hide "the divided face")—"the proud bridge and indignant nostril"; "the accosting profile, the erect carriage"; "the incorruptible eye"—are to be seen on all hands.

In this attack on a negative life in which the emotions are shrivelled, the influence of Lawrence is clear. But Lawrence was too anarchic, made too much of the dark subconscious, to be for Auden more than a stimulant that soon ceased to be effective. Auden has recently said that Lawrence was very useful to young men questioning their society in the 'twenties and early 'thirties, but that his value as a thinker was little more than that. Blake's influence is greater; he began to interest Auden at the same time as Lawrence, and his appeal has increased over the years—so much so that in 'New Year Letter' Auden, naming the tribunal which shall judge him, puts Blake second only to Dante. We remarked earlier that Blake's intuition led him to conclusions which Freud reached by observation and experiment. 'The Marriage of Heaven and

Hell', and especially 'The Proverbs of Hell' show most forcibly what Blake gave to Auden. There one finds the attack on frustration and fear, the call for liberation and energy, the insistence that the springs of feeling must not be allowed to run dry, e.g. from 'The Proverbs of Hell':

> "He who desires but acts not, breeds pestilence";
> "Shame is Pride's cloak";
> "Expect poison from the standing water";
> "Exuberance is Beauty";

—all of which inform 'The Orators'.

In 'The Marriage of Heaven and Hell', Auden found statements such as this: "For man has closed himself up till he sees all through narrow chinks of his cavern." He has closed himself up, Auden would add, through fear feeding on the sense of inadequacy, a fear which enfeebles the will, and renders its victims incapable of 'love':

> "Mourn rather for yourselves, and your inability to make up your
>   minds
> Whose hours of self-hatred and contempt were all your majesty
>   and crises."

Hence the constant neurotic dread, the awful sense of threat which Auden so often evokes, and which dogs "all those people round about us, leading / Their quiet horrified lives". Hence the cry "Alas" which recurs throughout his verse, the cry of the lost and inadequate, the cry of those who are unequal to the demands of life. Prinzhorn, one of Auden's healers, has a relevant passage on this:

> "A very high percentage [of people], partly out of defective constitution, partly through being overburdened with the free decisions which modern life demands of them, drive themselves to a standstill in neurotic crises."

An individual such as this is "afraid / of all that has to be obeyed"; he is unequal to the responsibilities of adult freedom, to the inescapable demands of the human condition. Rendered purposeless by the constant trickle of fears eroding the will, he becomes a hater of life, one who tries always to evade issues, to say "Not Now". This theme continues to appear in Auden's work, and is particularly well expressed in that brilliant speech by Caliban which forms the second half of 'The Sea and the Mirror':

> "We have never felt really well in this climate of distinct ideas; . . . O take us home with you, strong and swelling one, home to your promiscuous pastures where the minotaur of authority is just a roly-poly ruminant and nothing is at stake."

Many of us are therefore only half-alive, members of an "ashamed, uninteresting and hopeless race", a race of solitary individuals whose sickness increases their solitude, but who cannot rid themselves of that sickness except by a positive move towards communal life. Instead, we cry for a leader, a father, someone who will assume responsibility for us, will release and restore us. Hence so much of the spiritual Swedish drill in the early poems, the cries of "Repent-Unite-Act", the drum-beating in such work as 'The Orators'.

Most of us are lonely: "We have fallen apart / Into the isolated personal life." Our separation and our self-regard reduce human relationships to a series of shadows on a screen; we sit in the prison-house of our egocentricity, practising "the high thin rare continuous worship of the self-absorbed". Seeking peace from the strain of making personal decisions, from the constant readjustment which life seems to demand from us, we cling to the comparative calm of a fixed and rigid ethos, we become the "holders of one position, wrong for years". There is at least peace, almost a kind of pleasure, in remaining in one's cell.

We are of those whom Dante placed in his first group of sinners, the excessive lovers of self. Auden makes this specific allusion in the 'Address for a Prize Day' ('The Orators'), and gives more importance to self-regard as the root of psychological illness in the early works than in the later. Perhaps the problem seemed easier to solve that way at first; Auden probably felt more justified in chivvying people. And it is likely that some of the enthusiasm Auden had for Marxism as a creed of *community* was prompted by his suspicion that much of what currently passed for 'individualism' was really self-regard. One of his commonest symbols—it recurs in both 'The Sea and the Mirror' and 'The Age of Anxiety'—is the mirror, the symbol for self-regarding escape. In the mirror one stares only at oneself, and sees simply a reflection; panic clutches at the heart because there is no way through.

The defence-measures by which we conceal or compensate for this pervading sense of insufficiency take strange forms, but are all shaped finally by the desire to escape. In a chorus to 'The Dog beneath the Skin' Auden suggests that almost any activity may be inspired by this wish:

> "Some turn to the time-honoured solutions of sickness and crime: some to the latest model of aeroplane or the sport of the moment.
> "Some to good works, to a mechanical ritual of giving.
> "Some have adopted an irrefragable system of beliefs or a political programme, others have escaped to the ascetic mountains
> "Or taken refuge in the family circle, among the boys on the bar-stools, on the small uncritical islands."

There are numerous more private types of evasion, e.g. the desire to return to the irresponsibilities of childhood ("Pick me up, Uncle, let little Johnny ride away on your massive shoulders to recover his green kingdom"), to that childhood which yet dogs us with its vestigial tyrannies, and from whose terrors we rarely quite escape. In speaking of the 'lonelies' Auden almost always uses the image of frightened children, the children we become back at home, when the masks are off. Again—among the more private types of evasion—there is the lure of fantasy, of "the permanent daydream", of the "wishful-thinking sigh": we are too often those "for whom a slight cold is enough to create a day-dream of our death-bed with appropriate organ-music". More dreadful still is the emergence of a compulsive routine which so grips the sufferer that he is ridden by dread unless the obsessive ritual is carried out; he is:

> "Unable to taste pleasure unless through the rare coincidence of naturally diverse events, or the performance of a long and intricate ritual. With odd dark eyes like windows. . . ."

There is a parallel passage in Freud:

> "A third observation is provided by patients whose symptoms take the form of obsessive acts, and who seem to be remarkably free from anxiety. When we restrain them from carrying out their obsessive performances, their washing, their ceremonies, etc., or when they themselves venture an attempt to abandon one of their compulsions, they are forced by an appalling dread to yield to the compulsion to carry out the act. We perceive that the anxiety was concealed under the obsessive act and that this is only performed to escape the feeling of dread. . . . As we know, the development of anxiety is the reaction of the ego to danger and the signal preparatory to flight; it is then not a great step to imagine that in neurotic anxiety also the ego is attempting a flight from the demands of its libido."

As the obsessive routine emerges and hardens, the personality is gradually warped; the isolation is now almost complete: "the lonely are battered / Slowly like pebbles into fortuitous shapes."

Sickness may be cherished or even induced as both flight and compensation; we may nourish an illness as "a reaction against insecurity and shame". Minor ailments may be nervous defence-measures against difficult situations. So in 'The

Orators' colds, nail-biting and headaches are listed as aids of the Enemy; conversely, Mrs. Thorvald, the middle-aged bourgeois housewife in 'On the Frontier', finds her headache disappears when the excitement starts; and as recently as 'For the Time Being' a semi-chorus asks for help:

> "(for us) whose will
> To civil anarchy,
> Uses disease to disobey
> And makes our private bodies ill."

Klages, another of Auden's creditors, has a passage on the subject in which he says, "The hysterical interest in representing life is turned upon the ritual mutation of symptoms of disease". But it is to Groddeck that Auden owes most here; they share an intense interest in disease self-induced as compensation for a starved creative instinct, in that strange power of the human mind, forbidden normal creative activity and twisted back upon itself, to produce a sickness and to support and care for it with what would, under other circumstances, be admirable skill and vigour:

> "Only the challenge to our will,
> Our pride in learning any skill,
> Sustains our effort to be ill."

Groddeck investigated over a long period the mental induction of physical ailments. He also shares with Auden a strong sense of the symbolic character of the apparently commonplace, an upthrusting energy, and a habit of postulating an idealised 'Love' as the solvent for our troubles. His statements are always vigorous and often brilliantly suggestive:

> "Such ideas [fantasy, romance, the personal myths created to satisfy our illusions of our own importance—R. H.] are the foundations of human life, but why the It builds out of them for this man the religion of God the Father, for another rheumatism, for a third the founding of a kingdom or a mental illness, for

brides the bridal crown, for us all the striving after perfection, these are questions which each man must seek to answer for himself."

In the notes to 'New Year Letter', Auden quotes Groddeck's *Book of the It* at length on the same subject.

Auden himself sometimes takes an adolescent pleasure in mocking the 'queer' victims of neurosis. The ballad 'Miss Gee' scoffs at a religiously inclined spinster who produces her own cancer in place of the child which is denied her. Here, too, there is a parallel in a report by Groddeck:

"My experience with cases of tumour has convinced me that there, too, a symbolism of pregnancy is involved (and I have used this line of approach in treating cases with some success)."

Elsewhere Auden treats the theme more adequately :

"That which was creative (becomes) a stalking destruction:
That which was loving, a tormenting flame
For those who reject their gifts choose here their punishment."

Since Blake, a succession of writers have deplored a divorce between reason and imagination, a neglect of the 'id', of the emotional side of man. Blake had centred his attack on the rejection of the Newtonian universe ("May God us keep / From single vision and Newton's sleep"). In our period D. H. Lawrence in particular has reiterated that, since Newton, Western Europe has followed its head to the neglect of its heart. This view is clearly informing the whole of Auden's approach to individual psychology, though he would not be so ready to trust the 'id' as Lawrence, and he has to leave Blake at the point where examination ends and belief begins. More than once he echoes Blake on the evil of 'Will', notably in the Abbot's speech to Michael Ransom on F.6: "Government requires the exercise of the human will and the human will is from the Demon"; which has its counterpart in an obscure note of

Blake's: "There can be no good Will. Will is always Evil."
Auden may never have seen that note, and in any case the
Abbot speaks in character. But Auden is, I believe, largely in
agreement with Blake on the evil effects of 'Will', *in the sense in
which Blake defines it*. Mr. Bernard Blackstone defines clearly
what Blake meant by it. Blake, he says, here "anticipates the
findings of modern psychology":

> "By will here he means the faculty by which we try to change
> ourselves according to a pattern prescribed by the reason, by
> moral codes, and by religious organisations. This attempt must
> always end in disaster (even if the victim does not always recog-
> nise it as disaster) for the reason has no faculties for understanding
> the whole of personality. It is concerned with a very limited por-
> tion of the human totality. Only the understanding, drawing its
> life from the senses, the instincts, the obscure physical processes,
> as well as from the reason and the intuition, is fitted to deal with
> that whole. The imposition of the will ends in disaster in one of
> two ways.

> "The less serious disaster is that the totality rejects the pattern
> proposed to it by the reason, and there is what the religious used
> to call a backsliding, which may be repeated over and over again
> if the will is persistent and the personality strong. This happens
> in the case of men of decided intellect and powerful passions; and
> the result is a worse chaos than before. Much more serious, how-
> ever, is the case of the man of weak passions and intellect (the
> two always go together) who does allow his personality to be
> crushed into an alien mould, and goes through life thenceforth
> as a mutilated being. There is always a feeling of frustration."

So 'Will' in Blake's sense aggravates the split between intuition and reason, presents special problems to the exceptional
man, and helps to create the warped and lonely. On all these
points Auden would agree with Blake.

Though all such sickness is at bottom an individual matter,
it cannot be considered in isolation from the society in which

it thrives. We live in a period in which it is very easy for a personality to become lamed: "the lost and injured live in mechanized societies." Indeed, a society may exhibit a sort of communal neurosis, may fashion large-scale forms of escape from fear not different in kind from the rituals and routines of the individual:

> ". . . our cities predict
> More than we hope; even our armies
> Have to express our need of forgiveness."

So war may be partly an attempt to lay the demon, the "last attempt to eliminate the stranger / By uniting us all in a terror of something known". War, and many other social phenomena which few question, may be as much symptoms of the Fear as any little nervous tic: the roots are the same, only the disguises differ

> "What have we all been doing to have made from Fear
> That laconic war-bitten captain addressing them now."

And just as we may in fantasy escape to a dream of a childhood garden where all was good and easy and friendly, so our crowding together is more than a matter of practical convenience. "Our cities predict more than we hope", for:

> "All the conventions conspire
> To make this fort assume
> The furniture of home;
> Lest we should see where we are,
> Lost in a haunted wood,
> Children afraid of the night
> Who have never been happy or good."

Auden makes a good deal of play with the Freudian concept of the death-wish, especially in its communal forms:

> "We present to you this evening a picture of the decline of a class, of how its members dream of a new life, but secretly desire the old, for there is death inside them."

Freud had divided the instincts into two:

> "And now the instincts in which we believe separate them-
> selves into two groups . . . the erotic instincts, which are always
> trying to collect living substance together into even larger
> unities, and the death instincts which act against that tendency,
> and try to bring living matter back into an inorganic condition."

For Auden the distinction was useful. It helped to explain
the deadness of his society, the urge to violence which he
dramatised in 'Paid on Both Sides', the "unbreakable habits of
death" which he saw settling on so many faces, the death-
worshipping creeds which the 'twenties and 'thirties especially
cultivated. It gave him a stronger basis for the other force
which he set against the death-wish: that is, the force of 'Love',
the urge towards life, co-operation and unity. This 'Love' is
partly Freud's 'erotic instinct', but Auden gave it an importance
beyond any Freud would have thought legitimate.

It is this force which prompts man's unfailing desire to be
rid of his insanity:

> "O teach me to outgrow my madness.
>
> .   .   .   .
>
> Rally the lost and trembling forces of the will,
> Gather them up and let them loose upon the earth
>
> Till they construct at last a human justice,
> The contribution of our star, within the shadow
> Of which uplifting, loving, and constraining power
> All other reasons may rejoice and operate."

It is this force which ensures that "at moments—the trance
is broken . . . he believes in joy"; it is this force which may
eventually release man from his inhibiting stupor.

This major theme of the 'lonelies', who are in some ways all
of us, and of the power to help of 'love' (a word whose extensions of meaning mirror Auden's spiritual development), continues in Auden's verse to the present. He is still fruitfully

examining the nature of anxiety; but the process of discovering just what he means by the 'Love' which can oppose it has carried him to positions which, in the early 'thirties, would have seemed unthinkable.

(3) *Love*

It is impossible to define exactly what Auden means by 'Love' in the 'thirties, not only because he is vague, but because the meaning is continuously modified. There is often a generalised, a luminous air about his use of the word, a suggestion of the transcendental which inspires a lyricism otherwise expressed only in his poems of personal affection:

> "O Love, the interest itself in thoughtless Heaven
> Make simpler daily the beating of man's heart."

Or again:

> "Love, loath to enter
> The suffering winter
> Still willing to rejoice
> With the unbroken voice
>
> .   .   .   .   .   .
>
> Enter and suffer
> Within the quarrel
> Be most at home,
> Among the sterile prove
> Your vigours, love."

The root-idea—an intuition—is that men do wish to live together generously. This is clearly more than 'love' in either the sexual or the 'personal relations' sense, though it includes these senses. It always looks towards the larger community; yet it does not suggest that the individual should be submerged in the group. It has something in common with Bergson's theory of creative evolution and Shaw's notion of the 'life-force', although there is probably no direct debt to either of them. Most of Auden's 'healers' have contributed something to the general idea; it owes something to Groddeck, and perhaps a little to Klages who, speaking of bonds and their principal releases, says: "We comprehend them all (the releases from mental bonds) under the one name of Love." There are, as we have already said, debts to Freud's 'erotic instinct,' although Auden's 'Love' is much vaguer at the edges —yet it is, in one aspect, a form of mental therapy, a gloriously effective psycho-analysis, a liberator, a cleanser, a releasing and enlarging power:

> "The word is Love . . .
> Surely one fearless kiss would cure
> The million fevers."

It is partly Blake's 'energy' (in 'The Marriage of Heaven and Hell', for example): it owes something to Lawrence and a lot to Homer Lane. Auden first heard of Lane's theories in Berlin and found them immensely attractive. Lane made Love central to his psychology:

"All organic life may be represented as a wish. Man, the highest form of organic life, is in himself the cumulative wishes of all organic life in past ages. Man is the embodiment of the master-wish for perfection of the universe, and is therefore essentially good. The motive power of goodness is love, and love is compulsory. If a man does not love mankind and the universe, he is not true to his nature. Man does not choose to love: he must love.

"If he hates, his behaviour is untrue to himself, to mankind and to the universe, but the energy is still love, for his act of hatred is love perverted. The hateful act is destructive of the man's self and also of the happiness and welfare of mankind, thus retarding the perfection of the universe. It is wholly unnatural.

"The loving act is hopeful behaviour, the hateful act is fearful behaviour. And he who serves his fellow men by effort of will is making love a virtue; it is unnatural to mankind. According to his conception of authority man will either progress towards perfection, obeying the master-wish, or regress to the primitive. The only true authority is love, and the only true discipline is founded upon hope. The authority that is based upon force will transform love into hatred and hope into fear.

"If a man's love be not extended to all mankind and all communities, he cannot be completely happy; for love is dynamic and universal. Any distrust or fear of another community than his own, will infect his own community with hatred and destroy its harmony. For hatred makes a community sick, as it makes each human sick. Every man must choose for himself. No man can be compelled to love, for love is itself the highest form of compulsion."

'Love', then, is in all men, but only finds itself in community—it is "the flood on which all move and wish to move". It is partly a biological urge towards co-operation. An object is doing good when it is fulfilling its function in society (again the central place is given to man in society), that is to say, when it is living creatively, that is to say, loving.

'Love' is the source of all that is 'lucid' and 'civilised' (both favourite words of Auden's) in human societies; it encourages —and for this Auden almost always finds a landscape image— a "natural climate", the "birth of a natural order".

And since 'Love' is a creative force it will out: refused a normal growth, it may take a horrible disguise. So many psychological oddnesses are at bottom "the false attitudes of Love", e.g. the excessive love of self, the transformation of the need for love into an insane striving for worldly recognition ('If I do well I shall be loved'), and Groddeckian sickness:

"Love, that notable forked one . . . transforms itself to influenza and guilty rashes."

In each of those cases, the error has been that love was really self-love. Since 'Love' can flourish only in the field of *relationships*, the greatest obstacle to its free growth is self-regard. If that rules, "the hard self-conscious particles collide": to the self-absorbed, all men are enemies; only with extreme difficulty can there be any moving out to a relationship, any submission of the ego in friendship. But not until the ego is forgotten in love can there be an escape from the prison cell:

> "No personal experience, no scientific knowledge, gives any other verdict than that what you can self-forgetfully love, you can cure."

Thus, by the operation of love, the will may be cleansed, and the personality, freed from undue preoccupation with itself, be rendered less likely to breed strange obsessions. Yet the self need not lose its identity or importance by being merged into a larger unit; the new relationship includes and transcends the old:

> "Every eye must weep alone
> Till I Will be overthrown.
>
> . . . .
>
> Then all I's can meet and grow,
> I Am become I Love,
> I Have Not I Am Loved
> Then all I's can meet and grow."

(Again, the 'Will' here is Blake's 'Will'.)

The same theme is the core of the Airman's message in 'The Orators': "Of kindness to one another for likeness, of love for each one's uniqueness"; the Airman calls it there the message of "the central awareness", but it stems from the Christian tradition.

The important, the cardinal point about 'Love'—and the reason for much of Auden's drum-beating ("choose therefore that you may recover")—is that it is the one thing needful, that it is there, that it needs only to be sought with care and, when found, nourished and developed:

> "O can you see precisely in our gaucheness
> The neighbour's strongest wish, to serve and love."

And at the prospect of building the city where "the will of love
is done", and where "grace may grow outward / and be given
praise / Beauty and virtue be vivid there", the lyricism rises
again, very strong—but still conditioned:

> ". . . Love finally is great,
>   Greater than all: but large the hate,
>   Far larger than man can ever estimate."

It is conditioned exactly because Auden has not up to this
point fully faced that 'large hate'; nor did he face it until the
late 'thirties, although he knew all along that a conception of
love which did not include and transcend sin was inadequate.
He might cry in 1935, "O Love, the interest *itself* in thought-
less Heaven / Make simpler daily the beating of man's heart";
but as far back as 1930, in Paris, he had admitted, and continued to admit to himself intermittently, that simple affirmation such as that is not enough, that 'Love' has its stern duties
and necessities: "We know it, we know that love needs more
than the admiring excitement of union." He knew, much as it
attracted him, that Homer Lane's euphoric afflatus, by cavalierly
dismissing the problem of evil, over-simplified the real
dilemma. In his twenties Auden found it impossible to accept
the Christian answer; he was too much the child of the destructive last half-century for that. He tried instead to stiffen
the vague concept 'Love' by uniting it to positive action, to a
scientific and a social discipline. Conversely, and probably
more importantly, he *had* to have such a concept exactly because Freud and Marx taken together did not give a complete
answer. 'Love' gave some sort of harmony to the separate and
incomplete themes of Freud and Marx. But, as Auden knew, it
did a good deal more than that. It stood in its own right; it
suggested themes profounder than any Freud or Marx had
conceived. Auden could not leave 'Love' alone; he has continued to talk of it insistently. And when he says now:

"The course of History is predictable in the degree to which all men love themselves and spontaneous in the degree to which each man loves God and through Him his neighbour"

'Love' obviously means something very different from what it meant at any point in the 'thirties. To find just what it does mean has been Auden's chief endeavour in the four long works from America.

In thus extracting the main themes in Auden's work up to the war, we have greatly simplified—and perhaps over-simplified—for the sake of clarity. His views were, it need hardly be said, never so cut-and-dried; they were shot through with modifications which it would require a chapter much longer than the poems themselves, and much less valuable, to describe. But from this and the later chapter on the American work a not too inaccurate pattern should emerge.

Nevertheless, Auden did tend to oversimplify in the 'thirties; he was often youthful in his enthusiasms, often lacking in humility. For this the pressure of his times was partly to blame, and there were, he knew, personal reasons:

> "I know that I am I, living in a small way in a temperate zone, blaming father, jealous of son, confined to a few acts often repeated, easily attracted to a limited class of physique, yet envying the simple life of the gut, desiring the certainty of the breast or prison, happiest sawing wood, only knowledge of the real, disturbances in the general law of the dream; the quick blood fretting against the slowness of the hope; a unit of life, needing water and salt, that looks for a sign."

His philosophy was not coherent, but was patched up from three main influences—Freud, Marx and 'Love'—combined in a precarious union in his own imagination. He was, we have said, largely in agreement with the Marxist social analysis, though the orthodox rightly suspected him; he thought much of Freud's analysis of the psyche correct, but was never ready to think it sufficient; he was not a Christian, but he talked of

'Love' and asked for pardon. In all these things he was, essentially, tackling the problem of the moral will, and his answer was eclectic. It was the sort of answer which an intelligent, concerned and forceful young man in the 'thirties might readily find, but would not be likely to accept for long.

Its value to Auden's work is that it did for the time being set up creative tensions, give him some sort of thesis, a positiveness with which to challenge the malaise which he hated in so much around him. And though he is now a good deal more doubtful about the final value of

> ". . . the same
> Old treatments for tedium vitæ,
> Religion [by which he means a soothingly final view of life],
> Politics, Love,"

he never fails to reassert that we are committed to our times, and to doing therein the best we can, inadequate though that will always be—since in our social forms we try to shadow forth truths not in themselves man-made. So, in the final section to 'The Age of Anxiety', Malin says:

> ". . . the noble despair of the poets
> Is nothing of the sort; it is silly
> To refuse the tasks of the time
> And, overlooking our lives,
> Cry—'Miserable wicked me'."

CHAPTER V

AMERICA AND LATER THEMES

(1) *The Need to Emigrate*

AUDEN emigrated to America early in 1939, and has therefore spent half of his poetic life there; he now lives in one of the districts of New York. He has deliberately cut himself off from the ties of family, race and the English scene, all of which meant much to him. He is alone in a crowd. He left partly out of disgust with the mess England had made of her affairs in the 'thirties, but more importantly for reasons connected with his art.

The whole bent of Auden's mind, and the kind of work to which it prompts, require him to be in a position of the kind he has chosen:

> "From now on the poet will be lucky if he can have the general living-room to himself for a few hours and a corner of the kitchen table on which to keep his papers. The soft carpets, the big desks, will all be reserved by the Management for the whopping liars. . . . Every poet stands alone. This does not mean that he sulks mysteriously in a corner by himself; on the contrary, he may perhaps lead a more social life than before, but as a neighbour like his neighbours, not as a poet."

As the 'thirties advanced and as Auden's understanding of his own purposes grew, it became clear that he would have to leave Europe's cultural domesticity. Cyril Connolly says of a conversation with Auden in 1947: "He reverts always to the same argument, that a writer needs complete anonymity, he must break away from the European literary happy family . . . and he must reconsider all the family values." The appropriate isolation for Auden is urban isolation, isolation in a vast anonymous metroland such as New York; isolation in a position from which one can observe and yet not be caught up, to the detriment of the power of analysis and reflection.

In such a position one may be lonely in the way that so many people are lonely today: one is never likely to forget there that "aloneness is man's real condition". And a writer is not likely to forget, as he might if he lived among writers, his relationship to the rest of society. American literature, says Auden, is a literature of lonely people. On another occasion he told an interviewer:

> "The attractiveness of America to a writer is its openness and lack of tradition. In a way it's frightening. You are forced to live here as everyone else will be forced to live. There is no past. No tradition. No roots—that is, in the European sense. . . . But what is happening here is happening everywhere. The general effect of the trends of machinery has been to de-root people. . . . With history moving so fast, people are so afraid! People feel, what is the permanent thing?"

Metropolitan New York exhibits these tendencies of Western civilisation in their most advanced form, makes it impossible to ignore those spiritual problems which such technologically competent societies aggravate. The issues are more obscured in Europe, where the remnants of a religious tradition still provide some spiritual capital to live on, even though that capital is not being renewed:

> "More even than in Europe, here,
> The choice of patterns is made clear
> Which the machine imposes, what
> Is possible and what is not,
> To what conditions we must bow
> In building the Just City now."

Auden's social interest can best be expressed from a position of isolation inside a city of eight million souls. But this situation makes Auden less than ever certain of exactly whom he is addressing; he lacks the sense of having a moderately identifiable body of readers. If he had stayed in England he would not have lost that at least. Nevertheless, one cannot for that reason wish his decision reversed: he is a spiritual exile, and his geographical exile gives point to that fact. He will write less quixotically when he is emotionally as well as intellectually sure of his beliefs, and meanwhile he will be finding gradually the audience, neither simply American nor simply European, which he now needs—and which needs him. Auden is faithful to what he believes important. 'The Age of Anxiety' is at times exciting, at times disappointing; but that, given the conditions outlined above, is not surprising in a long work. A short poem of roughly the same date—'In Praise of Limestone'—though still in places wayward, comes much nearer to being fully and successfully an expression of Auden's extremely significant present position. It is a poem which could only have been written in his kind of isolation. From it and from parts of the long works we may see what Auden, severed from all local cultures, as a poet of his type must be today, may yet produce.

(2) *The Place of Art*

"Analogy is not Identity,
Art is not enough."

Today, having left "the European literary happy family", Auden has set himself also "to reconsider all the family values". He enquires continually into the nature of creative art, not only in its social, but in its metaphysical implications; he is considering the purpose and scope of his own life. It is of the first importance to him now that he should be on his guard against as many as possible of the false attitudes towards art, and should decide what, if any, are its justifications. The question is not simply or most importantly concerned with art itself; it is inseparable from the problem of belief. The false attitudes of art are the false attitudes of faith.

Previously Auden had often discussed the function of the writer. He had agreed, for instance, that the artist today must be in some ways an émigré, but had refused to wear that title like a badge or indulge in the pride of the odd. He meant to indicate by it the necessity for the artist, as for any imaginative and critical personality, to refuse simply to accept the terms of life which his society offers, without questioning the ends which the terms subserve. Auden still thinks the attitude correct in principle: in 'New Year Letter' he quotes an extract from the Journals of Kierkegaard in support of it, and explores its application to the social value of art in Poem 23 of 'Another Time', which begins (the artist is being addressed):

> "Not as that dream Napoleon, rumour's dread and centre,
>   Before whose riding all the crowds divide,
>
>   .   .   .   .
>
>   Do not enter like that: all these depart. . . ."

Because he has always been aware of some of the peculiar temptations of the artist, Auden has expanded frequently, especially in his earlier essays, Freud's explanation of art as fantasy and of the artist as a neurotic who compensates himself through fantasy for what reality denies, whose art is a substitute for "honour, power, and the love of women". Michael Ransom is quoting the twenty-third of Freud's *Introductory Lectures on Psycho-Analysis* when he applies the phrase to Dante in that opening soliloquy on the Pillar Rock. But though he believed that art has a neurotic origin, Auden did not fully accept Freud's summing-up:

> "Art is almost always harmless and beneficent, it does not seek to be anything else but an illusion. Save in the case of a few people who are, one might say, obsessed by art, it never dares to make any attacks on the realm of reality."

He put Freud's view the more readily, however, because it helped to dispel the pretentious mystification which can arise from the idea of the artist as an exile.

In one section of 'New Year Letter' and in 'The Sea and the Mirror' Auden has made his closest and most subtle examinations of the nature of the artistic process. His starting-point today is that art is a game, a matter of knack and skill. Periods in which Christian belief is weak tend to overvalue art:

"The romantic movement has been, *au fond*, an attempt to found a new non-supernatural Catholicism, and because art is a shared thing and so in this sense Catholic, one of the romantic symptoms has been an enormous exaggeration of the importance of art as a guide to life. . . . The modern artist is in a dilemma. If he has beliefs, realising that he cannot assume them in his audience, he is tempted to underline them in his work and to become a preacher. . . . If he has none, he is drawn [to] evading the problem of belief by presenting something which is as ambiguous as life itself and so putting the audience *vis à vis* his work in the same situation as he is toward life."

The danger of over-emphasising the importance of art threatens both audience and artist, but in particular the latter, since he feels the force of his own gifts. So the poet is tempted to practise indefinitely his "old innocent game of playing God with words", especially since he thereby puts off more difficult tasks: "He would like to be religious," quotes Auden from Kierkegaard, who has most influenced his thinking on this subject, "but remains a poet. Consequently, he is unhappily in love with God."

Art not only tends to distort life by imposing on it an unreal but tranquillising pattern, a false appearance of harmony and order, but it gives to both producer and consumer a satisfaction which hinders their study of more difficult questions, to which art itself can give no answers. Precisely because art does reflect these other questions, one may be tempted to suppose it answers them. Or it may make one happy to remain in an intensely aware but delightfully uncommitted condition: "As though an awareness of the gap is in itself a bridge." Thus may art be narcissism, mirror-gazing, a subtle and finished begging of questions, an escape from the important issues in life, in no matter how well-disguised a form. For the artist his activity can thereby become, as Caliban insists, a postponement of the moment when the inadequacies of his own personality have to be faced, when, in Kierkegaard's phrase, "a man must get out of the poetical and into the existential".

Auden is proscribing that fundamentally unserious attitude which attempts to elevate æsthetics into religion—the attitude which encourages a great *interest* in the 'necessities' of life as the material of art, but will not allow itself to be embarrassed by them. The error is particularly common among the more intelligent: they confuse the æsthetic with the spiritual and, when they begin to think about religion, they run the converse risk of regarding the spiritual life as a kind of æsthetic performance.

But though art may not be of the first importance, it has considerable value: Auden sums up what he calls the two theories of poetry thus:

"Poetry as a magical means for inducing desirable emotions and repelling undesirable emotions in oneself and others, or Poetry as a game of knowledge, a bringing to consciousness, by naming them, of emotions and their wider relationships.

"The first view was held by the Greeks, and is now held by M.G.M., Agit-Prop, and the collective public of the world. They are wrong."

And presumably the second view is right. It contains a wide mandate for art, according to which the creative imagination is the Ariel in man, not to be considered apart from the Caliban, the 'id':

"Never hope to say farewell,

. . . .

Both of us know why,
Can, alas, foretell,

141

> When our falsehoods are divided,
> What we shall become,
> One evaporating sigh
>
>   . . . I."

The view implies further that, so long as art is not regarded as an end in itself, it can by its patterning suggest a profounder order:

> "By significant details it shows us that our present state is neither as virtuous nor as secure as we thought, and by the lucid pattern into which it unifies these details, its assertion that order is *possible*, it faces us with the command to make it *actual*. . . . No artist, not even Eliot, can prevent his work being used as magic, for that is what all of us, highbrow and lowbrow alike, secretly want Art to be."

By its hints, then, of a severer and more splendid order, art suggests the extent of our fall:

> "What else exactly *is* the artistic gift which he is forbidden to hide, if not to make you unquestionably conscious of the ungarnished offended gap between what you so questionably are and what you are commanded without any question to become."

It points towards those necessities which, Auden repeatedly says today, all of us must recognise. Thus judged, art is not confined; it is rather released, strengthened, given new power, for:

> "[In Him] Imagination is released from promiscuous fornication with her own images. . . .
>
> "Nor is there any situation which is essentially more or less interesting than another. Every tea-table is a battlefield. . . .
>
> "Because in Him all passions find a logical In-Order-That, by Him is the perpetual recurrence of Art assured."

(3) *Moral Struggle, 'Love' and Social Ends*

> "Perhaps I always knew what they were saying:
> Even the early messengers who walked
> Into my life from books where they were staying,
>
> . . . .

Love was the word they never said aloud
As something that a picture can't return.

And later when I hunted the Good Place,
Abandoned lead-mines let themselves be caught;
There was no pity in the adit's face,

. . . .

While all their lack of answer whispered 'Wait',
And taught me gradually without coercion,
And all the landscape round them pointed to
The calm with which they took complete desertion
As proof that you existed.

It was true.
For now I have the answer from the face
That never will go back into a book
But asks for all my life, and is the Place. . . ."

The most striking characteristic of the considerable body of
work which Auden has produced in America is that in all of it,
whether in poems, general essays, critical articles, reviews or
lectures, and whatever his ostensible subject, he discusses religious belief. His most important creditors—as important as
Freud or Marx earlier—have been Kierkegaard and Niebuhr.
Neither influence is surprising. Not only are Kierkegaard's
examinations of profound relevance today, but he laid much
emphasis on the individual soul (rather than on the body of
the church), its suffering and arrival at faith, and on the
importance of moral choice. Niebuhr similarly discusses
matters of special interest to Auden, in particular 'the situation
of the time', the conflict between freedom and necessity, and
the exact nature of sin.

Many of the ideas which Auden repeatedly considers today
are therefore to be found in the work of these two theologians.
But to attempt to trace these debts in detail would not be
relevant to an essay of this kind. Some mention will be made
of them and of others who have here affected Auden, but only
as much as will help towards a better understanding of his

poetry or convey the eclectic nature of his borrowings. The particular Christian themes which Auden considers most insistently reflect—as do those of, say, T. S. Eliot's 'Four Quartets'—the special bent of his personality. He enquires most commonly into the moral dilemma, into the nature of Love and into the social implications of his Faith. 'The Meditation of Simeon' in 'For the Time Being' is the best introduction to the main lines along which the discussion usually develops.

Auden's acceptance of the Christian presuppositions dates roughly from the time of his emigration. But the process by which he arrived at that acceptance had begun by the time he left Oxford. He has always, for example, insisted that man is not free, but must obey certain necessities. In the 'thirties Marxism supported that insistence by its definition of freedom as "the knowledge of necessity".

All through Auden's earlier work prayers, invocations, admissions of humility before an unknown God recur. Thus Ode 6 of 'The Orators' begins: "Not, father, further do prolong / Our necessary defeat"; a chorus in 'The Dog beneath the Skin' denies that it is sufficient to have "adopted an irrefragable system of beliefs or a political programme", and demands repentance; as the Abbot leaves him, Michael Ransom cries, not naming a Christian God: "Oh, you who are the history and the creator of all those forms in which we are condemned to suffer, to whom the necessary is also the just, show me, show each of us upon this mortal star the danger that under his hand is softly palpitating. Save us, save us from the destructive element of our will, for all we do is evil." The final chorus of Eric and Anna in 'On the Frontier' presents an interesting blend of Christian attitudes with left-progressive generalisations about the two young lovers helping, through their deaths, to build the greater future. There is talk of "tiny separate lives" (i.e. less important than the social whole), and of the mastering of necessity; there is the early idea of 'Love'; the reference is throughout to man and his earth, not to any higher power. But the note of humility and constant striving ("Pardon them their mistakes / The impatient and wavering will") is one from the Christian tradition. It is, in fact, a prayer, but to whom addressed is not stated:

> "*Eric.* 'Now as we come to our end,
>   As the tiny separate lives
>   Fall, fall to their graves,
>   We begin to understand.
>
> .   .   .   .
>
>   With our last look we bless
>   The turning maternal earth.'
> *Anna.* 'Europe lies in the dark
>   City and flood and tree;
>   Thousands have worked and work
>   To master necessity.'
> *Eric.* 'To build the city where
>   The will of love is done
>   And brought to its full flower
>   The dignity of man.'
> *Anna.* 'Pardon them their mistakes,
>   The impatient and wavering will.
>   They suffer for our sakes,
>   Honour, honour them all.'
> *Both.* 'Dry their imperfect dust,
>   The wind blows it back and forth.
>   They die to make man just
>   And worthy of the earth.'
>   "FINAL CURTAIN."

Throughout, the call is always for "a change of heart", the vision always of "The Good Place" (a much-repeated phrase), the place of 'Love'. Auden's spiritual history is the history of his growing realisation of how much this change of heart implied, and just what "the place of Love, the Good Place" might mean. That hazy concept 'Love' contained the beginnings of his faith: it had been introduced, we have seen, to fill a vacuum which neither Marxism nor Freudianism could fill; it gradually assumed supreme importance, and in the process put both the other main influences in their places.

So there has not been a sudden reversal of outlook, but rather a continuous development in a mind of great honesty and subtlety applying itself fruitfully to its field of experience. The road which led from Marxism and Freudianism in the early 'thirties to Christianity today is a long, difficult and tortuous one; but, we have already suggested, it is a single road. Auden's Christian belief is rooted in the same kind of response to experience as prompted an earlier allegiance to Communism. In youth Auden's great purposiveness and his powerful analytic intellect led him to solutions which had not been tested against very much of his personality. The only explanation of Man which he now finds tenable is the Christian, and that requires not primarily social analysis nor psychological observation, though either may be relevant starting-points for some kinds of mind. It requires Faith, a wager, belief in 'the Absurd', 'a leap in the dark'.

The cardinal item of faith, "the absurd" itself, is the fact that "the eternal truth has come into being in time, that God has come into being". Certain other statements follow from it, and are matters of faith-knowledge, not susceptible of scientific proof, e.g. the statement, to which Auden assents, that "Man is a fallen creature with a natural bias to do evil", or the assertions contained in this passage from as early as 'In Time of War':

> "Men are not innocent as beasts and never can be,
> Man can improve himself but never will be perfect,
> Only the free have disposition to be truthful,
> Only the truthful have the interest to be just,
> Only the just possess the will-power to be free."

We cannot carry on our lives without believing certain

values to be absolute, much as we may hate the fact that they are not susceptible of proof as we know it. "I should not love because I had no proof," says Sebastian in 'The Sea and the Mirror'—"yet all my honesty assumed a sword." That the Way, the Law, Natural Order, exists can only be therefore "an absolute presupposition deliberately and consciously held". It is a matter of faith-knowledge, though the evidence of all our lives helps towards it:

> "The Way rests upon Faith and Doubt: Faith that Natural Law exists and that we can have knowledge of it; Doubt that our knowledge can ever be perfect or unmixed with error:
> > Our grounds for Faith: the unhappiness of Man
> > Our grounds for Doubt: the same."

Yet, though we can have some knowledge of these values, the knowledge will always be "distorted by the limitations of our historical period and our personal character".

Since these values exist and must be obeyed, man is not free: he cannot evade moral choice:

> "We live in freedom by necessity,
> A mountain people dwelling among mountains."

Man may insist that he does not recognise the existence of a field of moral decision; he is thereby making a moral decision, since the refusal to choose is itself a choice, a denial of necessity. He can therefore choose rightly or wrongly—so far he is free; he is not free not to choose—so far he is under necessity:

> "Dictatorship has been defined as a state where everything that is not obligatory is forbidden, and in that sense man has always lived under a dictatorship and always will. Our only choice lies between an external and false necessity passively accepted and an internal necessity consciously decided, but that is the difference between slavery and freedom."

Freedom has value, but is not "the corollary and ground of value"; our freedom is valuable because it is a freedom to be virtuous, a freedom which we cannot relinquish. We have therefore to be "conscious of Necessity as our Freedom to be tempted and of Freedom as our Necessity to have Faith".

There is a field of 'causal' Necessity in which we have no choice (we must eat to live; we must work to eat); but these are not to be confused with 'logical' necessity, the necessities of moral choice. This distinction is discussed at length in the notes to line 63 of 'New Year Letter'. By eating to live or working so that we may eat we do not acquire virtue; we simply obey 'causal' Necessity. By exercising our responsibility for moral choice we may acquire virtue. The material successes of one generation may lift some 'causal' Necessities from their successors. But the moral struggle is presented afresh to each person in every generation, and can never end in complete success. We are always "becoming" not "being"; we are never perfect ("an existing individual is constantly in process of becoming" —Kierkegaard).

Yet this is no reason for despair; "the distresses of choice are our chance to be blessed": since consciousness may be aided by grace, error and weakness may be redeemed. So is the inadequacy of man made adequate to its task. And in occasional moments—the moments of 'Being'—we are given some illumination of the end of the process of 'Becoming'. It is characteristic of Auden that, in his religious discussions, although he mentions the absolute necessity of grace for the redemption of man, he lays far more emphasis on that which man must himself do to correct error.

In revealing the truth of choice to man, Christianity freed him from an overwhelming necessity, by suggesting a sphere in which he is free: it took away the dream of an unlimited anarchic freedom by defining an inescapable necessity—he must choose morally:

"Greek tragedy is the tragedy of Necessity. . . . Christian tragedy is the tragedy of possibility. 'What a pity it is this way when it might have been otherwise.' . . . To say that a character is tempted means that it is confronted by possibility, that it is not a fixed state but a process of becoming; the possibilities are not infinite . . . but the possibilities are eternal; the past is irrevocable, but always redeemable now."

The responsibilities implied are so frightening that we often try to "slip out of our own position / Into an unconcerned condition". We long futilely for the womb ("as though a fœtus could refuse to be born!"); we try to hand our wills over to an *alter ego* (as Shawcross to Michael Ransom); we are glad when a dictator promises to assume for us the weight of our consciences; we deny that "being chosen, we must choose", and we rail against a blind 'fate', or we suggest that there are several orders, each with different values and each right (e.g. "the sentimental businessman").

Hence our unhappiness, for "liberty to be and weep has never been sufficient"; hence Auden's persistent cry that life gives you nothing, that its terms cannot be escaped: "The rules are necessary, for they do not cease to exist if you disobey them but operate within you to your destruction."

Paradoxically we feel both too small to assume the limited responsibility offered, and too important to be limited anyway. We deny necessity because it lowers our pride; we find it hard to "stretch imagination to live according to our station". We commit gratuitous acts simply because they are gratuitous, and so an assertion of the freedom of our ego from necessity:

"Sin is occasioned precisely by the fact that man refuses to admit his 'creatureliness'; he pretends to be more than he is. . . . His essence is free determination. . . . His sin is the wrong use of his freedom and its consequent destruction."

This is the condition of pride, a lack of proper humility in the face of our own weakness, a refusal to discipline the hard self-regarding 'I':

> "Since Adam, being free to choose,
>   Chose to imagine he was free
>   To choose his own necessity,
>   Lost in his freedom, Man pursues
>   The shadow of his images."

In this state Man may say, not 'there are several orders', but 'there is one order—and it is *man-made*'.

The dilemma is the same for the gifted and the ungifted, and the possibilities of blessedness exist equally; for both, "the choice to love is open till we die". The self-deceptions and evasions of the simple person may differ from, and perhaps be less complex than, those of the more exceptional, but the roots will be the same. The passages at the Manger, in 'For the Time Being', between the three wise men (the exceptionally gifted) and the shepherds (ordinary people) treat this more thoroughly than any other section of Auden's work.

Auden stresses the point rather conscientiously, perhaps because of that special interest in the temptations of the exceptional man which we have already noticed. In examining those temptations he is examining some particularly troublesome aspects of his own personality.

For the exceptional man there will follow, from moral necessity, certain implications for his conduct towards the less gifted. He will be constantly tempted to ignore the latter, to react into power, to still the nag of conscience by imposing himself on others. Or he may reject, not only power, but any kind of responsibility; he may deny the necessity for any metaphysic, and retreat into a cold intellectual autarchy. The temptations will be the greater in a disordered world. So false intellectualism may become a form of escape from necessity; one may become subjectivist to avoid the difficulty of upholding objective values. That way lies madness, the glance of mirrors, panic and emptiness. The ego has been afraid to lose its cherished uniqueness; it has thus forfeited the possibility of profounder development.

Again, the gifted man may decide that he will, with his un-aided intellect, investigate all the possibilities of error before deciding whether to assent. But in those terms there can never be an answer—only the arrival at a state of chronic open-mindedness, the fascinating condition of informed indecision:

> "So that, far from being led to contrition and surrender, the regarding of your defects in his mirror (Caliban is addressing the 'important persons at the top of the ladder' in his audience), your dialogue, using his words, with yourself about yourself, becomes the one activity which never, like devouring or collecting or spending, lets you down, the one game which can be guaranteed, whatever the company, to catch on, a madness. . . ."

Fifteen years earlier Auden had written an elliptical poem on the same theme:

> "To ask the hard question is simple;
>
> . . . .
>
> The simple act of the confused will.
> But the answer
> Is hard and hard to remember. . . ."

The history of the last few hundred years alone should have made it clear that man's intellect is inadequate to solve the problem of evil, that the humanistic intelligence, for all its value, can never give final answers, that the idea of 'progress' in any other than a material sense, and the liberal dream of man's natural goodness, are delusions: "This is the epoch of the Third Great Disappointment"; 'the first came with the end of the Roman Empire, the second with the decay of Christian belief, the third on the collapse of the security of scientific materialism'.

Nevertheless, most of us, rooted in space and time, continue to deny what Kierkegaard called 'the Unconditional'; we continue to think that reason alone can put things right:

"as if it were only some trifling and easily rectifiable error, improper diet, inadequate schooling, or an outmoded moral code which was keeping mankind from the millennial earthly paradise. Just a little more effort, perhaps merely the discovery of the right terms in which to describe it, and surely absolute pleasure must immediately descend upon the astonished armies of this world and abolish for ever all their hate and suffering";

and:

"As the issue between virtue first and liberty first becomes clearer, so does the realisation that the cost to any society that accepts the latter is extremely high, and to some may seem prohibitive. One can no longer make the task look easier than it is by pretending, as the liberals of the Enlightenment believed, that men are naturally good. No, it is just as true as ever it was that man is born in sin, that the majority are always, relatively, in the wrong, the minority, sometimes, relatively, in the right (everyone, of course, is free at any time to belong to either), and all, before God, absolutely in the wrong, that all of the people some of the time and some of the people most of the time will abuse their liberty and treat it as the licence of an escaped slave."

It follows that Auden is much less ready today to accept, for example, Freud's conclusions than he was earlier. It has become insufficient to try to *explain away* guilt by reference to the unconscious, or to regard a preoccupation with virtue and sin as an aberration, particularly common among ascetics and certain artists. Auden had not previously much pursued the question of where psychotherapy ends and moral choice begins, although he had been aware of its importance. He now enquires into it often, and with particular cogency in the notes to line 1244 of 'New Year Letter'. Clearly some things which have been or are regarded as logical necessities (i.e. only to be faced in the field of moral choice) are really causal necessities (e.g. a mental sickness induced by a trauma may be in its origin as fortuitous as an infectious disease) and may be treated as such by psychotherapy. But thereafter moral choice remains; one cannot by any amount of deep analysis remove the necessity for that choice: about it, only religion speaks adequately.

So Auden remains deeply interested in the possibilities of psychotherapy, but regards Freud as a scientist, not as a philosopher, personal or social. While insisting on its final insufficiency, Auden does not try to deny the importance of reason or of reason's product, science. He recognises the scientific method as the only way of asking questions to obtain valid knowledge, but draws a distinction between belief, which is experimentally verifiable, and faith, which is an absolute presupposition. But because "the existence of absolutes implies the unity of truth, the truths arrived at in different fields cannot ultimately conflict": both science and art have value as "isomorphs of one common co-operative task", and, "because in Him abstraction finds a passionate For-The-Sake-Of, by Him is the continuous development of Science assured".

On this basis Auden is able to consider much more deeply and precisely the nature of 'Love'. He is able to dispel the rather romantic penumbra which has always previously surrounded it. To love is not simply to have a vague hope that all may be well; we all wish that. Such good intent may disguise any of several kinds of self-regard:

> "For the error bred in the bone
> Of each woman and each man
> Craves what it cannot have,
> Not universal love
> But to be loved alone."

The urge to love may therefore contain in itself contradictions preventing its realisation:

> "How much must be forgotten out of love
> How much must be forgiven, even love."

To love implies a discipline. Hence Jacopone da Todi's prayer, which Auden repeats after E. M. Forster, "O thou who lovest me, set my love in order." So today Auden continually enquires into both the severe requirements of love and into its false forms—and especially into those false forms which hide a wish to escape from the responsibilities of love ('if only people would love me just as I am, like Mother did'). To love is difficult or it is worth nothing, since we can all love what we already find pleasant; but we have to love in spite of our personal wish:

> ". . . we are *required* to love
> All homeless objects that require a world.
> Our claim to our own bodies and our world
> Is our catastrophe. What can we know
> But panic and caprice until we know
> Our dreadful appetite demands a world
> Whose order, origin and purpose will
> Be fluent satisfaction of our will."

And further:

"The only serious possession of men is not their gifts, but what they all possess equally, independent of fortune, namely their will, in other words, their love, and the only serious matter is what they love, themselves, or God, or their neighbour—in loving well, i.e. in loving one's neighbour, the pleasure/pain criterion does not apply. If the Good Samaritan is asked why he rescued the man who fell among thieves he may answer: 'because I like doing good'; but the answer will be a joking reproof to the interrogator for asking silly questions when he already knows the answer, which is, that to love one's neighbour as oneself is an order and whether I enjoy obeying an order or not is irrelevant."

So we need to *learn* to love . . . and our first lesson will be the realisation that to love properly is extraordinarily difficult:

> "O let none say I love until aware
> What huge resources it will take to nurse
> One ruining speck, one tiny hair
> That casts a shadow through the universe."

And immediately after that warning Auden calls "Rejoice" —rejoice that by grace we exist and that Love is possible. Otherwise we should be in a sad plight indeed, for only Love can help us in "this modern void". And as the love of God made Him send His Son to earth to reveal His forgiveness and grace, so now by grace we may be helped in the difficult task of loving. We are all alone yet never really alone ("never less alone than when alone"). This is the love of God, of which ours is a reflection, and from which it gains strength:

> ". . . beloved, pray
> That Love, to whom necessity is play,
> Do what we must yet cannot do alone."

And as Love is essentially a matter of relationship with others ("Love's a way of living / One kind of relation"), so by the practice of it we may have glimpses of that larger community which Charles Williams, to whom Auden acknowledges himself indebted, calls "the community of coinherence". The moment of love is the moment of being. Our earthly communities will remain inadequate unless informed by Love; we are therefore to seek a society "whose form is truth, whose content Love", and that can only grow "where Freedom dwells because it must / Necessity because it can / And man confederate in man". One might there expect Auden to go on to discuss the place of the Church on earth, but he does not: as we have suggested, his approach is Protestant, and his main concern the struggle of the individual will with its own conscience.

The effects on our secular groups of denying the necessities of Love are demonstrated with dreadful clarity today. "We must love one another or die", says Auden, and:

> "We are reduced to our true nakedness:
> Either we serve the Unconditional,
> Or some Hitlerian monster will supply
> An iron convention to do evil by."

He is ambiguous here. In emphasising that the times confirm the truth of the concept of Love, he lets it be implied that we should love lest worse befall, i.e. in obedience to a kind of expediency—instead of loving, whatever befall, because we are all children of God.

Auden probably slips into such an ambiguity the more easily because his interest in social life remains so strong. One of the three sections of 'New Year Letter', for example, is specifically concerned with the nature of right social action. It is a complete misreading of Auden, therefore, to suggest, as some do, that, having tired or become frightened of the problems of political reform, he has retired to cultivate the good of his own soul. He relates his social purposes to what he now believes are larger ends. The manner of our existence in Space and Time is of immense significance; that existence is the field in which our 'becoming' is tested and tried out:

> "Space is the whom our loves are needed by,
> Time is our choice of How to Love and Why."

Auden is no longer a near-Marxist, but he retains a great admiration for Marx's insistence on the importance of social life and the need for co-operation, and for his analysis of the economic forces in society. He does not, of course, agree with the Marxist valuation of the group to the point at which it has moral authority and may deny the rights of the individual conscience.

For we cannot be better citizens than we are individuals: social reform begins when we ask ourselves about the conduct of our private lives. This applies to all, and very obviously to those who set out to speak to others, to writers: to point out this fact, says Auden, is:

"... not a denial of the importance of political action, but rather the realisation that if the writer is not to harm both others and himself, he must consider and very much more humbly and patiently than he has been doing, what kind of person he is, and what may be his real function. When the ship catches fire it seems only natural to rush importantly to the pumps, but perhaps one is only adding to the general confusion and panic: to sit still and pray seems selfish and unheroic, but it may be the wisest and most helpful course."

A comparison of that with Auden's early allegory about sportsmen and villagers shows the extent of the change in his attitude towards direct commitment.

He concerns himself particularly, today, with the pressures which the business of living in large centralised groups imposes on the individual. He repeatedly enunciates the distinction between an 'open' and a 'closed' society. The open society is one in which the individual is free to decide on logical necessities. A society becomes more open as causal necessities are removed or made less of a nuisance, and as the individuals in it become more responsible. No individual or class can claim a right to impose its idea of good on others because all are sinful. And because all are sinful all must be able to fight individually with that sin: "Government must be democratic, the people must have a right to make their own mistakes and to suffer for them, because no one is free from error." The degree of responsibility which a people can assume is increased through the activity of experts, teachers and others like them: the exceptional in any society and any age have "an obligation to educate and persuade. Responsibility is in direct proportion to capacity." In closed (primitive or fascist) societies, individual moral choice is removed or minimised. A society becomes more open as 'causal' choices are made moral choices, e.g. if the fear of starvation is removed and so ceases to be an incentive to work, the only remaining incentive in a democracy is a moral decision that one ought to work as a member of the community.

Societies today become increasingly centralised and mechanised: they are therefore constantly tending to become closed.

The onus of moral decision tends to be taken from the individual and vested in an anonymous Authority which, by implication, suggests that personal moral judgment is secondary to conformity. This is "the lie of Authority / Whose buildings grope the sky". The Collective Man is required to live the Generalised Life.

The engineers of such a state are the new race of managers (again, the exceptional men), dedicated, over-worked, strained, brilliantly competent. We give them power, asking them also to take blame:

> ". . . far into the night
> Their windows burn brightly,
> And behind, their backs bent over some report
> On every quarter
> For ever like a god or a disease
> There on the earth, the reason
> In all its aspects why they are tired, the weak,
> The inattentive, seeking
> Someone to blame."

The dirge in 'The Age of Anxiety' reflects the same situation, the profoundly significant relationship between managers and managed. In other places Auden talks about the split between the 'doers' and the 'feelers', the separation of "the tender who value from the tough who measure".

In his beliefs Auden has traced a curve similar to that followed by many writers of the last century in particular, from Tolstoy onwards. His position now might be summed up in Charles Williams's question: "What is there anywhere but ignorance, grace and moral effort?" We have to acknowledge our sinfulness; we have also to remember the possibility of love, charity and brotherhood; we have to continue, striving and committed; we are saved from despair by the thought of grace.

So he is not pessimistic. As far back as 'Letters from Iceland' he had expressed thanks for:

> ". . . the quiet considerable spark
> Of private love and goodness which never leaves
> An age, however awful, in the utter dark";

and the first poem of 'Another Time' closed with this hope for "deliberate man":

> "To fresh defeats he still must move,
>   To further griefs and greater,
>   And the defeat of grief."

That note remains:

> "In the meantime
> There are bills to be paid, machines to keep in repair,
> Irregular verbs to learn, The Time Being to redeem
> From insignificance."

The Way is difficult, but we must have faith and act. We will make many mistakes and never produce an Eden. But we have to do the best we can, rejoice that some at least do well, and carry on without ever being quite despondent, for:

> "We know very well that we are not unlucky but evil,
> That the dream of a perfect State or no State at all
> To which we fly for refuge, is a part of our punishment.
> Let us therefore be contrite but without anxiety,
> For Powers and Times are not gods but mortal gifts from God;

> "Let us acknowledge our defeats but without despair,
> For all societies and epochs are transient details,
> Transmitting an everlasting opportunity
> That the Kingdom of Heaven may come not in our Present,
> And not in our Future, but in the Fullness of Time,
> Let us pray."

CHAPTER VI

AMERICA—THE LONG WORKS

(1) 'New Year Letter'

IN America, 'New Year Letter' was called 'The Double Man'.
That title is more appropriate, for the poem's subject is the
divided consciousness, that conflict between freedom and
necessity already noted as a frequent subject of Auden's later
work. Montaigne, who is quoted below the dedication, expressed the problem in a well-known epigram:

> "We are, I know not how, double in ourselves, so that what
> we believe, we disbelieve, and cannot rid ourselves of what we
> condemn."

We recognise necessities, but do not obey them, and are thus
aware of sin.

Auden examines this ambivalence as it is reflected in various
human activities . . . in metaphysics, in ethics, in art and particularly in social life. 'New Year Letter' appeared during the
recent war; it is pervaded by a sense of the world's misery, and
of the spiritual sickness of which that misery is, to Auden, a
symptom. Though the central theme is the conflict in the individual will, the applications are predominantly social.

Technically, the 'Letter' owes something to Samuel Butler,
to Dryden and to Pope, and there are parallels with Browning's
'Christmas Eve and Easter Day'. Browning uses the same
metre (octosyllabic couplets), though with considerably less
freedom, in a dispute between a Christian and a sceptic on the
grounds of belief:

> "So, the old process, I conclude,
> Goes on, the reasoning's pursued
> Further. You own, ' 'Tis well averred,

A scientific faith's absurd,
—Frustrates the very end 'twas meant
To serve. So, I would rest content
With a mere probability,
But, probable; the chance must lie
Clear on one side—lie all in rough,
So long as there be just enough
To pin my faith to'. . . ."

The manner encourages some of Auden's more superficial
faults, such as overloading with incidental material, and the
pursuit of interesting little byways in the argument. It lends
itself to gossipiness and a bright didacticism; it tempts to
skittishness like this (Auden is arguing that no man-made rules
can hold the Truth):

"The Lex Abscondita evades
The vigilantes in the glades
Now here, now there, one leaps and cries,
'I've got her and I claim the prize.'
But when the rest catch up he stands
With just a torn blouse in his hands."

But the style can also be pithy, epigrammatic and energetic:
at his best Auden employs it with flexibility and confidence (he
is speaking of writers who conquer a sense of inferiority by
their creative achievement):

"All the more honour to you then
If, weaker than some other men,
You had the courage that survives
Soiled, shabby, egotistic lives,
If poverty or ugliness
Ill-health or social unsuccess
Hunted you out of life to play
At living in another way;

. . . .

Yet the live quarry all the same
Were changed to huntsmen in the game,
And the wild furies of the past,
Tracked to their origins at last."

Passages as lucid as this are not infrequent; others make harder reading because their subject is harder; a few only yield after reference to the notes, and not always then.

The notes occupy as much space as the 'Letter' itself, are in both prose and verse, and vary in length from one line to several pages. They make clear, by frequent quotation, the main influences on the thought of the poem—Kierkegaard, Pascal, Blake, Goethe, Kafka, Rilke, Nietzsche, Charles Williams and others. They also include items as diverse as the statistics of the main killing diseases in the U.S.A., an old joke about the use of the navel as a salt-cellar when eating celery in bed, odd or fantastic anecdotes which Auden has enjoyed (e.g. the notes to II, 507 and 517), some individual poems which he has rightly thought worth a place in his collected poems, some seminal comments on a variety of subjects (e.g. the note on Wagner to I, 1432), and some erudite, long, obscure glosses on a text already in parts clogged with detail. The notes reflect Auden's wide-ranging, lively mind and his novelist's pleasure in curious 'human' snippets; they are pages from an unusually interesting scrapbook.

The poem opens by asserting the real presence of that which we all—"singing or sighing as we go"—are trying unsuccessfully to forget, THE THING—our own guilt and sin, which are made manifest in the disorder surrounding us.

Yet we all inevitably yearn throughout our lives for order and harmony, and strive in many mistaken ways towards it. The moments of personal illumination which art gives may suggest the possibility of harmony, but do not teach us how to acquire it: art has its own kind of order, analogous to 'life-order', but reached by abstraction from it and not a guide to it.

But though the work of art is "a medium's artifice", often contrived to master a neurosis, its value remains:

> "Now large, magnificent, and calm,
> Your changeless presences disarm
> The sullen generations, still
> The fright and fidget of the will,
> And to the growing and the weak
> Your final transformations speak."

In the notes to this part of the argument Auden, applying a distinction of Kierkegaard's, makes one of his numerous long comparisons between æsthetics, the most difficult of games but still a game, a "conjuring trick", and ethical activity, which is not a game, but always work. Art remains the greatest of vocations; to be a saint is not a vocation.

A sustained and elaborate rhetorical simile leads to the reaffirmation that our present situation everywhere reveals guilt and vast spiritual disorders, and the section closes with the reflection that under such conditions we are all tempted to surrender to "the grand apocalyptic dream", to admit moral bankruptcy, and relinquish humane values in favour of violence.

Part Two discusses the devil and his ways with mockery and aplomb—that is, various forms of doubt and treachery within the personality are melodramatically personified in a manner by now familiar. The devil's function is to lead us to deny that we are vulnerable and sinful and must die—and so, by bringing us to "a recurrent state / Of fear and faithlessness and hate", to help us finally to accept those necessities. Our first and best protection against his ravages is our sense that we "in fact, live in eternity", for, "all our intuitions mock / The formal logic of the clock".

Intellect which has become arrogant and begun to despise intuition is therefore one of the devil's main supports. Auden quotes Pascal on this classical point in the notes: "L'esprit a son ordre qui est par principes et demonstrations; le cœur en a un autre" ("The mind has its order, which is by principles and proofs; the heart has a different order"). Kierkegaard frequently says the same thing ("with the eyes of the heart I read it"); and the influence of Blake is evident:

> "In Blake's view sin is nothing other than the destruction of order, and reason divorced from imagination is the agent of that destruction."

Auden makes the point with an echo of his old exuberance about "new styles of architecture, a change of heart":

> "O foolishness of man to seek
> Salvation in an ordre logique!
> O cruel intellect that chills
> His natural warmth until it kills
> The roots of all togetherness!
> Love's vigour shrinks to less and less."

Perhaps remembering that when artists propound this argument it is usually oversimplified at the expense of the scientific attitude, Auden takes care to enumerate the great virtues of the spirit of scientific enquiry, but still—and the objection is to Auden's tone rather than to his matter—does not give them sufficient weight.

For artists the devil's special temptations are to esotericism, false isolation, bohemianism and other kinds of attitude-striking. In us all he is supported by, indeed can only live on, doubt, on the contradictions and attractions of the habitual open mind; he feeds on that ability to doubt which is the mark of our freedom under necessity:

> "He knows the bored will not unmask him
> But that he's lost if someone asks him
> To come the hell in off the links
> And say exactly what he thinks.
>
> . . . .

> ... Because he knows, were he to win,
> Man could do evil but not sin.
> To sin is to act consciously
> Against what seems necessity,
> A possibility cut out
> In any world that excludes doubt."

Or the devil makes great use of our habit, once we have embraced some philosophy, of expecting Utopia to follow from its application. Since Utopians are always disappointed, they end in deeper despair than ever. Since no man-devised system can ever contain final Truth and so perfect the world, we must recognise our deficiencies:

> "No codex gentium we make
> Is difficult for truth to break.
>
> .   .   .   .
>
> Meanwhile at least the layman knows
> That none are lost so soon as those
> Who overlook their crooked nose";

we must, in short, learn to "be ourselves", and ask "what acts are proper to (our) task". (Kierkegaard said, "A logical system is possible, a system of existence is impossible"; and "Existence must be content with a fighting certainty".)

But though the devil has a fine time with all our doubtings and refusals to decide, with "The moral assymetric souls, / The either-ors, the mongrel halves ...", yet he never tells us lies—only half-truths. Our doubts, if properly examined, contain their own answer; the devil can help to "push us into grace".

Part Three restates the dilemma, elaborates its application to our present situation and suggests a resolution, that is, an approach to circumstance.

The moment of illumination and of love comes to someone every day, and in that instant time is conquered:

> "Yet anytime, how casually,
> Out of his organized distress
> An accidental happiness,
> Catching man off his guard, will blow him
> Out of his life in time to show him
> The field of Being where he may
> Unconscious of Becoming, play."

But if we yearn for a state of continuous happiness, i.e. if we reject the terms of life by which we are constantly Becoming, not Being, we shall be miserable. This is expressed in typical Audenesque horror-story imagery:

> "For, if he stop an instant there,
> The sky grows crimson with a curse,
> The flowers change colour for the worse,
> He hears behind his back the wicket
> Padlock itself, from the dark thicket
> The chuckle with no healthy cause,—
> And helpless, sees the crooked claws
> Emerging into view and groping
> For footholds on the low round coping."

We are then fear-ridden, "locked / Each in a stale unique-ness,—Time-conscious for eternity"; we are in Hell. At this point the purposive optimistic Auden comes uppermost with the assertion that we must do our best with life, climb our "purgatorial hill" not miserably but with "a reverent frivolity", refuse to give our allegiance simply out of desperation to any of those who clamour for it, and be faithful in the first place to the small and intimate evidences of love. Still, social issues have to be faced; we have to decide "where to serve and when and how" in our necessary resistance to the crowd values with which the new machine barbarism in Europe is opposing the values of the heart. Both the personal and the social maps have to be followed: "Here all are kings, there each a brother."

Auden then employs Rilke's technique of using geographical

symbols for abstract ideas, in a sustained and detailed analogy of the slow but continuous drive in man "to civilise and to create", with the scenery of the Northern Pennines as its wildness yields gradually to the culture of the valleys.

Simply by being born we are committed: "We are conscripts to our age", and must act in support of what we believe right. We all know that we live at a time of decision, and must think out afresh our social forms:

> "We know no fuss or pain or lying
> Can stop the moribund from dying.
> That all the special tasks begun
> By the Renaissance have been done."

They have been done, these tasks of considerable value, by the child of the Renaissance, "Empiric Economic Man", hardworking, inventive, emotionally starved. He has removed many 'false' necessities' (e.g. famine, disease, etc.—'causal' necessities, as they were called earlier), and so made truly moral choices clearer; he has been affirmative towards Nature, has developed the scientific discipline of submission to the evidence, and has rejected any attempt to impose a final *formula* for salvation on the world. He has not succeeded in producing happiness, but:

> ". . . if his half-success broke down,
> All failures have one good result;
> They prove the good is difficult."

And now the prophecies of the pariahs and rebels like Blake and Rousseau are fulfilled:

> "We see, we suffer, we despair.
> The well-armed children everywhere
> Who envy the self-governed beast
> Who know that they are bound at least."

On this Auden makes his final assertion of the personal lesson of the times. The blame lies with each one of us—for our betrayals of love in our private lives ("O what can love's intentions do / If all his agents are untrue?"), for our fear of individual and social responsibility; for the self-regard which is really self-annihilation ("self-known, self-praising, self-attached"); and for our refusal to admit error. Our problems arise from what each of us makes of "the freedom of the will". In this we are all the same, and all alone; we are also each one specially and uniquely valuable, and from that conjunction our community begins:

> "We can love each because we know
> All, all of us, that this is so:
> Can live because we've lived; the powers
> That we create with are not ours."

There follows a rapturous cry of faith, a lyrical invocation to God, the only source of "order", in His majesty and mystery, an admission of humility and a prayer for help:

> "Convict our pride of its offence
> In all things, even penitence,
>
> . . . .
>
> Send strength sufficient for our day,
> And point our knowledge on its way,
> O da quod Jubes, Domine."

The 'Letter' ends quietly but still joyously on the thought that daily we see Love practised by some of those around us. A triolet with a lengthened line sounds a moving final chord:

> "O every day in sleep and labour
> Our life and death are with our neighbour,
> And love illuminates again
> The city and the lion's den,
> The world's great rage, the travel of young men."

'New Year Letter' is, it will be seen, in some respects a note-book of Auden's self-examination into the grounds and social

application of his religious belief. He seems, except in the final
pæon, to be arguing with himself, to be "trying to teach himself to believe", as Charles Williams said of Boëthius. He seems
to be trying to come to terms inside himself with different
orders of experience, with the intellectual and the intuitive,
with demonstration and faith. His struggle is also similar to
that of Origen as Charles Williams described it—though
Auden does not find his 'check' in the Church, understood as
a corporate body, but rather in her 'universal decisions', i.e. in
the 'absolute presuppositions' of faith:

> "[He,] like all intelligent readers then as now, realised that he
> needed a check upon his own brain, and he found it, where all
> Christians have found it, in the universal decisions of the Church.
> This authority he recognised; this relationship he desired. The
> recognition of authority is the desire for union, but also it is the
> knowledge that the individual by himself is bound to be wrong."

Auden does not seem to be, at this point, at ease in his
belief. That unease is reflected in the tricks of technique (some
of the images gloss over a problem rather than clarify it). The
'Letter' is not a religious poem; it is an argument in verse, perceptive, careless, suggestive, bookish, vivid, almost everywhere
competent, and in places brilliant and moving.

Auden's aim, in the sequence of twenty 'Quest' sonnets
which follows 'New Year Letter', is brought out very clearly
in an essay entitled 'K's Quest' (1946), in which he discusses
the different kinds of Quest in mythology, from the Golden
Fleece to Kafka's 'K'. He distinguishes there between—the
Fairy Story, whose hero succeeds because he is humble and
always answers a call for help; the Grail Story, in which the
sight of a sacred object is obscured by sin, in which that object can only be seen again by Grace and in which the hero is
tempted to give up the search for the sake of immediate
pleasure; the Dream Quest (*The Divine Comedy*), whose

purpose is not objective but spiritual knowledge, and in which the vision is granted by divine grace, not by virtue, or does not come at all; and the *Pilgrim's Progress*, in which the Quest is the journey of life itself which all must take, since its aim is salvation. All such journeys differ, and their result depends on us or our will—the Way is difficult but possible.

Auden's Quest is nearest to *Pilgrim's Progress*, but shares characteristics with each of the others. Its subject is, obviously, the search for the Way, for the secret of that Unknown which puzzles man all his life and which his philosophies are attempts to explain. By means of that kind of symbolic fable which was discussed earlier, each sonnet deals with one or other of the false trails on the Quest—with the special traps for the exceptional, the intelligent and the sensitive; with the steps we take to avoid going on the Quest at all (gregariousness, worldly success, cynicism, solipsism, fake religions, power, over-intellectualism and so on); with the emptiness, disappointment or horror which follow from all these; and with the freedom from fear and anxiety which the ending of the Quest, in faith, brings:

> "Within these gates all opening begins:
>
> . . . .
>
> And flesh forgives division as it makes
> Another's moment of consent its own.
>
> . . . .
>
> All journeys die here; wish and weight are lifted."

The 'Epilogue' to the whole volume, more even than the 'Letter', is obsessed with the thought of widespread and deep human grief, with:

> "The hard- and the soft-mouthed together
> In a coma of waiting, just breathing
>
> . . . .
>
> In a darkness of tribulation and death."

All our escape-routes are blocked, and we know it; today we are all prophets, mostly of doom:

> "The waste is a suburb of prophets,
>   But who have seen Jesus and who only
>   Judas the Abyss?"

The concluding stanzas call again for contrition, the full assumption of our duty in time, and a "resonant" acknowledgment of "the Word which was / From the beginning. . . ."

The 'Epilogue' is more certain of itself than either the 'Letter' or the sonnets. It is not intellectually examining the data of belief, or devising lively symbolic situations to communicate them (which sometimes, because of their brilliance, are more obviously than usual "a medium's artifice"—and suggest that the writer is taking more pleasure in his devices for managing his material [the 'interestingness' of æsthetics] than the material itself would appropriately allow). The 'Epilogue' communicates more nearly than either of the other two parts a felt, personal faith, newly arrived at, and under test in a time of special stress; it is less the work of an intellectual than the 'Letter', less that of a conscious artist than the 'Quest'.

(2) *'The Sea and the Mirror'*

The theme of 'The Sea and the Mirror' is the relationship of the creative imagination to the problems of existence. (The 'mirror' certainly signifies art, and the 'sea', presumably, life, the unknown depths over which we all journey.) Auden needed here, as in the 'Quest' sonnets, a symbolic framework which would present his abstractions concretely; he was seeking now for one whose parts had a close internal organisation. He might thus show the relationship and interaction of ideas better than had been allowed by the straight sequence of the 'Quest' sonnets. He found his shape ready to hand in the characters and situations of 'The Tempest'. So that, although Auden subtitles 'The Sea and the Mirror'—'A Commentary on Shake-speare's "Tempest" ', the fact that it suggests an illuminating symbolic interpretation of the play is secondary to Auden's use of the play's structure as a base from which to deploy his own themes.

He has tried further to mark the difference between characters—that is, between various kinds of attitude to ex-perience—by giving each a different verse form. Sometimes he uses an old and neglected form brilliantly, to suggest the character to whom he allots it, as in Miranda's villanelle; some-times he successfully invents a suitable form, as in Alonso's letter to Ferdinand; sometimes he wastes his great skill in exhibitionism, as in the use of the highly contrived but unsuit-able sestina for Sebastian's confession.

In a preface of superb polish and irony (irregular iambics in lines of only three feet, to give speed), the stage-manager re-minds the critics that art interests itself in, but does not explain the surprise and mystery of life:

> ". . . but how
> Shall we satisfy when we meet,
> The lion's mouth whose hunger
> No metaphors can fill?"

Immediately thereafter we meet the "personified type of the creative", Prospero, bidding farewell to Ariel, that is, resigning his creative activity after using it for the last time to prevent wickedness and promote love. He is enjoying the opportunity of playing the Great-Master-on-Life. His verse rhythm, deter-mined by the stresses and pauses of speech not by foot measure-ment, suggests the conversation of a slightly pontifical old man. He is glad, he says, to give up the mirror-world of art, for now, "at last I can really believe I shall die", a fact which art, by making everything about life so absorbing and interesting, hides. He adds that the real value of art lies in its power, not directly to alter life, but to extend imaginative sympathy; it helps to free both audience and artist. So, by the exercise of Prospero's art on this island, all but one of the characters now on ship and bound for Naples understand themselves better.

But Prospero's own freedom is limited by his failure with Caliban; on him he has exercised his wish for "absolute devotion" ("But the error bred in the bone / Of each woman and each man / Craves what it cannot have, / Not universal love / But to be loved alone"). The result is a savage creature who is occasionally dangerous. The artist has helped others to know themselves better, but has ignored, though not stifled, the claims of certain sides of his own character. In his prose address later Caliban elaborates the same point.

Prospero reverts in his last stanza to the point that the artist may be so occupied with describing the interesting details of the Quest that he neglects to go on it himself:

"And now, in my old age, I wake, and this journey really exists,
    And I have actually to take it, inch by inch,
    Alone. . . ."

Prospero, an old man:

"Just like other old men, with eyes that water
    Easily in the wind, and a head that nods in the sunshine,
    Forgetful, maladroit, a little grubby,"

has to forget the game—art, and face the reality—life:

"Can I learn to suffer
    Without saying something ironic or funny
    On suffering?"

The three lively and sardonic lyrics which punctuate Prospero's speech with comments on, respectively, the difficulty of following the Way and the small number of those who face it, the longings and deceptions of the weak ego, and the comfort art may bring on the journey, are in Auden's best light vein. They relieve the long peroration by making idiomatic asides on its own themes. Auden is fond of the gay lyric with the death's head inside.

As each of the other characters speaks, he reveals the changes in his personality that Prospero's art has effected. Antonio alone remains intransigent, and adds a mocking chorus to each of the other contributions.

For Antonio is "the spirit that denies", the permanent doubter and disbeliever, unsubmissive of will and proud of intellect, arrogant, cynical, nonconforming, efficient, individualistic, 'knowing', strong enough not to need art as fantasy and limited enough to be sure it can be nothing else, the seed of the man of power and the spiritual barbarian. In his hard self-regard he is glad, not fearful, of man's essential loneliness. So all his choral echoes end on the word "alone". Others may be won over to the side of Love, but never Antonio; he does not recognise Love's existence. So long as he exists—and he is a part of each of us—there can be no final peace (compare the description of the disciplines of Love and the impossibility of a continuous state of pure Love, above, in part three of chapter five). Antonio will always prevent us from ever quite returning to the imagined innocence of childhood: he is our tainted consciousness with which we are committed to a state of continual war.

Antonio's terza rima is followed by an irregular Petrarchan sonnet from Ferdinand, expressing joy at his love for Miranda and the conviction that this kind of union suggests a greater coinherence, "another tenderness. . . . The Right Required Time; The Real Right Place, O Light." Miranda's poem on the same theme is full of dramatic images; Ferdinand's is abstract and moves like a theorem.

Stephano, the drunken butler, gives thanks, in a ballade, for drink as a womb-substitute, a shelter from loss and fear. Towards him Antonio is properly scornful; he is too proud and courageous thus to abdicate personality. Nor will he recognise the truths of the decayed Gonzalo, once portentous, but now subdued and humbled. Gonzalo has never quite "trusted the absurd", he is one of those who, in his attempt to formalise life, has overvalued the intellect and neglected intuition and imagination. He therefore stands "convicted of / Doubt and insufficient love".

Adrian and Francesco make a brief appearance as a pair of precious knockabouts and sycophants; their couplet is surrealistically smart, presumably to suggest their preciosity and sophistication. They seem to be saying that now, having been shown a sounder way of life, they (the good little sunbeams, e.g. light and playful things) have to train themselves to follow it (must learn to fly), and that, understandably, they feel some regret at the loss of their polished and childish play ("It's madly ungay when the goldfish die"). Again, like a tolling bell, Antonio rejects this outlook, despising their gregarious play-acting: "My audience is my own."

The message of Alonso's letter to Ferdinand, which has been examined in detail earlier, is contained in the injunction: "Remember that the fire and the ice / Are never more than one step away." It is followed, as is the utterance of each of the weightier characters, by a lighter poem from one of the subsidiaries. Here a good Audenesque ballad from the Master and Boatswain reveals that his pair of rough, careless and cynical old sailors are nevertheless lonelies too. Antonio has no difficulty in rejecting the false toughness of their world.

In contrast Sebastian, brother to Alonso and previously his would-be murderer, is a complex person who has at last come to a sense of his own sin, is thankful for his exposure and glad to realise after all, naked though he is, that Love exists. He is fearful and joyous; ashamed and for the first time free of anxiety and able to live:

> "I smile because I tremble, glad today
> To be ashamed, not anxious, not a dream.
>
> . . . .
>
> In dream all sins are easy, but by day
> It is defeat gives proof we are alive;
> The sword we suffer is the guarded crown."

To that the self-sufficient Antonio gives his usual mocking denial—this time of the validity of conscience.

Sebastian's sestina treats some extremely subtle ideas. The sestina is an elaborate and difficult form, and to use it for metaphysical discussion is a feat roughly comparable to explaining the differential calculus whilst riding a bicycle backwards—and just as unnecessary. The virtues of the sestina arise mainly from its echoing rhyming pattern, and that does not assist this kind of subject.

On the other hand, the jester Trinculo's simple quatrains of iambic trimeters with one line to each verse are wholly suitable. Auden's Trinculo is, one might almost guess, really a tense and terrified child bringing back funny stories from his frightening fantasy world with which to win over the stern adults. Antonio understands that, as he understands so many evasions, but is too tough to need the brand of humour Trinculo offers, the humour which the gifted and timid produce so as to increase their contemporaries' sense of importance.

Miranda closes the chapter with an evocative villanelle of simple thankfulness for her union in love with another. She is no longer a mirror-gazer; her terrors ("The Black Man", "The Witch") have gone; she has a child's spontaneity and assurance again. Antonio rejects that as he has rejected her lover's and other evidences of Love (e.g. love in human communities; love of God), and as he has rejected the evasions of fear. He denies, as always. Prospero's art has foiled some wickedness and has helped to show the lonely and anxious the possibility of a finer harmony; Antonio does not acknowledge it. Art cannot in the end solve the problem of evil in the will. "Art is not enough."

Caliban's dazzling prose address to the audience occupies just over half of the whole work. Since it is, in addition, heavily weighted with material and extravagant with metaphor, it makes the structure lopsided. But to change to prose here, and to prose of this kind, is justifiable. Perhaps Auden let the speech overrun because he had so much to say about its themes, and because he was enjoying the exercise of his own virtuosity in this apparent parody of Henry James's later style. But the virtues of James's later prose—its ability to express nuances, to condition, to present involved and highly quali-fied ideas—are exactly what Auden needs at this point. It is true that poetry—assuming a sensitive reader—can do all this more immediately, but Caliban is addressing representatives of the unpoetic world. He does so in a manner they will recognise; he is confident, ironic, fluent and happily conversational.

Caliban symbolises the dark forces in man which (this is a popular topic of Auden's), if ignored, break out in terrible forms. This subtle and articulate 'id' discusses his own signi-ficance in the human personality and his relation to man's art and metaphysics. To begin with, he puts the audience's (humanity's) questions about the play (life), and especially about his own part in it, to the playwright (the Creator); he asks God the questions we all ask about our own drama, and about the untamed part of ourself.

He outlines the limits of art in an elaborate metaphor sus-tained over four pages, in which "our native muse" figures as a cultured society hostess. And he reiterates, even more rhetorically, Prospero's complaint that although art develops our insight by its sympathy, communality and wit, it also collaborates with our attempt to forget the "unrectored chaos" outside. It goes very near to that "forbidden incoherence", but then, happily, "on the shuddering edge of the bohemian standardless abyss", neatly turns and satisfies us with some formal æsthetic pattern. It never dares quite to face Him, Caliban, "the represented principle of *not* sympathising, *not* associating, *not* amusing", for He is the awful fact about man which makes æsthetics—if it is regarded as a source of values, as a religion—look irrelevant and silly.

But most of us—Caliban continues to address the Maker on

behalf of his audience—do not want to elevate art into a religion. We want it simply as an escape, full of nicely unreal conventions, with all its problems beautifully solved, "the manifestations of the inner life—always—so easy and habitual", and with all the great questions tidily answered, in a world of "freedom without anxiety, sincerity without loss of vigour", a world of endless compensations for the lonelies. For though we would all like Love and unity in real life, few of us are equal to their demands. We only love when our love can feed our self-regard. (The passage dealing with this, which begins, "So, too, with Time . . .", is a particularly good example of Auden's command of vivid symbolic detail.) Therefore, we are happy for art to omit crude Caliban in order to make its soothing patterns ('a false appearance of harmony and order'—chapter five, section two). We would not even want art to intrude into life itself. There, of course, we know Caliban well, and get on rather more easily with him than with his imaginative brother Ariel. Let the present arrangement continue, "for, if the intrusion of the real has disconcerted and incommoded the poetic that is a mere bagatelle compared to the damage which the poetic would inflict if it ever succeeded in intruding upon the real."

Here Caliban inserts the familiar warning to any "gay apprentices in the magical art" that they may, by giving their all to Ariel and ignoring Caliban, not so much develop their personality as distort it ("Christianly conceived, every poet-existence is sin, the sin to poeticise instead of to be"—Kierkegaard). And since they will not have taken into account one important factor in personality, any conclusions they may reach about 'Truth', 'Beauty' and the rest will be false.

Caliban divides the remainder of his audience into two groups, the ordinary and the exceptional, and addresses each in turn. Towards the "general popular type" his irony is the sharper, his satiric images more forceful. He reminds them that they have to accept both of their disturbing gifts, their brutishness and their imagination, and with them take the journey to Nowhere (the Quest). The journey begins when we realise that the childhood dream has broken, and that we are each in the cold air, and each required to set out alone. Most of us find the prospect frightening, for "we have never felt really well in this climate of distinct ideas"; we long to get back to the child's state of pure self-regarding egotism in a world of friendly, concrete things. This is expressed in a sort of modern version, witty and dreadful, of Traherne's evocation of the state of *Being* in childhood ("The corn was orient and immortal wheat . . ."):

"Give me my passage home, let me see that harbour once again just as it was before I learned the bad words. Patriarchs wiser than Abraham mended their nets on the modest wharf; white and wonderful beings undressed on the sand dunes; sunset glittered on the plate-glass windows of the Marine Biological Station; far off in the extreme horizon a whale spouted. Look, Uncle, look. They have broken my glasses and I have lost my silver whistle. Pick me up, Uncle, let little Johnny ride away on your massive shoulders to recover his green kingdom."

The dream is that of Rosetta in 'The Age of Anxiety', and the moment of realisation that we are in the cold air is Stage One of the Seven Stages described there. Caliban's final warning is that if we continue to wish for this kind of world our reward will be to have it. The call for liberty and freedom "to be oneself" ends in emptiness ("liberty to be and weep has never been sufficient"):

"Your existence is indeed free at last to choose its own meaning, that is, to plunge headlong into despair and fall through silence fathomless and dry."

To the exceptional Caliban outlines the dangers by now well known. They too try to escape, but with more finesse . . . they enlist Ariel's help rather than Caliban's. Troubled by the detail and the mess and the loose ends of life, they long to make everything abstract and general; they yearn for absolute freedom, freedom from necessity. They too reach the logical goal of their wish—in a world of constant change and motion, but with no direction and no end. Their fear of decision leads them to the horrors of the totally subjective and highly intellectualised—but utterly purposeless.

These, then, concludes Caliban, addressing them all, are the two main ways of failing to meet life, the unquestioning acceptance of it (taking the good-fellow ticket), or the refusal to be committed in any way—"the facile glad-handed highway, or the virtuous averted track". If the artist depicts the dilemma, his audience enjoy the picture but don't apply its lesson—they use art as a substitute for the spiritual Quest to which it may point. Hence the central problem for the serious artist—if he produces æsthetically satisfying patterns, he must fail to express the real difficulty and inadequacy of human life. Nevertheless, there is "the real Word", the "wholly other Life". In the midst of all our deficiencies, and not dependent on us, Grace, Justice, Mercy, exist; they speak and they save:

> "The working charm is the full bloom of the unbothered state; the sounded note is the restored relation."

As a postscript Ariel reminds Caliban, in a sad lyric, that neither can ignore the other. They are inextricable; our imaginative side may often wish to forget our brute side, but finds its most fascinating material there. Together they comprise that puzzling and astonishing thing, human personality, the 'I'. So, as each stanza closes, the prompter echoes 'I', and the sixth and last lines of each stanza repeat the echo in a rhyme on the same syllable.

It is not surprising that 'The Sea and the Mirror' was written at this stage in Auden's spiritual journey; many of the "false attitudes" in art which he discusses there have been held by him. The poem's considerable success is due to the finding of a structure which would carry his themes and give scope for detailed allusive comment around them and for a free use of dramatic symbols. It also allows him to exhibit, on the whole successfully, his abundant technical skill. So obviously has Auden enjoyed all this highly conscious artistry that one is left wondering (as after reading the 'Quest', though now in a greater degree) whether the manner is not, for a believer, in some ways a betrayal of the matter, whether Auden has not been so *interested* in the exercise of his skill that he has not sufficiently hoped, as Caliban says any 'dedicated' artist must, that "some unfortunate mishap will intervene to ruin his effect."

(3) *'For the Time Being'*—a Christmas Oratorio

The setting of 'For the Time Being' is Palestine under Roman rule, and its movement in time extends from the moment immediately before Christ's Advent to the Flight into Egypt. It is dedicated to the memory of Auden's mother, who died in 1941: in June of that year Auden wrote a review entitled 'The Means of Grace', which shows the nature of his interest in that particular setting:

"The special Christian revelation, the Incarnation, occurred precisely at that moment in history when an impasse seemed to have been reached. The civilised world was now politically united, but its philosophical dualism divided both society and the individual personality horizontally, the wise from the ignorant, the Logos from the Flesh."

". . . precisely at that moment in history when an impasse seemed to have been reached . . ."; the analogy with our own time is clear. In examining the impact of the Advent on representative members of Herod's unhappy society, Auden is examining attitudes to the Christian revelation particularly common today. As in 'The Sea and the Mirror', he has provided himself with a strong structure inside which to develop his arguments. Here, too, he uses different metres (but not, usually, established forms), wide variations of tone and alternations of prose and verse to suggest various kinds of approach to the whole matter of belief. Thus, the prose passages are given to Simeon—for his long Meditation, which is really a *statement* of faith, and to Herod—for his outburst on seeing his reasonable world threatened by this irruption from a sphere he regards as fantasy ("the real incommoded by the poetic"). The Narrator, a kind of disembodied broadcasting voice, reproduces the attitudes of the prevailing ethos, and also calls for prayer and faith (as one who accepts the truth of the Incarnation), in a matter-of-fact conversational metre.

The first movement, the Advent, describes the despair which has invaded every department of life. Chorus and semi-chorus express this in general terms, using verse whose pace and images—the hard grip of ice and the muffling remorseless fall of snow—powerfully reinforce the sense of awful deadness before the Birth. An age is ending; none of the old gods avail; the pagans face the Void; Fear and Doubt seep everywhere:

> "Darkness and snow descend
> On all personality."

Immediately the key changes to the conversational, with the narrator admitting that the situation cannot be approached in the usual eminently sensible and practical way. As he continues his tone becomes shrill: here is a horror people do not know how to manage; this is the "Abomination. This is the wrath of God".

This first change of manner from chorus to narrator shows Auden's purposes in such changes clearly. He is anxious, not only that differences of approach shall be suggested, but that his readers shall not fail to see their relevance today. So he often chooses for his contrasts styles which have very little 'literary' air (e.g. Herod's idiomatic "administrator-talking-to-friends" speech), and he loads each section with modern allusions.

Parts of the Narrator's speech here and of the recitative which forms part four of the first movement illustrate something of Mr. Eliot's present influence on Auden. That there should be an influence is not surprising, since they are today dealing with similar problems, though with widely different technical equipment and profoundly different personalities. In this particular section Auden uses the same kind of 'pointing' as Eliot to describe the moment when the Horror strikes, when we see the Abyss beneath—in T. S. Eliot there is the waiting-room at the country junction, the moment of silence in the Tube train, and Charles in 'The Family Reunion', who sometimes feels:

"As if the earth should open, as I was about to cross Pall Mall."

For Auden's Narrator:

"It's as if, waking up with a start, we discovered
Ourselves stretched out flat on the floor, watching our shadow
Sleepily stretching itself at the window. I mean
That the world of space where events recur is still there,
Only now it's no longer real."

And in the fourth section Auden uses the 'garden' and 'desert' symbols which occur so often in Eliot.

The chorus now comment again on the general dread to which the Narrator's speech has given particular application:

"Alone, alone, about a dreadful wood
Of conscious evil runs a lost mankind."

Man is utterly hopeless, but cannot bring himself to believe. If only proof were given without the need for Faith ("There is no direct transition to the thing of becoming a Christian"; "Faith is against understanding"—Kierkegaard):

"We who must die demand a miracle."

The Recitative which follows asserts that one can only believe when there is no alternative *but* to believe, when, having tried all other solutions, one is capable of imagining, nothing else makes sense:

"As long as the self can say 'I', it is impossible not to rebel;

. . . .

For the garden is the only place there is, but you will not find it
Until you have looked for it everywhere and found nowhere
    that is not a desert."

Simeon later elaborates the same idea, and Auden has considered it in several other places, notably in some notes on the Faustian and Peer Gyntian personality. Personalities of this type, he says, are looking for a Way through life, but have no religious authority to guide. They want "certainty without faith, that the subject is 'in the truth'. This can only be acquired by exploring *all* the possibilities of one's nature, good *and* evil, for it is only when a man knows them all that he can be perfectly certain which is the right one; as long as there is a single possibility untried, he cannot *know* that it should be rejected, he can only *believe* it should." And the condition may become one of sinful pride. "He was a very great scoundrel", says Auden much more recently, "who said to himself early in life: 'I will explore every possibility of sinning and then repent on my deathbed'." The point is subsumed in the verse from Romans vi. which introduces the Oratorio: "What shall we say then? Shall we continue in sin, that grace may abound? God forbid."

The first movement ends with a chorus on man's inescapable urge to believe in spite of all, to find Home, to know the End.

The four faculties (Intuition and Sensation—the unconscious faculties—and Feeling and Thought—the conscious faculties) appropriately introduce the Annunciation movement, since their separate existences symbolise man's lack of wholeness. Before he erred they were united, but now struggle with one another and lure man to error by each telling him the truth partially and ambiguously; each of them is isolated and each misused by a creature no longer 'in the truth'. As they end, the first note of hope and expectancy is sounded; Gabriel is about to come to Mary with the message that to her is given the opportunity of being an instrument for the redemption of man. Through her the possibility of Love and of the integration of his warring elements is to be revealed. A chorus again closes the movement, this time rejoicing—with music-hall tag refrains ("There's a Way. There's a Voice")—that God is to manifest Himself.

The music-hall element is continued into the next movement, The Temptation of St. Joseph, which opens with Joseph harassed by doubts about Mary's honour. Is she pure or has she deceived him? Is he being led up the garden? If only he could have one "important and elegant" proof that she was acting at God's will! The chorus prompts him not to believe, to be 'knowing' and say, 'Such things just don't happen'. But there will be no proof: he must simply believe. So he stands for all who would believe if they could be given firm proof beforehand, so that they need never wonder thereafter whether they were being 'had'. The revue choruses are sly voices from the world of the 'wide' boys, too 'knowing' to be taken in.

The Narrator directly attacks that attitude, the attitude which becomes defiant or resentful or querulous in face of the demand to believe without safe assurances, which would like to keep the Truth down to its own cynical level, and which reduces any manifestation of Love to a bar-room joke. Joseph, says the Narrator, is paying in his person:

> ". . . for all
> The pay-off lines of limericks in which
> The weak resentful bar-fly shows his sting."

The choruses then develop the general theme of the whole

movement—the temptations not to trust God—but this time in a mood of sadness and loss:

> "Joseph, Mary, pray for those
> Misled by moonlight and the rose,
> For all in all perplexity. . . ."

They mention, not only the cynical evasions, but those of higher intent; not only Love derided, but the false forms of Love, the mistakes of those who, whilst feeling that brutishness is not enough, are yet unable to move beyond one or other of the first stages after its rejection—beyond putting their all on love for another human being (like the lovers in Paradise Park in 'The Dog beneath the Skin', who live for one another); or beyond playing for safety by being strictly conventional ("the bourgoisie"—"O pray for our salvation / Who take the prudent way, / Believing we shall be exempted / From the general condemnation"); or beyond one of the many forms of *self*-regard. These are the temptations of the "common ungifted natures", who now cry for help to face the Summons which is the theme of the next movement.

The Summons is to all kinds of men, simple like the Shepherds, or more sophisticated like the Three Wise Men, or great men of power like Cæsar. It is a summons to face the Truth, alone, and without the sort of proofs we are accustomed to. This the Star announces to the Wise Men who are now following it, each for a different reason—the first because he has failed to discover Truth by the scientific examination of nature; the second because he was a progressive, but found living in the future made the present no better; the third because he put his trust in abstract intellect and found himself still incomplete. They are really three rather silly and pathetic old men, who finally join their complaints in a variety chorus in the mood of 'Show me the way to go home'. To them the Star, closing the section, gives the advice Prospero had given himself:

"Descend into the fosse of Tribulation,

. . . .

O do not falter at the last request
But, as the huge deformed head rears to kill.
Answer its craving with a clear I Will."

The Narrator introduces Cæsar with an official proclamation—an example of his kind of authority. Cæsar has conquered Necessity; only follow him (Hitler; the Leaders in the plays) and you need no other God. Let us praise him, says the Narrator, and so introduces the brilliantly idiomatic and witty Fugal Chorus in Cæsar's honour. The totalitarian masses are eulogising their power-giant, the representative of man's overweening pride in his own achievements and possibilities. Cæsar has given them truths and has conquered chaos by his power of abstract thought, by his skill, science and high organisation. He has assumed responsibility for and removed fear from the little man:

"When he says, This is good, this is loved.
When he says, That is bad, that is hated.
Great is Cæsar: God must be with Him."

Again the Narrator begins boldly and confidently, by reciting the successes of Cæsar's man-centred world (our world, as the manner and the detail make it impossible to miss), only to switch suddenly to an expression of the emptiness underneath:

"If we were never alone or always too busy
Perhaps we might even believe what we know is not true."

Nevertheless, the moments of warning come, "In the bath, or the subway, or the middle of the night" (again, the same kind of 'pointing' as in T. S. Eliot), and we know we are sinners; let us therefore be contrite and pray, "that the kingdom of Heaven may come". The movement ends with an uncomfortably clever chorale of prayer to God for help.

The Three Shepherds of the next movement are about to be granted their vision. Although simpler than the complicated magi, they are shrewd enough to be ironical, in an appropriate conversational metre, about the status accorded to them by the powers of this world. They too are being summoned as the wise men were; they are the representatives of the ordinary people who are as much God's children as the great figures of the earth. They unite their voices to say that, though their life is hard and monotonous, they never despair; they are always sure that there is something at the end. That something, says the chorus of Angels, announcing the Birth, is Love. . . . Love has come to rule the world in place of Authority:

> ". . . the old
> Authoritarian
> Constraint is replaced
> By his covenant,
> And a city based
> On love and consent
> Suggested to men."

From today we may know that the Unknown is not a Horror but a friend.

So the setting changes to the Manger, where Mary sings a lullaby over the sleeping child to whom she can give nothing—the human legacies are fear and anxiety. The Wise Men and Shepherds follow her and alternate their voices in the sort of incantation which Auden had attempted with less assurance in 'The Ascent of F.6' and 'On the Frontier'. The exceptional and the ordinary have completed their separate Quests which are yet the same: now they believe: "Released by Love from isolating wrong, / Let us for Love unite our various song." But their other journey is only just beginning and will never end on this earth, that is, the journey they must take in their efforts to live up to the Truth they have now accepted. They each cry for help—the first against intellectual pride, the second against sensual escapism—and give thanks for the choice now offered to them:

> "O living Love replacing phantasy,
> O joy of life revealed in Love's creation
> Our mood of longing turns to indication."

The Meditation of Simeon which follows is, we have indicated earlier, Auden's most clear and full single *statement* of his belief. The figure of Simeon is understandably attractive to writers whose convictions have traced a curve similar to that of Auden—he symbolises the man to whom Truth came late, but with great consolation, and who thereupon gave praise. So Eliot wrote 'A Song for Simeon' during the period of his conversion to Anglo-Catholicism. His Simeon is old and tired, part Gerontion, part Tiresias; Auden's Simeon, on the other hand, expresses himself energetically and idiomatically. He is Auden in his middle thirties, after a search not long in time but intensive.

The Meditation falls into two parts, each with several sections interspersed by single-line choruses. In the first part, in which Simeon describes man's unavailing efforts to be self-sufficient, the chorus variously echoes his loss:

> "When we woke it was day: we went on weeping."

In the second part, where Simeon expresses the fullness of the answer in God, the chorus reflects his joy:

> "Now and forever, we are not alone."

The themes have all been separately met before—the urge not to admit man's fundamental inadequacy until every rational explanation of his failures has been examined; the refusal to admit sin; the over-confidence in the scientific and material ("This is the epoch of the Third Great Disappointment"); the results which flow from realising the possibility of our salvation—that our freedom and our necessity are made explicit; that the unknown Horror is removed, each personality given value, but freed from the tyranny of self-regard; art and science not rejected, but given a place in the whole order, the Way made clear: "Therefore at any moment we pray that, following Him, we may depart from our anxiety into his peace."

The Massacre of the Innocents opens with a long outburst by the liberal rationalist and humanist Herod, going through agonies of indecision before he decides to order the Massacre. He begins by enumerating the positive achievements of his rule, and ends on a wail of despair before the irrational and absolute (cf. "Around them boomed the rhetoric of the time, / The smells and furniture of the known world / Where conscience worshipped an æsthetic order / And what was unsuccessful was condemned; / And, at the centre of its vast self-love, / The emperor and his pleasures, dreading death"). That this immediately follows Simeon's assertion of faith emphasises that the struggle is never won outright.

Herod's times, like our own, have seen enormous material improvements and ameliorations of manners; he has been a great planner and a staunch upholder of the Rational Life whose good results are plain for all to see. He has tried hard to be self-sufficient, and he objects to the introduction of the element of mystery. Nor are his grounds of objection trivial or altogether selfish—he fears that in an era of faith, all the values for which he has striven, and especially such values as hard effort and responsibility, will be lost. He is afraid that God will be just a woozy dream, pie-in-the-sky, to his subjects, sapping their initiative and self-respect. He rejects a God which he thinks can only be a projection of soft self-regard, whose followers are really saying: "Be interesting and weak like us, and we will love you as we love ourselves." He is a proud rationalist, of great fidelity to his own lights. He has the scorn of a man of strong character for a God which is only a refuge from inadequacy and which demands nothing. And to him the faith Christ brings can be only that; he is able to imagine no other. This God must be simply another manifestation of the cheap and messy emotionalism of the masses. It can't possibly be allowed, he almost screams. One daren't allow it; anyway, it's impossible. Clearly, "the notion of a finite God is absurd". Herod is, after all, afraid inside himself, afraid of the emotional and subjective, the imaginative, the spiritual. For suppose, he ends, suppose, for one awful moment, that God exists and has come to earth—what an awful responsibility for him. And he has to decide all by himself, completely on his own; and all his intelligence and learning and efficiency do not help. He ends on a wail of despair, with the cry of every man who realises that he can "destroy God" by not believing, who feels dreadful doubts, but who cannot bring himself to believe without proof, and so, clinging to reason alone but getting no final answer from it, is, in his considerable partial honesty, utterly miserable:

> "I've hardly ever taken bribes. How dare he allow me to decide? I've tried to be good. I brush my teeth every night. I haven't had sex for a month. I object. I'm a liberal. I want everyone to be happy. I wish I had never been born."

His soldiers, just getting ready to carry out the Massacre, follow him with one of Auden's best cynical ballads. These are the cheerful, cynical, humorous, valueless gang who carry out the orders of the man of power. Here is yet another facet of the whole complex situation, another aspect of the world of Herod: the change of style is brilliantly justified.

Rachel, the mother of Joseph, closes the movement quietly and unhappily with a summing-up of the two main ways in which man is misleading himself and so failing to accept the Advent—the way of satisfied sensuality ("grinning dogs"), and the way of proud reason ("sensible sheep"). Between them, and unregarded, is the Son of God, "a lost child". So today there must be grief, "and her coldness now is on the earth for ever."

That constant grief and the ceaseless journeying of man are epitomised in the final movement, The Flight into Egypt. There, Joseph and Mary crossing the desert are all those of good intent called to leave the world they know—a bad world, but one in which they felt at home (the world of space and time):

> "The Kingdom of the Robbers lies
>   Between Time and our memories;
> Fugitives from Space must cross
>   The Waste of the Anonymous."

By crossing the desert they may reach the garden; but they are not at ease:

> "Safe in Egypt we shall sigh
>   For lost insecurity;
> Only when the terrors come
>   Does our flesh feel quite at home."

The voices of the desert interject at intervals, speaking in both the four-beat alliterative line which Auden used in 'The Age of Anxiety', and in a cheap ballad metre. They sing the pleasures of the spiritual desert which Joseph and Mary are leaving, the desert inside the sophisticated and rootless, the desert where even sin is streamlined:

> "Come to our well-run desert
>   Where anguish arrives by cable,
>   And the deadly sins
>   May be bought in tins
>   With instructions on the label."

But though the cheap tone of the voices is meant to echo the civilisation they represent, these choruses are unpleasant. They are clever, bitter, and cynically amused at the culture whose cynicism they deplore.

The Narrator's final long conversational section is a comment on the oratorio, addressed directly, not by analogy, to us today:

"Now we must dismantle the tree,
   Putting the decorations back into their cardboard boxes—
   Some have got broken—and carrying them up to the attic."

The short vision is over, and our ordinary twentieth-century life goes on, not much affected. We are back again in Herod's world, "in the moderate Aristotelian city / Of darning and the Eight-Fifteen, where Euclid's geometry / And Newton's mechanics would account for our experience". But things are not quite the same, for:

". . . To those who have seen
   The Child, however dimly, however incredulously,
   The Time Being is, in a sense, the most trying time of all."

The moment of joy has gone, but so, too, has our brash confidence in ourselves, "the guilt remains conscious". We long for the vision of coinherence again, and are tempted to ask to be allowed to suffer so as to come nearer to it; we almost ask for the opportunity to be tempted and to do evil, so that once again we may experience God's grace (again, the verse from Romans vi. is appropriate). But that is not the way: we will have our suffering all in good time, and without looking for it, and we will sense grace. Meanwhile, we must do as well as we can:

"In the meantime
   There are bills to be paid. . . ."

The final chorus reiterates that "He is the Way—the Truth—the Light—" and that he must be sought in our own day and in all parts of life. . . . "Follow him through the Land of Unlikeness; . . . Seek Him in the Kingdom of Anxiety; . . . Love Him in the World of the Flesh".

(4) 'The Age of Anxiety'

"Auden's is a poetry of the nerves," said G. W. Stonier nearly twenty years ago, and that is truer of 'The Age of Anxiety' than of any earlier work. For this is an unhappy book, and, in parts, excessively difficult to read. There are some memorable passages—notably the last long speeches of Rosetta and Malin—and some of the bright aperçus one has learned to expect; but much is perverse and much batters at the reader. Auden has come "back to the hands, the feet, the faces", back to the close detail of life in the twentieth century more thoroughly than at any date since 'Another Time'—and finds them now less interesting as items for observation and more unpleasant as symptoms.

He is so preoccupied with the dullness, dryness and barrenness ("dowdy they'll die who have so dimly lived") of many lives that he becomes harsh and bitter. His analytical brain, his tendency to classify people, and his lack of simple sensuousness then operate so powerfully and astringently that he quickly has his subject wriggling, naked and unpleasant, dead-centred on the pin.

Nevertheless, his theme is a terrible one—no less than the condition of civilised man in 'The Age of Anxiety'. By anxiety here Auden means, as always, partly what psychologists intend by the term, neurotic dread, *angst* . . . a condition common today; more particularly, he means something in its nature unamenable to psycho-therapy—Kierkegaard's 'dread' or 'despair', that fear of the Unknown which is the condition of lacking Faith: "Both Catholicism and Protestantism," he says, "agree in maintaining that only faith can conquer man's original anxiety", and later, in 'The Meditation of Simeon': "Therefore at every moment we pray that, following Him, we may depart from our anxiety into His peace."

That "original anxiety" is increased by the anonymity and fragmentariness of life in the Waste Land. The chromium-

plated metropolis is the "Kingdom of Anxiety" in the final
chorus of 'For the Time Being'—"Seek Him in the Kingdom
of Anxiety" was the injunction—and it indicated that in such
a place the lack is so apparent that one can hardly be blind to
the need for some personal concern, since one is unlikely
simply to *accept* the terms of life. The point is one Auden frequently makes, and is, we have seen, connected with his own
emigration to America:

> "[The Good Place may be] nearer to the anonymous country-
> side littered with heterogeneous *dreck* and the synonymous
> cities besotted with electric signs, nearer to radio commercials
> and congressional oratory and Hollywood Christianity, nearer
> to all the 'democratic' lusts and licences, without which, perhaps,
> the analyst and the immigrant alike would never understand by
> contrast the nature of the Good Place nor desire it with sufficient
> desperation to stand a chance of arriving."

So the scene for a work such as this must be a time-ridden,
newspaper-headline-obsessed, 'superhet' city; the local setting
(other writers, e.g. Graham Greene, have used it for similar
purposes) a bar, a place in which the unhappy ego is given a
boost; the period most suitable, that of the recent war; the
characters, some typical 'lonelies'.

Auden has supplied himself with three men and one woman,
two of the men not far from middle age, the third and the
woman young. The young man and one of the older men are
in the Services, the other two civilians. This disposition of
characters has presumably been chosen so as to allow the impact of the situation on different kinds and types of personality
to show. Thus the young naval man Emble is sexually successful, but profoundly lacking in confidence; the girl Rosetta, a
buyer for a big department store, is physically attractive,
professionally successful and has a good public mask, but lets
her profound dissatisfaction leak away in fantasies of a return
to innocence and grace, all of which she pictures as the upper-

middle-class English landscape of her childhood—a landscape of rectory gardens and tea on the lawn (possibly a landscape for which Auden is sometimes homesick, the setting of "the untransfigured scene, / My father down the garden in his gaiters, / My mother at her bureau writing letters"). Rosetta is a Jewess, and unlike Emble has deep racial roots from which she is finally able to draw strength for the solitary journey she realises is to be her lot. Quant, a dusty middle-aged clerk, is tired, empty and not particularly intelligent; Malin, a Medical Intelligence Officer in the Canadian Air Force, is the shrewdest of the four, and leads most of the discussion.

In one sense all four are exiles; not artistic or intellectual exiles, but the ordinary exiles who "lost a world they never understood" ("Loss is their shadow-wife, anxiety receives them..." Auden added in this poem, written a few years earlier and sometimes called 'Exiles'). They are without purpose and without faith, all trying to forget the "Hidden Law". They establish some sort of communion *faute de Dieu*; they are huddling together for warmth and with a kind of pity for one another, since all are caught in the same predicament. The action in which they are involved is a simple one: they meet in the bar, fall into conversation about the state of the world, create a semi-drunken intimacy and go for drinks to the girl's flat; after some dancing by the young couple, the two older men leave them to sleep together. But Emble passes out straightway, and the girl goes to bed alone. The older men go separately home. Each of the four is alone again, and day is breaking.

Auden's purpose is to create neither character nor dramatic incident, but states of mind. He takes a commonplace happening, a chance encounter in wartime, and works outwards from it through the personalities of the people involved until it is revealed as containing, behind the slightly glittering euphoric exterior, the misery of a whole society. His biggest problem has been here, as it was in the three preceding works, to find an effective form. This time he has not found it. He has provided himself with representative personalities, set them in the required place, made them reveal their condition in highly stylised dialogue and called the result a baroque eclogue (ironically, since an eclogue is usually a pastoral dialogue). He has adapted some short forms to hold the poem's separate parts—a dirge, a masque, the Seven Ages of Man, the Seven Stages—but the result is not a whole.

The metre is predominantly the alliterative line of the Old and Middle English poets which Auden had used occasionally during the 'thirties. More recently it had been used for the Voices of the Desert in 'For the Time Being':

> "It was visitors' day at the vinegar works
>   In Tenderloin Town when I tore my time."

There the object was to suggest the deadness of the world of bars and anxiety, the world from which the voices came, and in which 'The Age of Anxiety' is set. Most traditional metres would not give the necessary hollowness and the right kind of looseness; yet a conversational metre might not be rigid enough and a certain rigidity is needed since this world, although without grace, is not loose and easy, but fast-bound in its own misery. This broken line with its four hammer-beats can suggest, firstly, a grim acceptance or hanging on. The spirit and the movement are both well illustrated in the chorus to the Anglo-Saxon poem 'Deor':

> "That passed away: so may this"

which is echoed in 'The Age of Anxiety':

> "Many have perished: more will."

It is the mood of 'Paid on Both Sides', where the ellipsis and the metre suggest a tightlipped determination:

> "Guns shoot Hot in the hand
>   Fighters lay Groaning on ground
>   Gave up life Edward fell."

But this is not exactly the mood Auden wishes most frequently to convey in 'The Age of Anxiety'. Here he needs primarily a regular monotonous beat, a kind of dull *dribbling away* of existence; too much ellipsis would unduly stiffen the back:

> "Consider rather the incessant Now of
> The traveller through time, his tired mind
> Biased towards bigness since his body must
> Exaggerate to exist, possessed by hope,
> Acquisities, in quest of his own
> Absconded self yet scared to find it
> As he bumbles by from birth to death
> Menaced by madness";

and:

> "In hot houses helpless babies and
> Telephones gabbled untidy cries,
> And on embankments black with burnt grass
> Shambling freight trains were shunted away
> Past crimson clouds."

Whilst the line is free from the demands of syllabic metre or rhyme, it is, as the above extracts show, closely disciplined by the demands of alliteration and cæsura. It achieves some variety by alternating pauses of sense with the pauses demanded by the metre, e.g. by running the sense over the end of the line. More importantly, the demands of alliteration tend to the creation of a special poetic language, especially through the use of synonyms and formulæ for periphrasis. The Anglo-Saxon poets, who had not as extensive a vocabulary as Auden to draw upon (he seems to have used a lexicon) and who were concerned to be immediately and orally intelligible to a general audience, made a wide use of compound words and kenning.

Auden does use synonyms and periphrasis freely here, but his most interesting reaction to the restrictions of the metre is his experimenting with verbs—especially since he has always previously seemed to turn more naturally to nouns for his effects. Often he dislocates his verbs to produce the necessary alliteration. But sometimes, instead of being badly misused, the verb's area of meaning is extended; thus:

"the light collaborates with a land of ease";
"lightning engraves its disgust on engrossed flesh";
"[he] grows into a grin" [of a small boy, learning the uses of a social face—cf. 'acquires a grin'].

And the same process sometimes, though not so frequently, takes place with nouns:

"For down each dale industrious there ran
A paternoster of ponds and mills,
Came sweet waters, assembling quietly
By a clear congress of accordant streams
A wild river that moseyed at will."

The more successful instances—many are showy and startling —promise to have a useful effect on Auden's language even after the alliterative demand has been lifted.

Auden's use of periphrasis, on the other hand, reveals that he still finds it very difficult to resist the opportunity for verbal gymnastics:

". . . desert dogs reduced their status
To squandered bones."

". . . plains winced as punishing engines
Raised woeful welts."

The Prologue, in Auden's favourite involved prose, presents the characters grouped round the bar, each alone and unhappy, and each thinking firstly of himself and then, after the wireless has broken in with the war news, of the state of the world. So Quant thinks of his own "soiled soul" and, in a passage of perverse periphrasis, of the horrors of war; the more intelligent Malin reflects on the troubled consciousness of man and, in unsuccessful verse, recalls a bombing raid; the career-girl Rosetta yearns for her lush English landscape "where work and law and guilt are just literary words", and thinks of Europe, where there is now appearing the new impersonal "odourless" society in which "they investigate / In soundproof cells the sense of honour"; Emble broods on the psychology of the "sad haunters of Perhaps," the lonelies such as himself. Dread grips them all: they feel that their society has somehow failed them and, as acquaintance ripens, agree to discuss that failure, to examine fallen Western man:

> ". . . in quest of his own
>   Absconded self yet scared to find it."

They will consider the Seven Ages of man today.

Of childhood Malin, always concerned with the double man, recalls the growth of the sense of guilt and the increasing betrayal of the "inner life"; Emble recalls the miserable years of being tortured by other boys and Quant a magic urban landscape of gas-lamps, embankments and old mills ("the view from Birmingham to Wolverhampton"); Rosetta remembers that graceful world into which she so often escapes from the present cold air:

> ". . . a still world of
>   Hilarious light, our lives united
>   Like fruit in a bowl."

For them all adolescence was the time of fantasy, of themselves imagined as Byronic intellectual exiles, or as the focus of splendid public obsequies, or as the commanding lover of many chorus girls, or as the self-regarding centre of a setting always gay, friendly and perfect.

So the examination proceeds through early maturity and marriage, the period of coming to terms with the hard, unappetising realities of life, the mid-point of successful arrival, or of the final realisation of failure, and the falling-away into a glassy old age. In each Age the individual contributions are designed, not only to comment on the condition of society to-day, but to reveal something of the type of personality making them. Thus Quant is bottomlessly cynical, a bored failure for whom life is a meaningless wheel-like succession, for whom there are no values, but only facts. He sums up his whole story in an elaborate and fantastic account of the Quest as it is made by the "ignored" such as himself, for whom the journey's culmination is one distant glimpse of "The Good Place" before they relapse for good into disillusion. Malin has known some success, and recalls its temporary pleasures in verse which uses the metre with effective curtness:

> "His body acquires the blander motions
>   Of the approved state. His positive glow
>   Of fiscal health affects that unseen
>   Just judge. . . ."

And in each Age Malin reverts to his insistence on the deceptions of the ego. He recognises one of those deceptions in what he calls Rosetta's longing for "some nameless Eden". But hers is not simply a selfish longing; in part she is re-creating in her dreams a place where the intimate personal values, which her tawdry, machine-existence disregards, will be reinstated. Her ideal is not false, but her belief that she may realise it in a human love-relationship is false, and her relapses after successive disappointments into further fantasy are a sign of weakness. She is yet stronger than Emble, who alternates between cheap mockery and the longing of a frightened boy for a closed world superficially similar to the one Rosetta wants. He expresses his dreadful uncertainty in that passage of brilliant dramatic imagery which has already been quoted ("To be young means / To be all on edge . . ."). Each of them is too young to have let regret freeze into the dead-end philosophy of Quant, and insufficiently experienced to be able to analyse it like Malin. They share with the other two a feeling of being somehow reproached from a "Hidden Centre" (that centre Sebastian, of 'The Sea and the Mirror', recognised "I should not love because I had no proof, / Yet all my honesty assumed a sword").

As the section ends, Quant sings an occasionally witty but over-spry ballad on the sad fate of Homo Vulgaris, and delivers some pathetic-ironic home-truths to his ageing self; Rosetta continues to regret the graceful life: "poor and penalised the private state"; Emble brings into the open his real fear—that he may succumb to the routine which he now mocks; and Malin describes the very last age:

> ". . . He is tired out;
> His last illusions have lost patience
> With the human enterprise. The end comes. He
> Joins the majority, the jaw-dropped
> Mildewed mob, and is modest at last,
> There his case rests: let who can disprove."

They have recited what seems to be the inevitable pattern of life in time, and found it miserable and meaningless. They are ready to look farther, to consider now, not the Seven Ages, but the Seven Stages in the search for "The Quiet Kingdom", which all begin to trace:

> "the sole essential a sad unrest
> No life can lack."

The Quiet Kingdom is not the Good Place, though it may be contained in it. It is the human dream of perfect peace and happiness which may yield, once it has met its inevitable disappointments, to the Quest for the Good Place.

Although one may be clear as to the general import of the Seven Stages, the significance of each stage is unjustifiably difficult to discover—partly because so much of the verse is baroque, partly because some of the symbols seem susceptible of several contradictory interpretations and partly because the whole section is excessively contrived. I offer very tentatively an explanation of the symbolism which seems to interpret each section fairly satisfactorily, though odd lines call it in question. It is not simply an excuse, however, to suggest that Auden may well have left his symbolism inconsistent.

The Seven Stages, then, are not chronological stages in the life in time—indeed, the characters "lost the sense of time" before starting on them—but stages of realisation about the nature of life through which it is necessary to pass before one may come to the edge of that desert which is faced on the second half of the last stage. This mixed quartet all start on the journey because they have "a feeling . . . of having lost their bearings, of a restless urge to find water", and move through successive stages of greater awareness until the final issue is before them—that if they want to reach the only real conclusion to such a journey, they must submit to a difficult discipline. The Stages, then, are not so much stages to God or to spiritual awareness or even to faith, so much as stages *from* a largely selfish unrest to the point where that unrest becomes a determination to try to find faith and God.

The first stage, of climbing gradually from a primitive landscape through an increasingly familiar countryside until they reach the summit and are in the contemporary world, may signify—in a rapid survey of the history of Western Society from prehistoric times (the primitive landscape—the monks of the Middle Ages—the lead mines of the beginnings of industrialism, etc.)—that the dream of a prehistoric bliss is a myth, that primitive people were, as Rosetta says, "the first to feel our sorrow", and that that sorrow has been a feature of all man's history, is indeed an inescapable part of his life. The climb would indicate the "urge to civilise and to create" of 'New Year Letter'. Perhaps there is also implied the concept that the individual runs through the history of the race from childhood until he has developed to the point of becoming part of his contemporary society and sharing its attitudes. Quant's remark as they near the top, that he has been given some advice on how to win favours by bribery once up there, would then indicate his brash and none too scrupulous confidence as he stepped into the adult world.

This leads logically to the Mariners' Tavern of the next stage, the point of departure for all those who, for many different reasons, begin to question the values of their society:

> "And one finds it hard to fall asleep here
> Lying awake and listening
> To the creak of new creeds on the kitchen stairs."

That the four separate into pairs, youth with youth and age with age, for their journey to the ports, presumably indicates that, though one may begin the journey at any time of life, one's reasons for going are likely to be different at different ages. Thus Emble is driven by his sense of not-belonging:

> ". . . must everyone see himself
> As I, as the pilgrim prince
> Whose life belongs to his Quest
> For the Truth, the tall princess."

Rosetta is driven by dissatisfaction engendered at the contrast between her dreams of "a land of ease" and the depersonalised life around her. Quant goes because in his middle age, at the root of all his overt cynicism, he feels guilt; Malin wants to understand more about the troubled heart and will. He speaks for all as they set out:

> "For wind and whining gull
> Are saying something,
> Or trying to say, about time
> And the anxious heart
> Which a matter-snob would dismiss."

The ports at the end of the second stage—I do not know why each couple should arrive at a different stage unless to underline their different starting-points (e.g. the port as a frontier, as in 'Dover')—the ports, those "queasy juncture[s] / Of water and earth", bring to the travellers' notice also how small a thing man is in comparison with the vast unknown universe; they carry the same reminder as Alonso gave to Ferdinand, of "the cold deep that does not envy you"; they recall "the vast waters of the petrel and porpoise" which surge in the background of Eliot's 'Dry Salvages', and against which man's life is played out. Here, says Quant:

> "The desperate spirit
> Thinks of its end in the third person,
> As a speck drowning
> In those wanton mansions where the whales take
> Their huge fruitions."

Against this background all four go now to look at man's attempt to make the world less terrifying, safer, predictable: they set off, appropriately by train, for the town. The journey gives Auden the opportunity for some socio-psychological detail reminiscent of the 'thirties, in his description of those who rush to the gregarious life of the city because they are afraid of their personal freedom, "the faded and failing in flight towards town", and of those who happily evolve a technique for making the most of their culture: "The successful smilers the city can use."

Thus they arrive at Herod's world, anthropocentric, godless, highly organised, the world also of the bourgeois in the Temptation of St. Joseph section of 'For the Time Being', a glossy and "facetious" culture, our culture. Quant's description of it is fantastic, quixotically high-lighted, in parts witty, but not so effective as similar descriptions from the 'thirties. The road out of town calls to their minds all the unhappiness (accidents; crime; death) which man's culture cannot remove or make easier to bear; the human city is not the Quiet Kingdom. Nor is the Big House at which they now arrive, and which represents the wish for the womb, or human love regarded as the justification of existence (again, one is reminded of the lovers in Paradise Park and of the first semi-chorus from part three of the Temptation of St. Joseph). This illusion, of being able to "love ourselves and live / In just anarchic joy" is particularly Rosetta's. It is fitting therefore that she should rush eagerly into the house, only to find its joys founded on cruelty, its happiness hollow. She returns slowly. She has idealised human love, wanted to believe it sufficient; now her landscape with figures is dissolving:

> "The significant note is nature's cry
> Of long-divided love."

As they race to the next point, something more of the weakness of each of their natures is revealed. Once there, at the graveyard, they are reminded of "death's eternal gap", in the face of which all our "quotidian joy" becomes occasional; they are reminded that, as someone has said, though the wise man does not fear the fact of death, he never forgets it. The lesson is again the same as Alonso's to his son: "How soon the lively trip is over."

When they split into pairs again, Malin with Emble, Quant with Rosetta, the new combination satisfies no one—there can be no peace in human relationships. More, the unfortunate grouping emphasises, even more markedly than the race had done, the impure motive behind each one's setting-out on the journey ("the desires of the heart are as crooked as corkscrews"). So far the moral of each stage has been a fairly generalised one, applicable to most human beings, e.g. we all sometimes want the warmth of the herd; we all die, and so on. But no Quest, as Michael Ransom discovered, becomes serious until the individual has examined his own crooked heart.

It is in this state—becoming aware, not only of generally applicable truths, but of their peculiar errors—that they reach the Hermetic Gardens. I do not know why this unpleasantly baroque place should be "hermetic", unless the adjective is

meant to indicate its magical character. The same garden symbol occurs before, with its opposing symbol of the desert, in
the Advent and Flight to Egypt movements of the Oratorio.
More particularly these gardens are the Kierkegaardian "Field
of Being" described in 'New Year Letter' (II, 860–97). The
same image of the wicket-gate is used and the same characteristics noted—as that in the Gardens man ceases for a
moment from Becoming, in order to Be. They are, Quant
says:

> ". . . a theatre where thought becomes act
> And . . .
> The ruined rebel is recreated
> And chooses a second self."

In the gardens there occurs the moment of illumination and
Love, the indication of what may be striven toward. Here
man's—

> ". . . hardened heart
> Consents to suffer, and the sudden instant
> Touches his time at last."

'The sudden instant' is Eliot's "moment out of time" and "the
moment in the rose-garden"; it is also Kierkegaard's 'instant'.
The "hero's . . . sudden leap into love" is Kierkegaard's
'leap in the dark'.

To the four, whose consciences are by now aware of weakness and insufficiency, it seems "like an accusation"; they are
afraid of what is demanded ("afraid / Of all that has to be
obeyed"). So Rosetta speaks for them all when she says, "I
would stay to be saved, but . . ." Now they understand that
they must in the end travel alone. Stripped of all excuses, they
wander the "solitary paths" of that wood which the chorus in
'For the Time Being' had described:

> "Alone, alone, about a dreadful wood
> Of conscious evil runs a lost mankind."

They are "abandoned souls" in the moment of utter loss before they come to the edge of the desert.

There they converge, "with only the last half of the seventh stage to go." But now the doubts of the double man are renewed and aggravated. Have they the necessary courage, for "it takes will to cross this waste"? Worse—is there really anything on the other side?—are spiritual questionings meaningful? If only they could be given proof before they cross, they say, echoing the cry from the Oratorio:

> "The Pilgrim Way has led to the Abyss
>
> . . . .
>
> We who must die demand a miracle."

Even the records of those who have crossed and returned provide no proof (see the Quest sonnet, No. XVI).

So the doubt, which is the devil of part two of 'New Year Letter', engulfs them, and thereupon their world,

> "from which their journey has been one long flight, rises up before them now as if the whole time it had been hiding in ambush."

They are back, not altogether unhappily, in the world they know; after all, one is used to Caliban; better confusion than commitment:

> ". . . indifferent tongues
>
> . . . .
>
> . . . recite in unison
> A common creed, declaring their weak
> Faith in confusion."

With this the mood is broken, and the four find themselves once again in the bar, now closing. As they walk to Rosetta's, they lament the absence of the Father God they have lately been seeking and failed to find.

This dirge is typical of much of Auden's recent verse. It is baroque, experimental, extremely skilful. The object is presumably to suggest the atmosphere of the cockeyed, disrupted world from which it emerges. And, in spite of its obvious faults, the dirge is both arresting and pathetic. The group are voicing, not only the general wish for a father, but also the loss of a particular father, scientific humanism, which had made the world so secure:

> ". . . thanks to him
> Brisker smelles abet us,
> Cleaner clouds accost our vision
> And honest sounds our ears.
> For he ignored the Nightmares and annexed
> their ranges."

Now chaos is come again: father the authority and father the healer are both gone.

At Rosetta's they try to be cheerful, in a Masque whose grotesque ironic fancies are meant to fit the situation, but are overstrained. There are a few good lines and some of the usual instances of extraordinary perceptiveness, but the total effect is of clever silliness.

The attraction between Rosetta and Emble develops until gradually all share that sense of hazy well-being in which the troubles of the world seem easily remediable, and sin only an aberration or the result of ignorance. They have failed to meet the demands of a higher love, and are deceiving themselves once again into thinking that human love will do. They are hymning something far more unreal, in its vagueness and innocence of guilt, than Auden's 'Love' of the 'thirties. So, before they leave, the two older men sing a hymn of dedication, hailing this pitiful little temporary affair as a proof that man may find peace without having to meet the greater demands to which they have so recently found themselves unequal; they ask that it may:

> "Redeem with a clear
> Configuration
> Of routes and goals
> The ages of anguish."

But when Rosetta returns to her room, she finds that the other half of this wonderful partnership has fallen into a drunken stupor. Over his prostrate body she delivers a soliloquy which is, in spite of its Joycean punning and some other tricks, both intelligent and moving.

She understands well that he is a child, and will soon settle down and cease to question himself so much; may he have "Christian luck". She, a Jewess, is the permanent exile and wanderer:

> "More boys like this may embrace me yet
> I shan't find shelter."

She is leaving her fantasies, realising without regret that there is no "Innocent Place where the Law can't look", no escape from Jehovah's eye. The image of Jehovah merges into that of her "poor fat father" whom she left to make a career for herself, but who, in a deeper sense, she can never leave; the racial roots hold. She ends on the line of prayer most frequently used by believing Jews:

> "Hear, O Israel, the Lord our God, the Lord is One."

The Quest for the Good Place is, Auden is apparently indicating, common to both Jew and Gentile. Except for Malin's soliloquy at the close, 'The Age of Anxiety' is not specifically a Christian fable any more than is Kafka's *The Castle*. Both deal with the urge to find the Way, and the sense of guilt.

As the two older men walk home Quant, semi-drunk, comments cynically on life and the times: he remains much as he was. Malin broods on the moral dilemma. Do we ever learn from the past? Will decision and action ever make things better? How reluctantly, he cries, echoing the last part of the Seven Stages, we shake off illusions:

> "We would rather be ruined than changed
> We would rather die in our dread
> Than climb the cross of the moment
> And let our illusions die."

Neither intuition nor imagination can bring about the possibility of order—only Faith. He had failed at the Seventh Stage, but now, as dawn breaks, he recognises necessity and delivers a soliloquy which, in its management of the Anglo-Saxon line, is as impressive as Rosetta's. In it he acknowledges the evil in the will as the source of the present horror, and ends—as Auden's poems usually do today—in a cry of thankfulness for the Descent of the Dove, and the evidence of God's ever-present mercy. But how small a space that cry of faith occupies after so much anguish; how much it seems like a saving incantation against madness at the end.

'The Age of Anxiety' is poetically a failure, and all the greater a disappointment for the expectations aroused by 'The Sea and the Mirror' and 'For the Time Being'. What distresses most is that Auden worries his themes, that he seems not to have the patience to let them emerge, but has to thrust them at the reader. The Seven Stages, for example, which forms the core of the book, is altogether too consciously developed: the symbols rarely do anything to reinforce and extend the meaning; after a lot of effort we recognise, or think we recognise, what they are meant to signify—but our response is not deepened. The weakness is an old one aggravated: the images into which Auden translates his abstractions are liable to be less clear than the abstractions themselves.

CHAPTER VII

CONCLUSION

IN trying to assess the peculiarly uneven work which Auden is producing today, one has to remember, first of all, that it is natural for him to experiment in poetry. He is at present experimenting even more than he was during the 'thirties—as, for instance, in his use of Anglo-Saxon metre and the baroque manner in 'The Age of Anxiety'. It is characteristic of Auden, too, that he is today assimilating American idiom in an even more living way than he did the English. He now frequently employs it, not so much to jar, as it so often used to, as to startle the reader into feeling the contemporary importance of the ideas he is discussing—by a sudden switch from abstract comment to an appropriate colloquialism. Though perversity and carelessness remain, they do not represent a falling-away of his unusual technical skill or an exhaustion of his imaginative powers. The good parts of the later works would, in any event, forbid that conclusion.

As wholes, these works reveal the major technical problem before Auden today. He needs to write long works if he is to examine adequately modern life in its breadth and complexity. He needs in each instance to find a *coherent* form within which he may modify and develop his ideas, set them in various lights, and reveal their connections. He needs structures in some ways analogous to those of music. His task therefore is similar to that undertaken by Eliot in both 'The Waste Land' and 'The Four Quartets', though Auden's cast of mind places him nearer the earlier work. His structure should allow him to embody his ideas in personalities—like those of 'The Age of Anxiety'—seen as states of mind and as subjects for analytic comment; it should also afford him large scope for dramatic gesture.

In some degree this problem has affected him since he began writing: 'The Orators' was his first attempt to solve it. From one point of view, the plays were another; he hoped in them to have extended scope for his use of significant detail: they failed because he is not otherwise dramatically competent. He needs the long, closely articulated poem, not the play. Since 1940 this has become clearer to him as well as to his readers. He cast 'New Year Letter' in a loose metre, and thereafter let the argument decide the form; much of the matter is incidental, and there is some repetition. The 'Quest' sonnets presented their themes dramatically and economically, but not organically. Both 'The Sea and the Mirror' and 'For the Time Being' were more successful: the one because Auden married a fairly strictly defined main subject—the place of art—to a ready-made symbolic pattern; the other because he found for a wider subject an historical framework, the events immediately before and after the birth of Christ. In 'The Age of Anxiety' he needed a form capable of comprehending, even more than the others he had used, the *detail* of modern life and the peculiar stresses the present situation puts on the individual; as we have seen, he did not find the form.

Nor has he yet found his audience. In the early 'thirties it was often assumed, because Auden's poetry was obscure, that he wanted to write only for a clique. Later he became more intelligible, and surer of his larger audience—the audience of the "decent" weeklies. At the same time, we have seen, he wrote a good deal of verse aimed at a very much wider audience and with an unmistakable intention to reform. We have seen, too, why that effort was bound to fail under existing conditions. Today he has lost also a large part of that other audience, the audience drawn from the 'intelligentsia'. Perhaps he would have kept more of those by stopping at a certain point in his examination. Many of them are today thoroughly disappointed or sincerely puzzled; Auden seems to have gone sour, depressingly religious, forbiddingly absolutist. He has, unfortunately, rejected their world, the world of forward-looking, intelligent, liberal humanism; for him now, as for Quant,

> "the decent advice
> Of the liberal weeklies [is] as lost an art
> As peasant pottery."

There are no journals with a weekly circulation of one hundred —or even twenty—thousand whose editorial outlook is austerely Christian.

Auden's popularity, then, is suffering from the change of country, the change of subject and the constant experimenting. He said recently that the poet's audience is tending for a number of reasons to be a "specialised" one, "perhaps of fellow poets". But Auden has not written, and does not write in 'The Age of Anxiety', primarily for fellow-poets. That statement was probably inspired by discouragement at not seeing with any degree of assurance exactly what is his audience today. Certainly he would like it to be largely non-literary; his whole cast of mind demands that. Yet it will be a minority audience— not because Auden's poetry requires an esoterically cultured set of readers, but because only a minority at any time is likely, so far as our present experience leads us to expect, to raise those questions about their individual and social life which Auden most frequently poses. If we assume that the better educated are likely to be more conscious in this way than others, then they will predominate. But they will not be alone: Auden's real audience, as the discussion of popular verse showed, will be from the "concerned" in all parts of society.

But neither the constant experimenting nor the doubts about his audience wholly explain the unequal character of Auden's verse today. Much of his verse suggests a mind still a long way from being "delivered from mistrust". And what is one to conclude from his apparent compulsion to hammer at the tenets of his belief, not only in his poems, but in essays on almost any subject? He sometimes seems, as we noted earlier, like a man who is *teaching* himself to believe, as though he were having for the first time to establish every detail of belief, having to construct it from a variety of sources. Sometimes the assertion of faith seems to be repeated almost as a charm. The mood of:

> ". . . the whirlwind may arrange your will
> And the deluge release it to find
> The spring in the desert, the fruitful
> Island in the sea . . ."

is uncomfortably near that of:

> "New styles of architecture, a change of heart";

and:

> "the lolling bridegroom, beautiful there."

We have seen that there are exceptions to this in some poems from the same period. But very often Auden seems to be fighting his own personality: the struggle is objectified in those frequent discussions on the relationship between the simple and the exceptional, or on the relative claims of intuition and intelligence, or on the secondariness of art.

The recurrence of that last topic suggests, too, an unsettled relationship between the poet and the believer. The side of Auden which assents to certain religious presuppositions seems not to be in what he has called, in another context, a 'one to one relationship' with the side which produces poetry; there seems to be a lack of harmony between the private and the poetic personality. Part of his character has always drawn him to metaphysical enquiry, but other parts are in opposition. Many of his early poses have gone, but he is still not free enough for his own peace of mind from that "old game of playing God with words". He was, earlier, particularly *interested* in all manner of things, and the interest was often 'æsthetic' in the sense which he declared insufficient in the notes to 'New Year Letter'. Thus, the pleasure he took in Brueghel's

Icarus—in Brueghel's noting that what makes the scene so dramatic is the fact that normal life goes on unconcernedly whilst the tragedy takes place in its midst—is largely an æsthetic pleasure, a pleasure in pattern, contrast, gesture. That kind of pleasure—which it is one of the objects of 'The Sea and the Mirror' also to declare inadequate and perhaps dangerous—seems to remain rather more powerful than the religious side of Auden can feel happy about.

So does Auden's pride in his skill at the literary "game", the kind of pride which will let some writers allow almost anything for the sake of a good phrase. In Auden this shows itself now in exhibitions of cleverness at places where they are not simply irrelevant, but almost a denial of the subject. He is, perhaps, thinking of himself when he makes Prospero say:

> "Can I learn to suffer without saying
> Something ironic or funny
> About suffering."

His poem 'At the Grave of Henry James' makes the fullest of all his direct statements on this theme:

> "All will be judged. Master of nuance and scruple,
> Pray for me and for all writers living or dead;
> Because there are many whose works
> Are in better taste than their lives; because there is no end
> To the vanity of our calling: make intercession
> For the treason of all clerks.
>
> Because the darkness is never so distant,
> And there is never much time for the arrogant
> Spirit to flutter its wings,
> Or the broken bone to rejoice, or the cruel to cry
> For Him whose property is always to have mercy, the author
> And giver of all good things."   (1943.)

This issue—between Auden the poet (singer and word-user) and Auden the moralist—has a further important aspect. The moralist in him seems to have strengthened that already powerful abstracting tendency in him, his tendency to *make statements* in his verse rather than to explore his experience and let the verse affect the reader in a less direct way. This abstracting and relation-finding quality in Auden's verse is thrown into sharp relief by a comparison—even though we admit the differences of character and do not ask Auden to write like either Eliot or Hopkins—of, say, parts of 'The Four Quartets' with the Seven Stages in 'The Age of Anxiety', or by a comparison of the Quest sonnets with the 'terrible' sonnets of Hopkins. Latterly, Auden's tendency towards abstraction seems to have increased, exactly because he does now assent to a whole view of the nature of life. He seems to be aware of the danger; in 'New Year Letter' he says, as though advising himself, "the poetic mood is never indicative", and in a later essay:

> "art is not metaphysics any more than it is conduct, and the artist is usually unwise to insist too directly in his art upon his beliefs."

All these things—the experimenting, the search for a form, the uncertainty about his audience, the difficulties in belief and the split between the poet and the moralist—account for the unsatisfactoriness of so much of Auden's recent work, for the disconcerting changes of tone, the switches, say, from subtle wit to childish crudity (e.g. in the love-duet in 'The Age of Anxiety'), or from an obviously *clever* manner to a somewhat heavy seriousness. Such blemishes are not likely to disappear until he has ceased playing so many successive parts. But, however the issues are finally resolved, he is not likely to cease writing poetry. Poetry is his natural way of speaking, and he is too concerned with man in society and too anxious to communicate ever to let himself be silent for long.

Meanwhile, his achievement is not slight. He has written a few poems memorable by the strictest standards. By his skill and energy he did much to enliven English verse in the 'thirties, and his present experiments may well do even more

for the 'fifties. He has produced some fine songs, and been unusually successful in light ironic verse. Much of his work is
faulty, but almost all of it reveals important qualities of
imagination, e.g. his extraordinary social and psychological
perceptiveness, and his command of the dramatic image.

We may sometimes feel that his view is distorted, that, for
example, he thinks more are frustrated today than are in fact
frustrated, or that he does not give sufficient weight, especially
at present, to the surrounding evidence of human goodness as
against the evidence of human sin. He is, after all, an "intellectual of the middle classes"; he may possess certain personal
characteristics which make him hardly a representative contemporary individual. Nevertheless, he is a significant figure,
and in nothing more than in his sensitivity to the tensions of
the age. It is not fortuitous, nor simply a consequence of
differences in temperament, that, of the two considerable
poets now writing in English, one felt it necessary, forty years
ago, to leave America for the civilisation of Europe, and the
other, ten years ago, to leave England for New York. Both are
particularly occupied with the pressures society puts upon
the inner life of the individual.

Whatever the relative status of these two poets on other
counts, Auden is nearer to the detail of most peoples' lives
than is Eliot. He may be neither profound nor prophetic, but
he is an intelligent, sensitive, fluent and generous man of his
day. He said in a recent paper that as the poet matures he asks
himself, not so much "how can I express myself?" as "how
can I express this novel experience of mankind?" Certainly
Auden himself asks that question, and is thus representative,
particularly responsive to experiences which in some ways
affect us all.

It would be pompous to apply to him without qualification
his own couplet on the Novelist, who:

> ". . . in his own weak person if he can,
> Must suffer dully all the wrongs of man."

Yet it does partially apply. Auden is at one of the frontiers of this anxiety-torn world; he is one of those who play out in themselves, with unusual and revealing clarity, struggles to which, whether we recognise it or not, we are all committed. He is, in spite of all his facetiousness, profoundly serious about his work (without being so no one could remain a poet after thirty-five today). It is that seriousness which impels him to a discipline of loneliness and of endless self-examination:

> "The alternative [to a new form of Catholic belief which Auden thinks could only be imposed crudely today] is the acceptance by every individual of his aloneness and his responsibility for it—and a willingness continually to re-examine his absolute assumptions in the light of his own experience and that of others."

Here is one of the functions of the writer at any time—not to present potted metaphysics or brisk social commentary, but, working in his own way, to be fully and sensitively implicated in the concerns of men. On this aspect of the relationship between poetry and morals, Auden has always been cogent in his prose statements, even though the issues sometimes become confused in his poetic practice. He said fifteen years ago:

> "Poetry is not concerned with telling people what to do, but with extending our knowledge of good and evil, perhaps making the necessity for action more urgent and its nature more clear, but only leading us to the point where it is possible to make a rational and moral choice."

Auden's work, then, is a civilising force. It will not solve the problems before us, but may, if we read it with due attention, help us to find better solutions, solutions that are more humane and sensitive.

Although 'The Age of Anxiety' is an unhappy book, it is, we have seen, closer than any other of Auden's recent works to his main preoccupation—the sense of loss and the anxiety in modern life. He is not relinquishing that interest, is still purposive, still engrossed in the Quest of Quant, and Emble, and Rosetta, and Malin, and himself for the Good Place, still eager and hopeful:

> "After so many years the light is
> Novel still and immensely ambitious."

His concern has not lessened. The "fight for privacy and isolation" which led to New York is only a move in that larger battle for better understanding and expression of our common grief; for all the time—

> ". . . germs besiege
> The walled towns, and among the living
> The captured outnumber the fugitive."

*

CHRONOLOGICAL TABLE

Auden was born in 1907, and educated at Gresham's School, Holt, and Christ Church, Oxford

1926.   Edited 'Oxford Poetry' (with Charles Plumb).
1927.   Edited 'Oxford Poetry' (with Cecil Day Lewis).
1928.   'Paid on Both Sides'—a charade in verse.
1928–9.   In Berlin.
1930.   'Poems'.
1932.   'Poems'—second edition—with six omissions and seven additions.
      'The Orators'—an English study—in verse and prose.
1933.   'The Dance of Death'—a dramatic poem.
1935.   'The Dog beneath the Skin' (with Christopher Isherwood)—play in verse and prose.
      'Look Stranger'—poems.

1936. 'The Ascent of F.6' (with Christopher Isherwood)—play in verse and prose.

Visited Spain.

1937. 'Spain'—a poem.

'Letters from Iceland' (with Louis MacNeice)—verse and prose.

Awarded King's Medal for poetry.

New Verse devoted double number to his work.

1938. 'On the Frontier' (with Christopher Isherwood)—play in verse and prose.

Visited China.

1939. Went to live in America.

'Journey to a War' (with Christopher Isherwood)—verse and prose.

1940. 'Another Time'—poems.

*1941. 'New Year Letter'—a long poem and a sonnet sequence, with prologue and epilogue.

*1945. 'For the Time Being' ('The Sea and the Mirror'; 'For the Time Being').

'Collected Poems' (American edition only).

Received the Award of the American Academy of Letters.

*1948. 'The Age of Anxiety'.

*1950. Collected Shorter Poems, 1930-1944 (all the poems Auden wishes to keep except 'New Year Letter', 'The Sea and the Mirror', 'For the Time Being', 'The Age of Anxiety' and the plays in verse and prose).

Appointed Assistant Professor of English Literature at Ann Arbor University, Michigan.

1951. 'The Enchafèd Flood' (not consulted).

* Dates of first English editions.

SELECT BIBLIOGRAPHIES

A. THE 'THIRTIES

(Contemporary works which provide useful background)

Lions and Shadows (autobiography), Christopher Isherwood. Hogarth Press, London, 1938; New Directions, Norfolk, Conn., 1947.

Enemies of Promise (autobiography), Cyril Connolly. G. Routledge & Sons Ltd., London, 1938; rev. ed., Macmillan Co., New York, 1948.

A Hope for Poetry (exposition), Cecil Day Lewis. Basil Blackwell, Oxford, 1934; Random House, New York, 1935.

Life and the Poet (exposition), Stephen Spender. Secker & Warburg, London, 1942.

Subject in Modern Poetry (in *Essays and Studies*, Oxford University Press, 1936), Louis MacNeice.

Modern Poetry (exposition), Louis MacNeice. Oxford University Press, London, New York, 1938.

Critique of Poetry (exposition), Michael Roberts. Jonathan Cape, London, 1934.

The Destructive Element (Part 3) (criticism), Stephen Spender. Jonathan Cape, London, 1935.

Journey to the Border (novel), Edward Upward. Hogarth Press, London, 1933.

The Wild Goose Chase (novel), Rex Warner. Boriswood, London, 1937; A. A. Knopf, New York, 1938.

New Verse (periodical), ed. Geoffrey Grigson. London, 1933–9. (Especially the double number on Auden, November 1937, and on 'Commitments', Autumn 1938.)

New Writing (afterwards *New Writing and Daylight*) (periodical), ed. John Lehmann, Hogarth Press, London, 1936–45.

New Signatures (anthology), ed. Michael Roberts. Hogarth Press, London, 1932.

New Country (anthology), ed. Michael Roberts. Hogarth Press, London, 1933.

The Mind in Chains (anthology), ed. Cecil Day Lewis. Frederick Muller, London, 1938.

The Arts Today (anthology), ed. Geoffrey Grigson. John Lane The Bodley Head, London, 1935.

Poems for Spain (anthology), ed. Lehmann and Spender. Hogarth Press, London, 1939.

B. Introductions, Surveys, Criticism

Survey of Modernist Poetry, Laura Riding and Robert Graves. Heinemann, London, 1927.

Poetic Unreason, Robert Graves. Palmer, London, 1925.

Axel's Castle, Edmund Wilson. C. Scribner's Sons, London, New York, 1931.

New Bearings in English Poetry, F. R. Leavis. Chatto & Windus, London, new ed., 1950; G. W. Stewart, New York, 1950.

The Trend of Modern Poetry, Geoffrey Bullough. Oliver & Boyd, London, 1934.

The Victorians and After, Dobree and Batho. Cresset Press, London, 1938; R. M. McBride & Co., New York, 1938.

The Present Age, Edwin Muir. Cresset Press, London, 1939; R. M. McBride & Co., New York, 1940.

Background of Modern Poetry, C. M. Bowra. Oxford University Press, London, 1946.

Modern Poetry and the Tradition, Cleanth Brooks. The University of North Carolina Press, Chapel Hill, 1939; Editions Poetry, London, 1948.

(*Most of the following books mention the Auden group in general rather than Auden alone*)

New Writing in Europe, John Lehmann. Penguin Books, London, New York, 1940.

Auden and After, Francis Scarfe. G. Routledge & Sons Ltd., London, 1942.

Sowing the Spring, J. G. Southworth. Basil Blackwell, Oxford, 1940.
(The only complete book on the Auden group.)

Post-Victorian Poetry, Herbert Palmer. J. M. Dent & Sons, London, 1938.
(An attack by a Georgian poet.)

The Personal Principle, D. S. Savage. G. Routledge & Sons Ltd., London, 1944.
(Criticism by a later poet with a radically different point of view from that of Auden.)

The Literary Outlook, S. L. Bethell. Sheldon Press, London; Macmillan Co., New York, 1943.

Man and Literature, Norman Nicholson. S.C.M. Press, London, 1943.
(Both these writers, in a general survey of modern literature from a religious point of view, fit the Auden 'group' into their map.)

C. Anthologies

(Most of these contain a fair selection of poems from the Auden group and from Auden in particular)

The Modern Poet (has useful notes), ed. Gwendolen Murphy. Sidgwick & Jackson, London, 1938.

The Century's Poetry, Vol. 5, ed. D. Kilham Roberts. Penguin Books, London, 1938.

A New Anthology of Modern Verse, ed. C. Day Lewis and L. A. G. Strong. Methuen & Co. Ltd., London, 1941.

Introducing Modern Poetry, ed. W. G. Bebbington. Faber & Faber, London, 1944.

(Contains a useful number of poems by a few poets.)

The Little Book of Modern Verse, ed. Anne Ridler. Faber & Faber, London, 1941.

The Faber Book of Modern Verse, ed. Michael Roberts. Faber & Faber, London, 1936.

(Has a valuable contemporary preface.)

New Verse Anthology, ed. Grigson. Faber & Faber, London, 1939.

Oxford Book of Modern Verse, ed. W. B. Yeats. Oxford University Press, London, New York, 1936.

A Little Treasury of Modern Verse, ed. Oscar Williams. C. Scribner's Sons, New York, 1946; Routledge, London, 1948.

Poetry of the Present, ed. Grigson. Phœnix Press, London, 1949.

Some Poems, W. H. Auden. Faber & Faber, London, 1940.

(A cheap and useful selection.)

Contemporary Verse, ed. Kenneth Allott. Penguin Books, London, 1950.

D. Auden

W. H. Auden, Francis Scarfe. Lyrebird Press, Monaco, 1949.

NOTES AND REFERENCES

CHAPTER I

P. 14. "Time and again . . ."—'New Year Letter,' II, 219–22.

P. 14. Quotations from pastiche of Hopkins: 'Poem' from *New Country*, and Ode II 'The Orators' respectively. Hopkins was recognised by the Auden group as an 'ancestor', an uncle, a brother in spirit.

P. 14. "debts to . . . Housman", e.g.
> "Into many a green valley
> Drifts the appalling snow;
> Time breaks the threaded dancers
> And the diver's brilliant bow."

('Another Time', Poem XXVI, 'As I walked out'.)

P. 14. Rilke—Rainer Maria Rilke, an Austrian poet (1875–1926).

P. 15. "For us the mornes . . ."—'Music is International'— *Horizon*, Nos. 93/94, October 1947.

P. 15. "But your lust . . ."—Epilogue to 'Letters from Iceland'.

P. 15. "that knowing assurance . . ."—Compare Spender's manner in "My parents kept me from children who were rough / And who threw stones. . . ."

P. 15. Groddeck—George Walther Groddeck (1866–1934), a German psychotherapist who made a special study of self-induced disease. *Horizon*, No. 102, contains a useful article on his work by Lawrence Durrell.

P. 17. "the intolerable neural itch"—Poem 30 of 'Poems 1930' (2nd ed.). 'Petition.'

P. 19. "Can speak of trouble . . ."—Chorus from 'Paid on Both Sides'.

P. 19. "group paraphernalia . . . etc."—See especially poems 3 and 12 of 'Poems 1930'.

P. 20. "Pardon the studied taste . . ."—Poem 30 of 'Look, Stranger'.

P. 20. "The sense of menace . . ."—In part this explains the interest in schools. Schoolboys, it was felt, were still uncorrupted by society.

P. 20. "However far we've wandered . . ."—'Letters from Iceland' VII.

P. 21. "indulgence in clique . . ."—The clique included 'ancestors' such as Hopkins, Katherine Mansfield ('Kathy') and Wilfred Owen ('Wilfred').

P. 21. The Auden group—It has already been noted that this group fell apart roughly at the outbreak of the Second World War. The title was meant to indicate the loose unity of several poets who had certain beliefs, particularly social beliefs, in common. By the later 'thirties all the chief members had arrived at a much more personal emphasis in their writing.

P. 22. "In grasping the character . . ."—Essay by Auden, on 'Henry James's "The American Scene" ', in *Horizon*, No. 86, p. 80 (first published by Scribners). The whole essay is illuminating on this subject.

The quotation is introduced simply to make clearer the distinctive nature of creative writing. One cannot go much farther with these terms:

"The division of which we are aware is not between Reason and Imagination, but between the good and evil will, not between objectivity and subjectivity, but between the integration of thought and feeling and their dissociation, not between the individual and the masses, but between the social person and the impersonal state" ('Yeats as an Example', *Kenyon Review*, Spring 1948).

P. 23. "And nervous people . . ."—Opening chorus from 'The Dog beneath the Skin'.

CHAPTER II

P. 24. anthropomorphism—the ascription of human qualities to natural objects.

P. 24. "To me art's subject . . ."—'Letter to Lord Byron', Part II.

P. 24. "He likes the human element . . ."—Louis MacNeice, *I Crossed the Minch*, p. 19.

P. 24. "When he mentions the pollen . . ."—'The Dog beneath the Skin', Chorus, Acts III–IV (also called 'Prothalamion').

P. 25. 'a width of allusion which most of his contemporaries lack. . . .' —Frederick Prokosch (not a member of the Auden group) has similar preoccupations, but is not so concerned with the sociology beneath the tourism.

P. 26. 'In Praise of Limestone'—Printed in *Horizon*, No. 103, July 1948.

P. 27. "that drives / Us into knowledge . . ."—'New Year Letter', II, 1141–3.

P. 27. "One of the constant problems . . ."—Auden—Review of 'Duino Elegies', *New Republic*, September 6, 1939.

P. 28. "From scars where . . ."—Poem 24 of 'Poems 1930'.

P. 28. 'The airman, well-equipped . . .'—Auden was unusually interested in the airman figure. In the 'Auden Double Number' of *New*

Verse, there is a facsimile of a draft of 'The fruit in which your parents hid you, boy'. The last three lines read:

> "Send back the writer howling to his art,
> And the mad driver pulling on his gloves
> Start in a snowstorm on his deadly journey."

"Driver" is one of the only two words substituted as corrections (I do not know whether other drafts preceded this): it replaced, if I read correctly, "airman".

P. 28. "Here on the cropped grass . . ."—'Look, Stranger', poem 17.

P. 29. "a necessary impersonality"—In enunciating these rules, he was assisted by the precepts and practice of T. S. Eliot.

P. 29. 'Spender says of Auden . . .'—Stephen Spender. 'W. H. Auden at Oxford', *World Review*, August 1949.

P. 29. 'solipsism'—"The view or theory that self is the only object of real knowledge or the only thing really existent" (*Shorter Oxford English Dictionary*).

P. 30. 'Whereas Spender is terribly involved . . .'—There are some poems by Spender in which this extreme personal sympathy, this sensibility of a kind which Auden lacks, does not spill over, but is held in a fine balance. These poems—such as 'The Two Armies'—seem to me among his best.

P. 30. "a stranger's quiet collapse . . ."—'The Sea and the Mirror', Chapter I, stanza 1.

P. 30. "he is all ice . . ."—Wyndham Lewis, *Blasting and Bombardiering*, 1937, p. 304.

P. 30. "Certainly, fidelity . . ."—'Lay your sleeping head, my love'. See also 'Fish in the unruffled lakes' and the not so successful 'Dear, though the night is gone'.

P. 31. 'A comparison of the styles of Auden and MacNeice . . .'—e.g. MacNeice's 'Eclogue for Christmas' compared with Auden's 'Birthday Poem—to Christopher Isherwood'.

P. 32. "Equal with colleagues . . ."—Poem 2 of 'Look, Stranger'.

P. 32. 'Spender, talking of the same . . .'—Spender, *World Review*.

P. 32. Auden's 'brutality'.—From the incidents cited here there may be a danger of Auden seeming excessively severe and pontifical. Sometimes, of course, he was simply enjoying the game of ideas or trying to startle his friends. Once, when Spender was particularly disturbed by some such pronouncement, Auden asked, 'But why do you take everything I say so seriously?'

P. 32. "novel-writing is a higher art . . ."—'Letter to Lord Byron'. See also the poem, 'The Novelist'.

P. 33. 'he may tend to look at people as types . . .'—Auden's first remark to his matron at school was, he says, "I like to see the various types of boys."

P. 33. "O once again . . ."—'New Year Letter', II, 961–70.

P. 34. "traffic of magnificent cloud . . ."—Poem 16 of 'Poems 1930'.

P. 34. 'He uses, . . . particularly, "enormous"—e.g. "enormous ranges"; "enormous rooms"; "enormous silence"; "enormous elders"; "enormous simple grief"; "shadows with enormous grudges"; "enormous beauties round him move".

P. 34. 'Geoffrey Grigson . . . says'—*New Verse Anthology*, preface to second edition.

P. 34. "Nor ask what doubtful act . . ."—Poem 2 of 'Look, Stranger'.

P. 35. "Never before . . ."—Commentary at the end of 'Journey to a War'.

In all this there are debts by Auden to Eliot, Lawrence and others.

P. 36. "Without contraries . . ."—Blake, 'The Marriage of Heaven and Hell'. Blake is demanding here what Bernard Blackstone (*English Blake*, C.U.P., 1949) calls "the acceptance of the human totality".

P. 36. 'it probably derives also from Prinzhorn . . .'—pp. 159 and 177 of Prinzhorn's *Psychotherapy* are relevant.

P. 36. "There must always be two kinds of art . . ."—'Psychology and Art', *The Arts Today* (ed. Grigson, The Bodley Head, 1935).

P. 36. 'We pray the power . . ."—Auden and MacNeice, 'Their Last Will and Testament', in 'Letters from Iceland'.

P. 38. "In the hour of the Blue Bird . . ."—Opening chorus from 'The Dog beneath the Skin'.

P. 39. "What do you think of England . . ."—'The Orators' I, i (2nd ed.).

P. 40. "Drop those priggish ways . . ."—Poem 22 of 'Poems 1930'.

P. 40. *The Yellow Book*—A quarterly which appeared in the 'nineties and was predominantly associated with the work of the 'æsthetes' and 'decadents'.

P. 40. 'as Mr. R. G. Leinhardt has pointed out . . .'—In a review in *Scrutiny*.

P. 41. "We are created . . ."—'Canzone', *The Mint*, No. 1, 1946.

CHAPTER III

P. 42. "a symposium published for T. S. Eliot's sixtieth birthday . . ." —*T. S. Eliot*, a symposium published by Poetry, London, 1948.

P. 42. "Just as his dream foretold . . ."—Poem 11, 'Look, Stranger'.

P. 43. The translation of 'The Unicorn' is by J. B. Leishmann, from *Rainer Maria Rilke, Poems*, Hogarth Press, 1939. 'The Supper', from the same volume, might almost as usefully have been quoted. Auden's poem is number X of the 'Quest' sequence. There are, of course, great differences between the poems, as well as the similarities I have indicated.

P. 45. "since art by its nature is a shared, . . ."—"Criticism in a Mass Society", *The Intent of the Critic*, ed. D. A. Stauffer (Princeton U.P., 1941; London—O.U.P.); also in *The Mint*, No. 2, ed. Grigson (Routledge).

P. 46. "as if a magic-lantern"—From 'Prufrock', by T. S. Eliot. This quotation was used in a similar context by G. W. Stonier in *Gog and Magog* (1933).

P. 46. "The slides are held up . . ."—I think this may be an echo of someone else's explanation.

P. 46. "I was brought up . . ."—Nevill Coghill, 'Sweeney Agonistes', in *T. S. Eliot*, a symposium (Poetry, London, 1948).
The magic-lantern simile suggests a structure not sufficiently articulated: it would be better to say that the development is musical and emotional rather than logical.

P. 47. "I thought I saw . . ."—'The Ascent of F.6', II, i (2nd ed.).

P. 48. "It provides another approach . . ."—The approach becomes a headlong dive in a passage like that in 'New Year Letter' (I, 233 *et seq.*) beginning, "The situation of our time. . . ."

P. 48. "Prospero is apostrophising . . ."—'The Sea and the Mirror', Chapter I.

P. 48. "Abruptly mounting . . ."—'In Wartime'.

P. 50. "As a trombone . . ."—'Music is International', *Horizon*, October 1947.

P. 51. 'The Managers'—in *Horizon*, November 1948.

P. 51. "a modified form of Byron's ottava rima'—Byron's has 'eight five-foot iambic lines rhyming ababababcc' (Fowler, *A Dictionary of Modern English Usage*, O.U.P. ed. of 1937): Auden's has seven lines rhyming ababbcc.
In spite of its faults, it seems a pity that Auden altogether excluded the 'Letter to Lord Byron' from his collected poems.

P. 52. 'Yeats . . . "released regular stanzaic poetry . . ." '—'Yeats as an example', *Kenyon Review*, Spring 1948. At present Auden has much less command of this manner than Yeats had.

P. 52. "I want a form . . ."—'Letter to Lord Byron'.

P. 54. "Over the heather . . ."—'Roman Wall Blues', *Another Time*.

P. 55. Auden's use of ballad. See also the songs written for the opera 'Paul Bunyan', for which Benjamin Britten wrote the music.

P. 55. "the pastiche, 'O, where are you going',"—The poem from which it is derived is 'The Cutty Wren' (No. 209 of *The Oxford Book of Light Verse*), whose opening line is, "O where are you going, says Milder to Malder".

P. 56. 'George, you old numero'—Auden used to be called 'the Kipling of the left'. Certainly 'George' owes a lot to Kipling's 'Back to the army again'.

P. 57. "The important thing to notice . . ."—'Letter to Lord Byron'.

P. 59. "You cannot tell people . . ."—Essay on 'Psychology and Art', *The Arts Today*, 1935.

P. 60. "and I believe that Michael Roberts later came to think in this way . . ."—See his book, *The Recovery of the West* (Faber, 1941).

P. 60. 'There comes a Time', by Michael Carr and Horatio Nichols (The Lawrence Wright Music Co.).

P. 61. "What is real . . ."—'For the Time Being', *The Vision of the Shepherds*, I.

P. 61. 'Robert Burns . . .' Introduction to *The Oxford Book of Light Verse*.

P. 62. "from now on the only popular art . . ."—Essay "Squares and Oblongs," in *Poets at Work* (New York, 1948).

P. 63. "the acknowledgment that there are relations . . ."—'Opera Addict', in *Vogue*, July 1948.

P. 63. "the audience . . . are not likely to have much taste for ritual."—Nor are they likely to respond to the dramatised set-figures—the hump-backed scissors man, the woman in dark glasses, or the witnesses (the dreadful figures who come in the small hours to the worried soul).

P. 63. "to find comprehensive symbolic patterns . . ."—See T. S. Eliot's 'Waste Land', and his Essay 'Ulysses, Order and Myth'.

P. 63. Kafka—Franz Kafka, Czech novelist (1883–1925).

P. 69. G. Rostrevor Hamilton—*The Tell-Tale Article, a critical approach to modern poetry*, Heinemann, 1949.
Mr. Hamilton quotes Whitman using the definite article in much the same way. I am indebted to Mr. Hamilton's essay for some of the material used here.

P. 69. "The boarding-house food . . ."—'The Ascent of F.6', end of Act I, 2.

P. 70. "Auden has always had . . ."—Stephen Spender, 'W. H. Auden at Oxford', *World Review*, August 1949.

P. 70. "Old faces frosted . . ."—'An Eclogue for Christmas'.

P. 71. "They are cutting down . . ."—*Autumn Journal*, VII.

P. 72. "Auden does not aim at creating character, except perhaps with Michael Ransom, and that for personal reasons." Ransom, the exceptional man, seems to be partly Auden, partly T. E. Lawrence, partly Michael Roberts (himself a mountaineer) and partly Auden's brother, John Bicknell Auden. (Lamp may also be drawn partly from Auden's brother, who is, I believe, a geologist and climber. 'The Ascent of F.6' is dedicated to him, as one of the "ghosts whom honour never paid".) (See 'Michael Roberts and the Hero Myth' by Kathleen Raine, *Penguin New Writing*, 39.)

P. 73. "stichomythia"—'In verse-plays, interchange of short speeches consisting each of a single line' (Fowler, *Modern English Usage*).

P. 73. Mr. Eric Bentley—*The Modern Theatre* (Hale, 1948; U.S.A. and Canada—Harcourt, Brace.) The comparative table is on p. 189.

P. 78. "There is much changing of sides . . ."—It has been said that the figure of the curate, who will ally himself to neither side but goes away to pray, is introduced to hit at the Anglo-Catholicism of T. S. Eliot. Certainly it is aimed at those who took up that sort of position in the 'thirties.

P. 81. "the vice of pity . . ."—'A Note on Graham Greene', printed in *The Wind and the Rain*, Summer 1949, from an N.B.C. broadcast by Auden.

P. 86. "To ask the hard question . . ."—Poem 27 of 'Poems 1930'.

P. 87. Homer Lane—there is a later note on Homer Lane.

P. 87. John Skelton—1460–1529 (?).

P. 88. "What makes the man . . ."—'On a piece of Music', an undated fragment, No. 110 of Hopkin's poems in the third edition. There are two versions.

P. 88. Robert Graves—G. S. Fraser has pointed out this resemblance in an essay on the poetry of Robert Graves in *Changing World*, Autumn 1947.

Francis Scarfe, in *W. H. Auden* (The Lyrebird Press, 1949), says Graves has accused Auden of plagiarism. Mr. Scarfe's book appeared as this essay was ready to go into typescript. Where I have made use of any of his points, I have acknowledged them. Any other similarities are coincidental.

P. 89. "Laura Riding had been writing . . ."—It has not been possible to obtain permission to quote from Miss Riding's poems. The similarities may be seen in her *Poems—A Joking Word* (Cape, 1930). In particular, the resemblances between the poems, 'All Nothing, Nothing', 'Hospitality to Words', and 'Fellows', from Miss Riding's volume, and Poems 10 ('Too dear, too vague') and 14 ('Shut your eyes and open your mouth'), from Auden's 'Poems 1930', are striking.

P. 89. "agnomic concentration"—'Gnomic': "writing that consists of or is packed with maxims or general truths pithily expressed" (Fowler).

Emily Dickinson was an American poet who died in 1886. Her poems were not published until after her death.

The quotations are respectively poems LXVII and CXXXVIII of Pt. I of *Poems of Emily Dickinson*, ed. M. D. and A. L. Hampson (Cape, 1937; U.S.A. and Canada—Little Brown.)

P. 90. "Since the external disorder . . ."—Dedication to 'Look Stranger'.

P. 91. "the 'wit-writing' of the metaphysicals"—The 'Metaphysical' poets wrote during the seventeenth century. Johnson condemned them for, among other things, their use of "witty conceits". Their work is most easily accessible in H. J. C. Grierson's 'Metaphysical Poetry' (O.U.P.). The Audenesque simile is also a kind of wit-writing.

Other members of the loose group of poets with similar aims used the epithet in this way. There are many echoes among the better poets.

P. 93. "Enraged phenomena . . ."—'New Year Letter', *The Quest*, No. 19.

P. 93. "what Edwin Muir calls . . ."—Though I do not think Mr. Muir is referring to Auden when he uses the phrase.

P. 94. "This lunar beauty . . ."—Poem 17 of 'Poems 1930'.

P. 94. "the rough line of his poetic development"—I was first led to think in this way by an essay in *Scrutiny*, written by Mr. R. G. Leinhardt.

P. 98. Quotation from 'The Wanderer'—from 'Anglo-Saxon Poetry', trans. Prof. R. K. Gordon. Everyman edition of 1926.

P. 99. 'Sawles Warde'—for the information about Auden's borrowings from this Middle English allegory I am much indebted to a paper by Morton W. Bloomfield, of the Ohio State University, contributed to *Modern Language Notes*, vol. LXIII, No. 8, dated December 1948 (Johns Hopkins Press, Baltimore).

P. 101. 'Our Hunting Fathers'—In 1935, in an essay on 'The Good Life' (*Christianity and the Social Revolution*—Gollancz, 1935), Auden made a comment which might well have been the germ of this poem. He talks of "the nineteenth-century evolutionary doctrine of man moving

'Upward, working out the beast,
And let the ape and tiger die'."

P. 102. "the animals, whose evolution is complete . . ."—note to i. 607 of 'New Year Letter'.

P. 103. "the second stanza . . . closes briskly and firmly"—I think the last two lines may be a quotation from some Marxist work, but am unable to identify it.

P. 105. "the pattern of predominantly weak rhymes"—This is a debt to Owen. Similar debts occur in the final verses of 'On the Frontier', and in the Epilogue to 'The Orators'.

P. 108. "the line is generally nine-syllabled"—Malcolm Cowley, in *Poetry Chicago*, says it is based on a French model, and points out that the rhymes are sometimes accented, sometimes unaccented. Another critic, I think G. S. Fraser, says there are debts to the syllabic metre of Marianne Moore.

CHAPTER IV

P. 111. "he echoes the tone and the technique of Wilfred Owen"— e.g. in his use of assonance and half-rhyme, of which something has already been said. Owen's poems, 'Strange Meeting' and 'Insensibility', offer a good introduction to his work of this kind.

P. 112. "Smokeless chimneys, etc."—Poem 22 of 'Poems 1930'.

P. 114. "Louder today, etc."—Poem 30 of 'Look, Stranger'.

P. 114. "For men are changed . . ."—Poem 17 of 'Look, Stranger'.

P. 114. "They believed some public action to be necessary"—E.g. from 'Spain':
    "Today the expending of powers
    On the flat ephemeral pamphlet and the boring meeting."

P. 115. "The villagers replied"—'To Sportsmen', a parable, *New Verse*, Autumn 1938.

P. 115. "The missus came in"—Chorus of workers in 'On the Frontier'.

P. 116. "Brothers, who when . . ."—Poem 14 of 'Look, Stranger'.

P. 116. "These two had to abuse their natural gifts"—Like Spender, Day Lewis seems to me a particularly personal poet, with an unusually fine ear for gentle and evocative lyricism.

P. 116. "There is no use any longer"—Article in *Transformation*, 3, p. 178.

P. 117. "especially of that psyche when it is twisted"—E.g. 'The Letter to a Wound' in 'The Orators' in particular, and some of the ironic ballads.

P. 117. "all those ancestors"—Like the uncle in 'Journal of an Air- man'—"he invited me to his flat. We had champagne for dinner. When I left I knew who and what he was—my real ancestor."

P. 118. "Klages, Prinzhorn and many others"—The article on 'Psychology and Art' already referred to, is a useful guide to Auden's early preferences in psychology.

P. 118. "does not detract from his seriousness"—See the 'Ode in memory of Sigmund Freud'.

P. 118. "Freud's 'map of the mind',"—E.g. the division into ego, super-ego and 'id'; the two basic drives—eros (love) and the death instinct.

P. 119. Freud's lecture, 'A Philosophy of Life'—*New Introductory Lectures*, 1st English edition, 1933.

P. 119. "No wonder then so many"—Poem 30 of 'Another Time'.

P. 120. "Mourn rather . . ."—Epilogue to 'The Dog beneath the Skin'.

P. 120. "a very high percentage"—Prinzhorn, *Psychotherapy*, p. 121.

P. 122. "Pick me up, Uncle . . ."—'The Sea and the Mirror', Caliban's speech.

P. 123. "for whom a slight cold . . ."—Emble, in 'The Age of Anxiety', has a variant of this as his daydream:

> "Massed choirs would sing as my coffin passed,
>   Grieved for and great on a gun-carriage."

P. 123. "a third observation"—Freud, *Introductory Lectures on Psycho-Analysis*, impression of 1936, p. 338.

P. 124. "the hysterical interest"—Klages, *The Science of Character*, p. 186.

P. 124. "Only the challenge . . ."—Poem 12 of 'Another Time'.

P. 124. "the mental induction of physical ailments . . ."—Much work has been done in this field of 'psychosomatic medicine' during the present century. Groddeck's work was early and not always, it appears, scientifically sound.

P. 124. "Such ideas . . ."—Groddeck, *The World of Man*, p. 192.

P. 125. "My experience . . ."—Groddeck, *Exploring the Unconscious*, p. 80.

P. 126. "There can be no good will . . ."—Blake's annotation to Swedenborg's 'Divine Love', c. 1788, cit. Bernard Blackstone, *English Blake*, p. 385 (C.U.P., 1949).

P. 126. "By will here he means . . ."—Blackstone, pp. 385–6.

P. 127. "last attempt to eliminate . . ."—Prologue to 'New Year Letter'.

P. 127. "What have we all . . ."—Ode V of 'The Orators'.

P. 127. "All the conventions conspire . . ."—'September 1, 1939'.

P. 127. "We present to you . . ."—'The Dance of Death'.

P. 128. "And now the instincts . . ."—Freud, *New Introductory Lectures*, ed. of 1946, chapter XXXII, Anxiety and Instinctual Life, p. 138.

P. 128. "O teach me to outgrow . . ."—From the commentary at the end of 'Journey to a War'. 'Will' in the second line is used in a different sense from that discussed on pp. 125–6. The last two and a half lines repeat part of a speech by Ransom in 'The Ascent of F.6', II, ii.

P. 129. "Love, loath to enter . . ."—Semi-chorus from 'The Dog beneath the Skin'.

P. 130. "we comprehend them all . . ."—Klages, *The Science of Character*, p. 265.
Klages goes on to distinguish between different kinds of love.

P. 130. "The word is Love . . ."—Poem 30 of 'Look, Stranger'.

P. 130. "All organic life . . ."—Homer Lane, *Talks to Parents and Teachers*, 1930, pp. 177–8.
Most of Homer Lane's work was in educational psychology. It is a pity that the only reference to him here should point out his limitations. A full account of one of his experiments may be found in *Homer Lane and the Little Commonwealth*, E. T. Bazeley, 1928.

P. 131. "It is partly a biological urge . . ."—The biological assertion of this urge is discussed by M. F. Ashley Montagu, in *Horizon*, No. 114.

P. 131. "Love, that notable forked one . . ."—'The Orators', II, iii.

P. 132. "no personal experience . . ."—Review by Auden in *Scrutiny*, IV, 2, 1935.

P. 132. "Every eye must weep alone . . ."—Dedication to 'Another Time'.

P. 132. "O can you see"—Poem 23 of 'Look, Stranger'.

P. 133. "Love finally is great . . ."—Final chorus to 'The Ascent of F.6'.

P. 133. "We know it . . ."—Poem 16 of 'Poems 1930'.

P. 133. 'The course of history . . ."—The Meditation of Simeon in 'For the Time Being'.

P. 134. "I know that I am I . . ."—End of Journal of an Airman, 'The Orators'.

P. 134. "His philosophy was not coherent . . ."—A poet's philosophy need not be coherent for him to produce good poetry (though it seems unlikely that the response to experience of a man who is satisfied with a superficial philosophy will be adequate to the production of important poetry). But to a writer with Auden's type of mind, his conscious view of life may constantly affect his attitude to his art (see Chapter VII).

CHAPTER V

P. 136. "has therefore spent half his poetic life there"—After 'Another Time', which contains some poems written before he left England, and except for a few poems printed in periodicals, the English public saw only Auden's longer works until 1950. Then the volume of *Collected Shorter Poems* appeared, but contained only those poems written up to 1944.

P. 136. "from now on the poet . . ."—Essay 'Squares and Oblongs', *Poets at Work* (Harcourt, Brace & Co., 1948).

P. 136. "he reverts always . . ."—Introduction to *Horizon*, double number 93–4.

P. 136. "a writer needs complete anonymity . . ."—In 'New Year Letter' Auden speaks of Rilke, "whom der Dinge bless / The Santa Claus of loneliness".

P. 137. "The attractiveness of America . . ."—Quoted by Benjamin Appel in 'The Exiled Writers', *Saturday Review of Literature*, October 19, 1940.

P. 138. 'In Praise of Limestone'—In *Horizon*, No. 103, for July 1948.

P. 138. "Analogy is not identity"—Essay 'The Ironic Hero', *Horizon*, No. 116.

P. 139. "The necessity . . . for any imaginative and critical personality . . ."—The point has been treated by Prinzhorn (*Psychotherapy*, p. 177) and others.

P. 139. "the twenty-third of Freud's lectures . . ."—The lecture ends: "Before you leave today I should like to direct your attention for a moment to a side of phantasy life of very general interest. There is, in fact, a path from phantasy back again to reality, and that is—art. The artist has also an introverted disposition, and has not far to go to become neurotic. He is one who is urged on by instinctive needs which are too clamorous; he longs to attain to honour, power, riches, fame, and the love of women; but he lacks the means of achieving these gratifications. So, like any other with an unsatisfied longing, he turns away from reality and transfers all his interest, and all his libido too, on to the creation of his wishes in the life of phantasy, from which the way might readily lead to neurosis. There must be many factors in combination to prevent this becoming the whole outcome of his development; it is well-known how often artists in particular suffer from partial inhibition of their capacities through neurosis. Probably their constitution is endowed with a powerful capacity for sublimation and with a certain flexibility in the repressions determining the conflict. But the way back to reality is found in the artist thus. He is not the only one who has a life of phantasy; the intermediate world of phantasy is sanctioned by general human consent, and every hungry soul looks to it for comfort and consolation. But to those who are not artists the gratification that can be drawn from the springs of phantasy is very limited; their inexorable repressions prevent the enjoyment of all but the meagre day-dreams which can become conscious. A true artist has more at his disposal. First of all he understands how to elaborate his day-dreams, so that they lose that personal note which grates upon strange ears and become enjoyable to others; he knows too how to modify them sufficiently so that their origin in prohibited sources is not easily detected. Further, he possesses the mysterious ability to mould his particular material until it expresses the ideas of his phantasy faithfully; and then he knows how to attach to this reflection of his phantasy-life so strong a stream of pleasure that, for a time at least, the reflections are outbalanced and dispelled by it. When he can do all this, he opens out to others the way back to the comfort and consolation of their own unconscious sources of pleasure, and so reaps their gratitude and admiration; then he has won—through his phantasy—what before he could only win in phantasy: honour, power, and the love of women." *Introductory Lectures on Psycho-Analysis*, 1922.

P. 139. "Art is almost always harmless . . ."—*New Introductory Lectures on Psycho-Analysis*, chapter XXXV, 3rd ed., 1946.

P. 140. "The romantic movement has been . . ."—Essay 'Mimesis and Allegory', *English Institute Annual* (Col. U.P., 1940).

P. 140. Kierkegaard (1813–55), Danish Christian philosopher.

P. 140. "He would like to be religious . . ."—Quoted in *Poets at Work*, 'Squares and Oblongs'.

P. 141. "into the existential . . ."—"Existential . . . [denotes] a special quality or attitude of men. In 'the existence of the individual' the deepest demands of life, serious and inescapable, are faced and dealt with in grave choice. . . . Existential thinking is the kind of thinking which accompanies or constitutes the coming-to-be of 'existence'. It is realised through the inner decisions of the individual, who thereby comes in touch with reality at its deepest. It is a mode of thought which concerns, not the intellect merely, but the whole personality of the man who awakens to it and adopts it. To think existentially, therefore, is to think, not as a spectator of the ultimate issues of life and death, but as one who is committed to a decision on them" (note to p. 219, *Types of Modern Theology*, H. R. Mackintosh; Nisbet & Co., London, 1937).

P. 141. "Poetry as a magical means . . ."—'Squares and Oblongs'.

P. 141. "Never hope to say farewell . . ."—Ariel to Caliban: 'The Sea and the Mirror'.

P. 142. "By significant details . . ."—Review of T. S. Eliot's 'A Choice of Kipling's Verse', entitled 'The Poet of the Encirclement', *New Republic*, October 25, 1943.

P. 142. "what else exactly . . ."—Caliban, 'The Sea and the Mirror'.

P. 142. "Imagination is redeemed . . ."—*The Meditation of Simeon*, 'For the Time Being'.

P. 142. "Perhaps I always knew . . ."—Poem 9 of 'Another Time'.

P. 143. "many of the ideas which Auden repeatedly considers today are, therefore, to be found in . . . these two . . ."—E.g. in Kierkegaard: Being and Becoming; the Instant; Dread; the aloneness of man; the dangers of individualism; the attack on the overvaluing of reason, and the assertion of the whole 'existing' man.

Reinhold Niebuhr's *The Nature and Destiny of Man* shows how extensively he has influenced Auden's thought. Mr. Niebuhr is Professor of Christian Ethics at the Union Theological Seminary, New York.

P. 146. "Man is a fallen creature with a natural bias to do evil"—Auden is probably echoing the ninth of the Thirty-Nine Articles, 'Of Original or Birth-Sin'; "man is very far gone from original righteousness, and is of his own nature inclined to evil".

P. 147. "The Way rests . . ."—Note to l. 761 of 'New Year Letter'.

P. 147. "We live in freedom . . ."—Sonnet XXVII, *In Time of War*.

P. 147. "Dictatorship has been defined . . ."—Essay, 'Criticism in a Mass Society', loc. cit.

P. 148. "conscious of necessity . . ."—Meditation of Simeon, 'For the Time Being'.

"Free lives mutually coinhering, and necessity and freedom (dare one say) mutually coinhering. In the crucifixion of Messias, necessity and freedom had mutually crucified each other, and both (as if in an exchanged life) had risen again. Freedom existed then because it must; necessity because it could."—Charles Williams, *The Descent of the Dove*, pp. 174-5.

P. 148. "We are always 'becoming' not 'being' "—"An existing individual is constantly in process of becoming" (quoted in *Søren Kierkegaard*, by M. Chaning-Pearce, London, 1946, pp. 29-30).

P.148. "consciousness may be aided by grace . . ."—"We do not find grace by liberty, but liberty by grace"—Augustine, cit. Williams, p. 174.

P. 148. "In occasional moments . . . we are given some illumination . . ." —'In the instant a man, standing within his time and existence, takes his stand in the immutable and eternal essence or being which underlie them. Existence is a standing out or forth from that pure being; the instant is a return to it, a standing within it. Thus the existential movement, according to Kierkegaard, is from and through existence to the "instant", and that movement is one of inwardness'—Chaning-Pearce, pp. 72-3.

P. 148. "Greek tragedy . . ."—'The Christian Tragic Hero', review of *Moby Dick* in *New York Times Book Review*, December 16, 1945.

P. 149. "the rules are necessary . . ."—'Squares and Oblongs'.

P. 149. "sin is occasioned precisely . . ."—'The Means of Grace', review of Reinhold Niebuhr's, *The Nature and Destiny of Man* in *New Republic*, June 2, 1941. The thought closely follows Niebuhr.

P. 150. "the hard self-regarding 'I' "—The connections with Auden's attacks on self-regard in the 'thirties (chapter IV) will have been noticed. Kierkegaard said: 'It [Faith] is . . . a death, the death of the old self, the autonomous Ego. And at the same time it is a joy; it is the resurrection of a new Ego' (quoted Mackintosh, op. cit., p. 224).

P. 150. "Since Adam, being free to choose . . ."—Part III of *The Annunciation*, 'For the Time Being'.

P. 150. "for the exceptional man . . ."—'The more consciousness, the more will'—Kierkegaard, cited Chaning-Pearce, p. 50.

P. 151. "To ask the hard question . . ."—Poem 27 of 'Poems 1930'.

P. 152. "as if it were only . . "—*The Masque*, 'The Age of Anxiety'.

P. 152. "as the issue . . ."—*Horizon*, No. 86, 'The American Scene'.

P. 152. "all [are], before God, absolutely in the wrong"—Kierkegaard said: "We are always in the wrong as against God" (quoted Mackintosh, op. cit., p. 236).

P. 153. "because in Him . . ."—*The Meditation of Simeon*.

P. 153. "How much must be forgotten . . ."—'Canzone', *The Mint*, No. 1, 1946.

P. 154. "we are *required* to love . . ."—'Canzone', *The Mint* (italics mine).

P. 154. "The only serious possession . . ."—'Squares and Oblongs'. A passage in an essay written thirteen years before 'Squares and Oblongs' ('The Good Life', in *Christianity and the Social Revolution*, Gollancz, 1935) makes an interesting parallel: "The two commandments of loving God and thy neighbour imply that the good life is a product, and only a product, of an attitude of complete love and faith towards life." Auden was there examining Christianity's view of the good life; we have seen that he was not at that time a believer.

P. 154. "O let none say I love . . ."—'In Sickness and in Health', *The Mint*, No. 1, 1946.

P. 155. "never less alone than when alone . . ."—Kierkegaard, cited Chaning-Pearce, p. 84.

P. 155. "beloved, pray . . ."—'In Sickness and in Health', loc. cit.

P. 155. "Love's a way of living . . ."—Poem 1 of Part 2 of 'Another Time'.

P. 155. "where Freedom dwells because it must . . ."—This and the line following are, it will be recalled from an earlier note, derived almost exactly from Charles Williams' *Descent of the Dove*.

P. 155. "we are reduced . . ."—'Christmas 1940'.

AUDEN: AN INTRODUCTORY ESSAY

P. 156. "Space is the whom . . ."—Part III of 'At the Manger', 'For the Time Being'.

P. 156. "not a denial . . ."—Review of Duino Elegies (Rilke), *New Republic*, September 6, 1939.

P. 157. "an 'open' and a 'closed' society"—For some account of the history and meanings of the terms 'open' and 'closed' society, see *The Open Society and its Enemies*, I, 'The Spell of Plato,' by K. R. Popper (Routledge, 1945).

Bergson's *Les deux Sources de la Morale et de la Religion* is, I believe, more important in this connection, but is probably less accessible to the general reader.

P. 157. "Government must be democratic . . ."—'Criticism in a Mass Society', loc. cit.

P. 158. "far into the night . . ."—'The Managers', *Horizon*, No. 107, November 1948.

P. 158. "Charles Williams' question"—Williams, p. 232.

P. 159. "the quite considerable spark . . ."—Auden and MacNeice, 'Their Last Will and Testament', *Letters from Iceland*.

P. 159. "In the meantime . . ."—Final section of 'For the Time Being'.

P. 159. "We know very well . . ."—Part IV of 'The Summons', 'For the Time Being'.

CHAPTER VI

P. 160. "we are, I know not how . . ."—This is also quoted by Charles Williams in an illuminating chapter in *The Descent of the Dove*, entitled 'The Quality of Disbelief'. See also Romans 7, xix.

P. 160. Samuel Butler, 1612–80, author of *Hudibras*, a satire in octo-syllabic couplets, with three parts.

P. 160. "So, the old process . . ."—Browning, *Christmas Eve and Easter Day*.

P. 163. "the devil and his ways . . . are melodramatically personified"—Charles Williams has some perceptive comments on the value of the devil as a melodramatic villain, p. 165, *The Descent of the Dove*.

P. 163. "all our intuitions mock . . ."—"We have an incapacity of proof, insurmountable by all dogmatism. We have an idea of truth, invincible to all scepticism", Pascal, cited Williams, p. 197.

P. 164. "In Blake's view"—Blackstone, cited Kathleen Raine, *New Statesman and Nation*, May 14, 1949.

Blake's direct influence shows several times in the form of the notes, e.g. the note to l. 1059:

"New facts will not be known / Until we part and live once more alone: / New values will not be found / Until we meet again on common ground"; and also to l. 1366, "Who built the prison-state? / Free men hiding from their fate. / Will wars ever cease? / Not while they leave themselves in peace."

P. 165. "A logical system is possible . . ."—Chaning-Pearce, p. 35.

P. 167. "Empiric Economic Man . . . emotionally starved"—E.g. the note to l. 1213, a verse echo of Blake again:
> "When devils drive the reasonable wild,
> They strip their adult century so bare,
> Love must be regrown from the sensual child."

P. 168. "a rapturous cry of faith . . ."—which has much in common with the apostrophe at the end of Masefield's 'Everlasting Mercy' (ll. 1651 et seq. of Auden are those concerned).

P. 168. "O da quod Jubes, Domine"—'Give what thou commandest, Lord.'

P. 169. "[He] like all intelligent readers . . ."—Williams, p. 38.

P. 169. 'The Quest'—the journey of the wanderer, which we have seen recurring throughout Auden's verse, now takes on a clear significance. As so often, Kierkegaard helped to define it. He talks of the necessity for a Quest, and of the unavoidable loneliness of all who undertake it.

P. 169. 'K's Quest'—in *The Kafka Problem*, ed. A. Flores, New Directions (New York, 1946).

P. 172. "He is glad, he says, to give up the mirror-world"—Prospero's image for the venture now before him is that most characteristic of Kierkegaard. Prospero says he will be "Sailing alone, out over seventy thousand fathoms . . ."; Kierkegaard talks of being '"above seventy fathoms of water" on this voyage of "inwardness and faith"' (Chaning-Pearce, p. 63).

P. 173. "But the error bred"—'Sept. 1, 1939'.

P. 174. "Antonio's terza rima"—"Lines of five iambic feet with an extra syllable, so rhymed that every rhyme occurs thrice in alternate lines, etc." (Fowler). This example has speech-, not foot-stresses.

P. 174. "a ballade"—"An elaborate poem consisting of three eight-(or ten-) line stanzas and a four- (or five-) line envoy, all on three (or four) rhymes only, in the same order in each stanza, and with the same line ending each stanza and the envoy" (Fowler).

P. 174. Gonzalo—Speaks in trochaic tetrameters with very irregular rhyming and some spare syllables.

P. 176. sestina—"A poem of six six-line stanzas (with an envoy) in which the line-endings of the first stanza are repeated, but in different order, in the other five" (Fowler).

P. 176. "iambic trimeters"—Three iambics to a line.

P. 176. "villanelle"—'Five (or more) tercets and a quatrain, all on two rhymes, one that in the middle line of each tercet and the second line of the quatrain, the other everywhere else," etc. (Fowler).

P. 179. Traherne—Thomas Traherne (1634?–1704).

P. 179. "Give me my passage home . . ."—Auden had written a similar passage earlier, in the Vicar's sermon in 'The Dog beneath the Skin':
"Listen to the wooden sabots of Thy eager child running to Thy arms! Admit him to the fairs. . . . Mother is waving from the tiny door! The quilt is turned down in my beautiful blue and gold room! Father, I thank Thee in advance! Everything has been grand! I am coming home!"
The "pick me up, Uncle" section of the passage quoted from Caliban is like the end of Joyce's *Finnegan's Wake*: "Carry me along, taddy, like you done through the toy-fair."

P. 180. "Ariel reminds Caliban . . ."—A variant of the Ariel / Caliban relationship is suggested in an article, 'The Ironic Hero', in *Horizon*, No. 116, where Auden discusses the relationship between Don Quixote and Sancho Panza.

P. 181. 'The Means of Grace'—loc. cit.

P. 183. "the Abyss beneath"—"We must all found our lives upon a fathomless abyss" (Chaning-Pearce, p. 41).

P. 184. "the Faustian and Peer Gyntian personality"—In 'K's Quest', loc. cit.

P. 184. "He was a very great scoundrel . . ."—'Squares and Oblongs'.

P. 184. "the four faculties . . ."—Auden presumably has in mind Jung's "Four Psychological Basic Types".

P. 186. "The Summons is to all kinds of men"—"Passion and feeling are open to all men in an equal degree"—Kierkegaard, cited Chaning-Pearce, p. 37.

P. 187. Cæsar—Augustus Cæsar, 63 B.C.–A.D. 14; first of the Roman Emperors, an enlightened patron of the arts. Until 12 B.C. his rule saw great reforms. Thereafter occurred a succession of both public and private disasters.

P. 189. "The figure of Simeon . . ."—The story of Simeon occurs in the Gospel according to St. Luke, ii. 25–32.

P. 190. Herod—c. 73–4 B.C., 'King of Judea'; he was a strong enforcer of order and an able ruler. He developed a bureaucracy and promoted centralisation. He is said by St. Matthew to have been responsible for the Slaughter of the Innocents.

P. 191. Rachel—Rachel talks of "a solitude too deep to fill with roses". Roses are Auden's favourite image for a dream of sensual bliss.

P. 194. "Auden's is a poetry of the nerves . . ."—Stonier, *Gog and Magog*, 1933, p. 173.

P. 194. "Kierkegaard's 'dread' "—"The matrix of sin is fear; as a psychological event it springs from dread or anxiety. Despair, taken by (Kierkegaard) as the virtual equivalent of sin, is a universal condition. Men fear or dread when they hear the challenge of eternity, the call to be spiritual; they despair when they refuse it.

'As doctors could tell us (he writes) that there is perhaps no man living who is completely sound, so a real knowledge of men would compel us to say that there is no living man who is not in some degree the victim of despair; no man in whose inner life there does not dwell an unrest, a dispeace, a disharmony, the dread of something unknown, of something on which he dare not look, ...' "
(Mackintosh, op. cit.—pp. 236-7.)

P. 194. "Both Catholicism . . ."—'Means of Grace', loc. cit.

P. 195. "nearer to the anonymous countryside . . ."—*Horizon*, No. 86. preface to 'The American Scene'.

P. 195. "this disposition of characters has presumably been chosen so as . . ."—Here, as in 'The Sea and the Mirror' and 'For the Time Being', Auden's method is closely related to Kierkegaard's "indirect communication", whereby "he fabricates characters representative of various aspects or phases of contemporary life, letting each work out his own views" (quoted Mackintosh, op. cit., p. 222).

P. 197. "The alliterative line of the Old and Middle English poets" . . . —The following lines are from 'Beowulf', the most considerable O.E. poem (Klaeber's edition of 1936, ll. 320-3):

> "Strǣt wæs stānfāh,   stīg wīsode
> gumum aetgaedere.   Gūðbyrne scān
> heard hondlocen,   hringīren scīr
> song in searwum."

This is a rough translation, designed to retain the main effect of the metre whilst being intelligible:

> "Street was stone-decorated   Path kept
> Men together   War corslet shone
> Hard handlocked   Ringed-iron gleaming
> Sang in armour."

Langland's (M.E.) vision of Piers the Plowman begins,

> "In a sómer séson   whan sóft was the sónne,
> I shópe me in shróudes   as I a shepe were,
> In hábite as an héremite   vnhóly of woŕkes,
> Went wýde in þis woŕld."

They can be compared with Malin's opening speech in the Seven Ages section:

> "Behold the infant helpless in cradle and
> Righteous still, yet already there is
> Dread in his dreams at the deed of which
> He knows nothing. . . ."

P. 202. "The Seven Stages"—There is a mystical concept of the seven stages necessary to spiritual purity which Auden is no doubt remembering here.

P. 202. "the general import of the Seven Stages"—As the Seven Stages section is being announced, Auden says, "They sought that state of prehistoric happiness which, by human beings, can only be imagined in terms of a landscape bearing a symbolic resemblance to the human body".

Several critics have taken this to mean that the Seven Stages symbolise, secondarily, parts of the human body. Yet perhaps Auden, who does not say "can only be imagined in terms of a *journey* bearing a symbolic resemblance", but "can only be imagined in terms of a *landscape* . . .", is not referring there specifically to the separate stages, but is making a more general comment on the urge for "prehistoric happiness", imagined in terms of rest on mother's breast, or of a return to the womb, i.e. of a female body. I am not at all sure which view is right, and add, in case a body-symbolism would have more significance than I imagine, some suggested applications.

STAGE	'Spectator', review by H. A. L. Craig.	R.H.
1. Plains with tarns	face with eyes	face with mouth, eyes, etc.
Twin peaks	nose	breasts ("twin confederate forms") ("where the great go to forget themselves")
Rest of section		arms ("the long piers") ribs ("the saw-tooth range"), head and hair.
2. To ports	ears	arms ("from the high heartland")
3. To city	mouth	stomach (?)
4. To big house	navel	navel (womb)

George Every, *Poetry and Personal Responsibility*, p. 55 (S.C.M., London, 1949), thinks Auden may have been thinking of a map of Europe and Western Asia at the beginning of Charles Williams' *Taliessin through Logres*, which has superimposed on it a drawing of the figure of a naked girl. Mr. Every adds that 'The Age of Anxiety' derives from Charles Williams' *All Hallows' Eve*, but I find the debt slight.

P. 207. "the same image of the wicket-gate . . ."—The wicket also occurs in Kierkegaard:

> ". . . [a] swinging-wicket set
> Between
> The Unseen and the Seen";

And "beyond that 'swinging-wicket' of despair and faith is that land of light where God's lovers live in an 'immediacy'. . . ."—Chaning-Pearce.

P. 208. "There they converge . . ."—Emble's passage on p. 89, beginning, "But otherwise is it . . .", and discussing the urge in man to know, echoes the ideas of, and uses similar images to, ll. 1096–1152 of 'New Year Letter'.

P. 209. "Father the healer . . . gone"—This part resembles that section of 'In Memory of Sigmund Freud' in which Freud is described as one of man's healers.

P. 210. "Do we ever learn . . ."—Malin's cry echoes Eliot's 'Portrait of a Lady' and his chorus in 'The Family Reunion':

> "We're quite in the dark: we do not
> Know . . ."

says Malin; and Eliot's poems:

> "My self-possession gutters,
> We are really in the dark."

and:

> "We have lost our way in the dark."

CONCLUSION

P. 215. "the pleasure he took . . . is largely an æsthetic pleasure"—The qualification is important. Auden is also attracted to such incidents, because they throw into sharp relief important aspects of the human condition:

> "That is the way things happen; for ever and ever
> Plum-blossom falls on the dead, the roar of the waterfall covers
> The cries of the whipped and the sighs of the lovers
> And the hard bright light composes
> *A meaningless moment into an eternal fact*" (my italics)

—'Memorial for the City', *Horizon*, No. 119, November 1949.

P. 216. 'At the Grave of Henry James.'

P. 217. "art is not metaphysics . . ."—'Mimesis and Allegory', loc. cit.

P. 218. "he said in a recent paper . . ."—A broadcast talk, 'The Art of Thomas Hardy', B.B.C. Third Programme, September 16, 1949.

P. 218. "in his own weak person . . ."—Poem 20 of 'Another Time'.

P. 219. "the alternative is the acceptance . . ."—'Mimesis and Allegory', loc. cit.

P. 219. "Poetry is not concerned . . ."—Introduction with John Garrett to *The Poet's Tongue*.

P. 220. "After so many years . . ."—Epilogue to 'New Year Letter'.

P. 220. ". . . germs besiege . . ."—'Music is International', *Horizon*, Nos. 93–4, October 1947.

THE COLLECTED SHORTER POEMS

In the *Collected Shorter Poems* (1950) all reference to earlier volumes has been omitted. The poems are arranged in alphabetical order of opening lines. There are two main sections, 'Poems', and 'Songs and Other Musical Pieces'. Titles, most of them new, have been given to all the 'Poems'. If these titles do not already appear in the preceding notes they are given below:

Poem 3 of 'Poems 1930'—'Venus Will Now Say a Few Words'.

Poem 12 of 'Poems 1930'—'Let History Be My Judge'.

Poem 16 of 'Poems 1930'—'1929'.

Poem 17 of 'Poems 1930'—'Like a Dream'.

Poem 24 of 'Poems 1930'—'Missing'.

'Poem 27 of 'Poems 1930'—'The Hard Question'.

Ode 5 of 'The Orators'—'Which Side Am I Supposed to Be On?'

Poem 2 of 'Look, Stranger'—'A Summer Night, 1933—to Geoffrey Hoyland'.

Poem 11 of 'Look, Stranger'—'Nobody Understands Me'.

Poem 17 of 'Look, Stranger'—'The Malverns'.

Poem 23 of 'Look, Stranger'—'It's So Dull Here'.

Poem 30 of 'Look, Stranger'—'Birthday Poem—to Christopher Isherwood'.

'Roman Wall Blues'—'Over the Heather'.

Poem 1, Part 2 of 'Another Time'—'Heavy Date'.

Poem 3 of 'Another Time'—'The Creatures'.

Poem 9 of 'Another Time'—'The Prophets'.

Poem 12 of 'Another Time'—'Hell'.

Poem 20 of 'Another Time'—'The Novelist'.

Poem 30 of 'Another Time'—'Another Time'.

Poem 31 of 'Another Time'—'The Riddle'.

AUTHOR'S NOTE

THE English volume of *Collected Shorter Poems* 1930–44 differs in some respects from the American *Collected Poetry of W. H. Auden*. Some poems appear in the American volume, but not in the English, and vice-versa; some poems change their titles. Of the poems referred to in this book the following are affected. They are listed in their order of appearance in the volumes of collected poems.

First Line	English Title	American Title
'August for the people . . .'	Birthday Poem—to Christopher Isherwood	NOT INCLUDED (is Poem 30 of *Look, Stranger*)
'Can speak of trouble . . .' in *Paid on Both Sides*		Always in Trouble
'Doom is dark . . .'	The Wanderer	Something is Bound to Happen
'Enter with him . . .' (Chorus to *The Dog Beneath the Skin*)	Legend	I Shall Be Enchanted
'Here on the cropped grass . . .'	The Malverns	NOT INCLUDED (is Poem 17 of *Look, Stranger*)
'Not as that dream Napoleon . . .' (Poem 23 of *Another Time*)	Like a Vocation	Please Make Yourself At Home
Prologue to *New Year Letter*	NOT INCLUDED	Spring 1940
'Our Hunting Fathers . . .'	Our Hunting Fathers	In Father's Footsteps
'When devils drive the reasonable wild . . .' (notes to l.1213 *New Year Letter*, quoted in notes to p. 167 above)	NOT INCLUDED	Montaigne
Epilogue to *New Year Letter*	NOT INCLUDED	Autumn 1940
'This lunar beauty . . .'	Like a Dream	Pur
'To ask the hard question . . .'	The Hard Question	What Do You Think?
'Watch any day . . .'	A Free One	We All Make Mistakes

(In America *Look, Stranger* was called *On This Island*. *New Year Letter* was originally called *The Double Man* there, but was given its English title in the American volume of collected poems.)

INDEX

The sign '(n)' after a page number indicates that a subject is mentioned both on the page and in the 'Notes and References' to that page. 'Notes to . . .' indicates that a subject is mentioned in the 'Notes and References' to a page without being mentioned on the page itself.

248

INDEX

INDEX

INDEX

INDEX

Origen, 169

'Our Hunting Fathers', 101 (n) et seq., 109

'Over the Heather', 54 (n), 246

'Overtures to Death' (C. Day Lewis), 57

Owen, Wilfred, 14, 36, 51, 112 (n), notes to 21 (1st), 105

'O, what is that sound?', 55

'O, where are you going?', 55 (n), 98, 'O, who can ever praise enough?', 47

Oxford Book of Light Verse, The 55 (n), notes to 61 (2nd)

Oxford Book of Modern Verse, The (ed. W. B. Yeats), 224

Paid on Both Sides, 18, 19 (n), 20, 73, 128, 197

Palmer, Herbert, 223

Pascal, 22, 65, 68, 162, 163–164 (n)

'Past Values, The' (Stephen Spender), 29

Paul Bunyan, notes to 55 (1st)

Peer Gynt, 184 (n)

Penguin New Writing (ed. John Lehmann), notes to 72

Pennines, The, 26, 167

Personal Principle, The (D. S. Savage), 223

'Petition', 17 (n)

Petrarchan sonnet, 174

Piers Plowman (Langland), 48, notes to 197

Pilgrim's Progress (Bunyan), 170

Plumb, Charles, 220

Poems, 1930, 17 (n), 23, 24, 28 (n), 34 (n), 40 (n), 50, 51, 64, 86 (n), 87, 94 (n), 95, 97, 101, 103, 114 (n), 133 (n), 151 (n), 246, notes to 19 (2nd)

Poems—A Joking Word (Laura Riding), notes to 89 (1st)

Poems for Spain (ed. Lehmann and Spender), 222

Poetic Unreason (Robert Graves), 223

'Poet of the Encirclement, The', 142 (n)

Poetry and Personal Responsibility (George Every), notes to 202 (2nd)

Poetry, Chicago, notes to 108

Poetry of the Present (ed. Geoffrey Grigson), 224

Poets at Work, see 'Squares and Oblongs'

Poet's Tongue, The (ed. Auden and Garrett), 55, 219 (n)

Poland, 25

Pope, Alexander, 160

'Popeye,' 61

Popper, K. R., see Open Society and its Enemies, The.

'Portrait of a Lady' (T. S. Eliot), notes to 210

Post-Victorian Poetry (Herbert Palmer), 223

Present Age, The (Edwin Muir), 223

Prinzhorn, 36 (n), 118 (n), 120 (n), notes to 139 (1st)

Prokosch, Frederick, notes to 25

'Prophets, The', 246

Prose Style, Auden's, 53–54

Protestant approach, Auden's, 155

'Proverbs of Hell, The' (Blake), 120

'Prufrock' (T. S. Eliot), 46 (n), 65

Psychology, 34–36 (n), 117 (n) et seq., 152–153, 194, see also Freud, Groddeck, Jung, Klages, Prinzhorn.

'Psychology and Art', 36 (n), 59 (n), notes to 118 (1st)

Psychosomatic Medicine, 123–125 (n), see also Groddeck, Klages.

Psychotherapy (Prinzhorn), 120 (n), notes to 36 (2nd), 139 (1st)

'Quest, The', 26, 42, 43 (n), 45, 51, 63, 93 (n), 95, 169–171, 181, 208, 213, 217

Quest, The, 173, 179, 180, 188, 201, 202, 206, 210, 220, notes to 169 (2nd)

Raine, Kathleen, notes to 72, 164

Recovery of the West, The (Michael Roberts), notes to 60 (1st)

'Refugee Blues', 57

Rembrandt, 77

Renaissance, The, 22, 167

Rhetorical imagery, 47–48 (n)

254